Additional Praise for
Forms of Intersubjectivity in Infant Research and Adult Treatment

"*Forms of Intersubjectivity in Infant Research and Adult Treatment* is an outstanding achievement. Not only does it bring clarity to the confusing array of meanings attaching to the term 'intersubjectivity' in the discourse of contemporary psychoanalysis and infant research. This alone would be a singular contribution, but the book does so much more. In forging important links among the fields of psychoanalytic theory, developmental research, and therapeutic practice, it offers a comprehensive and integrated view of human interaction that will be invaluable to clinicians and academics alike."
—Robert D. Stolorow, Ph.D., coauthor, *Worlds of Experience*

"The authors have provided a thorough, clarifying, and immensely useful discussion of the research and conceptual attempts to model the forms of intersubjective processes occurring between infants and caregivers, enlarging and deepening the issues. The usefulness of these ideas for clinicians, namely the importance of attending to implicit as well as to explicit processing, is brilliantly demonstrated through a remarkable ten-year treatment of an adult woman presented by Beebe. This is an important book—breaking new ground in research methods, in theory building, and in therapeutic techniques!"
—E. Virginia Demos, Assistant Clinical Professor of Psychology in the Department of Psychiatry at Harvard Medical School

"I would recommend this volume on intersubjectivity to psychotherapists of all schools. Not only will it allow them to upgrade their theories about psychotherapist/patient interaction, it uses clear concepts and language to provide them with an extensive review of the literature on clinical and experimental studies of how psychoanalytic psychotherapies operate, and how patients can be helped. Clinical vignettes demonstrate how verbal and bodily, cognitive and emotional dimensions are combined to form a particularly clear vision of what is being experienced and enacted at each moment. One of the originalities of this model is the imaginative way in which a relation is perceived as a combination of interactive and auto-regulative strategies. Finally, this volume contains original and imaginative theoretical and practical suggestions about effectively combining scholarship and love in order to help wounded souls."
—Michael Coster Heller, Ph.D., editor of *The Flesh of the Soul*

"Moving their video camera from the studies of caretaker-infant interactions to the broad field of intersubjectivity, Beebe, Knoblauch, Rustin, and Sorter utilize dyadic systems theory as a panorama that integrates verbal and nonverbal, implicit and explicit dimensions of interactions. In a clear, eminently readable and concise manner, comparisons of five theories of intersubjectivity in adult treatment (Benjamin, Ehrenberg, Jacobs, Ogden, Stolorow) are explicated and enhanced with diagrams that emphasize similarities and differences among theorists. Close-ups of the work of three theorists of intersubjectivity (Meltzoff, Stern, Trevarthen) in infant research address their similarities and differences, focusing on the concepts of matching, the role of self-regulation, and the balance between self- and interactive regulation. The final section consists of a microanalytic description of Beebe's treatment of a fragile, traumatized woman. Beebe videotaped her own face during portions of this treatment so that the patient, unable to look at her at times during sessions, and later unable to see her in continued telephone sessions, could process her experience of the sessions under less pressure. The detailed discussions of this treatment makes not only for compelling reading but provides a model for a creative, yet rigorously disciplined treatment approach. The relevance of attending to nonverbal communication and forms of intersubjectivity from infant research are carefully documented in this adult treatment case. Discussions by Theodore Jacobs and Regina Pally provide additional perspectives on this exciting and rich material."

—Frank M. Lachmann, Ph.D., author of *Transforming Aggression: Psychotherapy with the Difficult-to-Treat Patient*

FORMS OF INTERSUBJECTIVITY IN INFANT RESEARCH AND ADULT TREATMENT

BEATRICE BEEBE, Ph.D.

STEVEN KNOBLAUCH, Ph.D.

JUDITH RUSTIN, M.S.W.

DORIENNE SORTER, Ph.D.

WITH DISCUSSIONS BY
THEODORE J. JACOBS, M.D.
and
REGINA PALLY, M.D.

OTHER

Other Press
New York

Permission to reprint chapters from *Psychoanalytic Dialogues* Part 1: 13 (6): 743–841, 2003; Part II: 14 (1): 1–51, 2004 is gratefully acknowledged. Reprinted by permission of the Analytic Press, Hillsdale, NJ.

Production Editor: Mira S. Park

This book was set in 11 pt. Berkeley by Alpha Graphics of Pittsfield, NH.

10 9 8 7 6 5 4 3 2 1

Library of Congress Cataloging-in-Publication Data

Forms of intersubjectivity in infant research and adult treatment /
 Beatrice Beebe ... [et al.].
  p. cm.
  Includes bibliographical references and index.
  ISBN 1-59051-151-4 (pbk. : alk. paper) 1. Psychotherapist and
patient. 2. Intersubjectivity. 3. Psychotherapy. I. Beebe, Beatrice,
1946-
RC480.8.F67 2005
616.89'14—dc22
                                        2005012813

Dedication

To Ruth and Gilbert Beebe
Edward McCrorie
and
Dolores

To Ingrid Roze and Giana Knoblauch

To Herb and Cara Rabin

To George Sorter

Contents

Acknowledgments

We would like to thank the psychoanalytic communities who have encouraged our study of the relevance of infant research for psychoanalysis. For all of us, we express a deep gratitude to the Institute for the Psychoanalytic Study of Subjectivity, out of which our association grew. We all thank our students and supervisees. In addition, Beatrice Beebe and Steven Knoblauch thank the New York University Postdoctoral Program in Psychotherapy and Psychoanalysis. Beatrice Beebe thanks the Columbia Psychoanalytic Center. Judith Rustin, Steven Knoblauch, and Dorienne Sorter thank the Psychoanalytic Psychotherapy Study Center. Steven Knoblauch thanks the Institute for Contemporary Psychotherapy and the National Institute for the Psychotherapies.

We are grateful to the editors of *Psychoanalytic Dialogues*, who first published the four core chapters of this book (entitled "Symposium on Intersubjectivity in Infant Research and Its Implications for Adult Treatment." Part I: *Psychoanalytic Dialogues* (2003) 13(6): 743–841; Part II: *Psychoanalytic Dialogues* (2004) 14(1):1–51). Particular thanks to Carolyn Clement, who invited the work and

encouraged Beatrice Beebe to add the case of Dolores, as well as to
Neil Altman and Lew Aron. We are particularly indebted to these
editors for their suggestion that we add a clinical case, which became the fourth chapter of this book. We wish to thank the staff at
Analytic Press, and particularly Eleanor Starke Kobrin and Meri
Freedman, for their editorial support in producing the original four
papers for the journal. We thank Paul Stepansky for permission to
republish the work in book form.

We would also like to thank many other people who commented
on the work and encouraged us as it evolved: Frank Lachmann,
Joseph Jaffe, Martin Bergmann, Stanley Feldstein, Michael Heller,
Ted Jacobs, Regina Pally, George Downing, Edward Tronick, Doris
Silverman, Barbara Kane, Estelle Shane, Alexandra Harrison, Lin
Reicher, Anni Bergman, Adrienne Harris, Fred Pine, Sid Blatt,
Michael Basch, Julie Gerhardt, Michael Eigen, Jennifer and Peter
Kaufmann. We thank our theorists of infant and adult intersub-
jectivity for their support and for reviews of portions of the manu-
script: Jessica Benjamin, Darlene Ehrenberg, Ted Jacobs, Andy
Meltzoff, Tom Ogden, Dan Stern, Bob Stolorow, and Colwyn
Trevarthen.

Beatrice Beebe would like to single out for special thanks Dan
Stern, her first teacher in infant research; Joe Jaffe, her research
collaborator who contributed so formatively to her systems views;
and Frank Lachmann, her psychoanalytic collaborator with whom
the project of integrating infant research and adult treatment began,
and continues. She is grateful to Lotte Kohler, Edward Aldwell and
Laura Benedek. Special thanks to Mary Sue Moore for her consultations on attachment and vocal rhythm. She also wishes to thank
all those who devoted thousands of hours to the second-by-second
coding of videotapes of mother–infant interaction, and to thinking
about what the research findings might mean: Diane Alson, Rhonda
Davis, Helen Demetriades, Lauren Ellman, Nancy Freeman, Donna
Demetri Friedman, Patty Goodman, Michaela Hager-Budny, Sarah
Hahn-Burke, Liz Helbraun, Allyson Hentel, Tammy Kaminer, Sandra
Triggs Kano, Limor Kaufman-Balamuth, Marina Koulomzin, Jerilyn
Kronen, Greg Kushnick, Paulette Landesman, Tina Lupi, Sara

Markese, Lisa Marquette, Kathleen Mays, Irena Milentijevic, Jillian Miller, Alan Phalen, Danielle Kramer Phelan, Jill Putterman, Michael Ritter, Jane Roth, Stephen Ruffins, Michael Singer, and Shanee Stepakoff.

Special thanks to Sara Markese, Michael Ritter, Emily Brodie, Claudia Andrei, and Matthew Kirkpatrick who ran the research lab. We are grateful to our creative and dedicated statisticians who have made such a contribution to the research: Stanley Feldstein, Patricia Cohen, Karen Buck, Henian Chen, Howard Andrews, Donald Ross, and Samuel Anderson. Our gratitude to the research assistants who devoted many hours to the preparation of the manuscript: Emily Brodie, Hwee Sze Lim, Heather Chan, Lauren Cooper, Jessica Sarnicola, Emlyn Capili, Sonya Sonpal, Eunice Lee, and Marina Tasopoulos. We also acknowledge the support of New York State Psychiatric Institute where Beatrice Beebe and Joseph Jaffe have conducted infant research since 1970.

We are grateful to Michael Moskowitz for introducing our work to Other Press. We would like to thank Other Press, and particularly Stacy Hague and Mira Park, for shepherding this work toward a book.

Finally, Beatrice Beebe thanks Dolores for trusting her, for sharing so intimately, and for giving her permission to write about their work together.

Contributors

In parallel to this collaboration, each of us has forged other collaborations and developed other interests.

Beatrice Beebe is a Clinical Professor of Medical Psychology (in Psychiatry) at Columbia University College of Physicians and Surgeons; and faculty at the Psychoanalytic Center, Columbia University; the New York University Postdoctoral Program in Psychotherapy and Psychoanalysis; and the Institute for the Psychoanalytic Study of Subjectivity. With Joseph Jaffe and a team of talented statisticians and graduate students, Beatrice Beebe pursues research at the New York State Psychiatric Institute on mother and infant self- and interactive regulation, and how both maternal and infant distress may affect these forms of regulation (Beebe et al. 2005). Using psychoanalytically informed video feedback, she has applied findings from infant research to mother-infant treatment (Beebe 2003; Cohen and Beebe 2002). With Phyllis Cohen, Anni Bergman, Kathryn Adorney, Helge Staby Deaton, Donna Demetri-Friedman, Naomi Hirschfeld, Kirsten Kupferman, Rebecca Melon, Sarah Moaba, Sally

Moscowitz, Kristen Peck, Rita Reiswig, Nancie Senet, Mark Sossin, Linda Taylor, and Suzi Tortora, she has applied findings from infant research to a primary prevention project for mothers pregnant and widowed on 9-11 and their infants and young children.

Steven Knoblauch is faculty and supervisor at the Institute for the Psychoanalytic Study of Subjectivity, the Psychoanalytic Psychotherapy Study Center, the Institute for Contemporary Psychotherapy; and faculty at the N.Y.U. Postdoctoral Program in Psychotherapy and Psychoanalysis, and the National Institute for the Psychotherapies. Building on his experience as a jazz musician, Knoblauch (2000) in his book, *The Musical Edge of Pychoanalysis*, uses the metaphor of the "musical edge" to illuminate relationships between implicit and explicit registers in psychoanalytic dialogue. Emphasizing the improvisational process between patient and analyst organized as rhythms, tone, pitch, cadence, and pauses, he seeks to expand analytic attention to the implicit register as a way of recognizing unconscious meaning and communication.

Judith Rustin is faculty and supervisor at the Institute for the Psychoanalytic Study of Subjectivity, and the Psychoanalytic Psychotherapy Study Center. She has explored the concept of the two-person field through her study of current neuroscience research. Despite increasing emphasis on genetics, much current research reveals that the fine-tuning of brain development relies on the early relationship between infant and caregiver. Using this metaphor for memory and emotion, Rustin and Sekaer (2004) have applied these ideas to the treatment dyad in a paper "From the Neuroscience of Memory to Psychoanalytic Interaction."

Dorienne Sorter is Co-Chair, faculty and supervisor at the Institute for the Psychoanalytic Study of Subjectivity; and faculty and supervisor at the Psychoanalytic Psychotherapy Study Center. She has pursued the application of concepts from infant research to clinical case material, focusing on the role of procedural knowledge and implicit relational knowing. In her paper, "Chase and

Dodge: An Organization of Experience"(Sorter 1996), she uses her knowledge of mother–infant spatial derailments to notice split-second spatial disturbances in an adult treatment, and to bring them into the analytic process.

Theodore Jacobs is Clinical Professor of Psychiatry, Albert Einstein College of Medicine, New York University School of Medicine; Training and Supervising Analyst, New York and New York University Psychoanalytic Institutes; Supervising Child Analyst, New York University Psychoanalytic Institute, Columbia Psychoanalytic Center; author of *The Use of the Self: Countertransference and Communication in the Psychoanalytic Situation*; and co-author of *On Beginning an Analysis*. He is currently working on a paper entitled, "The Adolescent Neurosis" for the American Association of Child Psychoanalysis, and putting together a collection of his articles for a book.

Regina Pally is Associate Clinical Professor of Psychiatry, University of California Los Angeles—Neuropsychiatric Institute; and Faculty, Los Angeles Psychoanalytic Institute. She is a practicing psychoanalyst intensely interested in the interface between adult treatment and neuroscience. She teaches about this interface in professional settings as well as in community settings with parent groups and parent educators. She is the author of numerous articles, as well as a book, *The Mind-Brain Relationship*. Her most recent publication is a paper, "Non-conscious Prediction and a Role for Consciousness in Correcting Prediction Errors."

Introduction

This book emerged from ten years of our collaborative study of verbal and nonverbal forms of interaction in the therapeutic encounter. We began with our interest in the interactive process and ways in which three decades of infant research on face-to-face communication might enrich our understanding of communication in adult treatment. Our goal was to integrate an understanding of interactions that operate prereflectively, out of conscious awareness, with those that operate through more usual verbal narrative.

The pivotal construct of intersubjectivity became the focus of our efforts to integrate these different forms of interaction. We were struck by important parallel developments in theories of intersubjectivity in the last decade by leading theorists in both infant research and psychoanalysis, though with little dialogue between them. Psychoanalysis has described intersubjectivity primarily in the verbal, explicit mode, whereas infant research has described intersubjectivity in the nonverbal, implicit mode of action-sequences, or procedural knowledge. Yet we became perplexed that the very same term is used by psychoanalytic theorists to describe a symbolic mind and by infant researchers to describe a presymbolic mind. We decided to study both adult and infant theorists of intersubjectivity to better understand this complex concept.

We used a dyadic systems view of communication as our framework to compare theorists of intersubjectivity. This view construes the dyadic system to be the basic unit of interest. This unit is defined by both self- and interactive regulation processes, with each form of regulation affecting the other. Systems views have a rich intellectual history in the twentieth century, but our dyadic systems view of communication was influenced more immediately by Joseph Jaffe, Louis Sander, Edward Tronick, Alan Fogel, and the team of Beebe, Jaffe, and Lachmann. This view links the individual to the dyad, emphasizing what Beebe and Lachmann have called the "co-construction" of inner and relational processes. Our dyadic systems view also integrates explicit and implicit realms of discourse. We note that our term "interactive regulation" is a neutral rather than "positive" concept. Moreover it does not imply mutuality (with its usual positive connotation), symmetry, or causality. It does mean that both partners affect the other's behavior moment-by-moment. But some other evaluation, such as attachment type, or presence/absence of maternal depression, is required to determine whether any particular pattern of regulation is "optimal" or "nonoptimal." For example, when degrees of vocal rhythm were used to predict attachment types, we discovered that degrees of interactive regulation could be excessive or insufficient, with mid-range optimal for secure attachment (Jaffe et al. 2001).

Two fundamental premises oriented our thinking. First, all theories of intersubjectivity are theories of interaction. Any theory of intersubjectivity can be evaluated in terms of the degree to which it articulates a systems view of interaction, a broader concept that can integrate the various forms of intersubjectivity described in both infant research and psychoanalysis. Second, for a theory of intersubjectivity to be most generally useful for psychoanalysis it must address both verbal and nonverbal, more recently reconceptualized as explicit and implicit, forms of intersubjectivity. We note that these two sets of terms, verbal/nonverbal and explicit/implicit, are not synonyms, a topic we address in Chapter 1.

We first compared a number of adult psychoanalytic views in which the concept of intersubjectivity was central to the theoretical perspective, or where a theory of interaction was clearly articulated. We chose Benjamin, Ehrenberg, Jacobs, Ogden, and Stolorow and colleagues. We are grateful to the late Stephen Mitchell (1997) for his articulation of the differences in the theories of Ogden, Jacobs, and Ehrenberg. Our review of these theorists revealed that each held different fundamental assumptions and had different relative emphases on self- and interactive regulation processes.

We then extended our study to three infant theorists of intersubjectivity, Meltzoff, Trevarthen, and Stern. We chose theorists who use intersubjectivity as a central theoretical construct. In so doing we omitted other theorists who have made important contributions to the concept of intersubjectivity in infancy, most notably Sander, Tronick, and the Boston Change Process Study Group. Although each of the three infancy theorists we chose addressed the question of how the infant could know the state of the partner and used crossmodal correspondences as central to the construction of intersubjectivity, again each emphasized different aspects of the dyadic system and held a distinctly different theory.

We found it remarkable that the term *intersubjectivity* is used with a wide range of meanings among both psychoanalytic and infant theorists. We were further impressed by the differences among the adult theorists, as well as among the infancy theorists. Given the widespread usage and appeal of the concept of intersubjectivity and the multiple uses of the term, the resulting difficulties of communication in our field are currently an important problem in psychoanalysis.

This book attempts to provide a framework within which to discuss these multiple uses of the term intersubjectivity. We arrived at several conclusions. First, the concept of intersubjectivity was not used in the same way from author to author. Thus we have proposed in this book that intersubjectivity as a universal term be discarded. In its place we offer *forms of intersubjectivity*. A central task of our collaboration has been the delineation of the different forms of intersubjectivity described by our infancy and adult theorists. Many more forms could surely be described. Second, presymbolic forms of intersubjectivity in infancy are very different from symbolic forms in adulthood. Third, within adult treatment, forms of intersubjectivity in the explicit, narrative realm are organized at a different level of discourse from those in the implicit dialogue.

The work presented in this book shares much with the work of Beebe, Lachmann, and Jaffe, particularly their emphasis on a dyadic systems view of communication, nonverbal dimensions of the co-construction of dialogue, and an array of interaction patterns. There is a continuity between our work, their work, and that of Stephen Mitchell and Lewis Aron, whose studies of an array of patient–analyst interactions have been seminal to the growth of a relational perspective. Although the terms of their discourse are different from ours, Mitchell and Aron have been similarly concerned with the balance between inner and relational processes: a dialectic between the intrapsychic and the interpersonal, each constituted by the other. Aron (1996) in particular has an important discussion of differences in the ways that various theorists have used the term intersubjectivity.

We would like to acknowledge the powerful and creative contributions of the Boston Change Process Study Group to the articulation of the relevance of infant research to adult treatment (Stern et al. 1998, Tronick 1998). This group was not chosen as one of the positions of intersubjectivity in infancy to study for two reasons: they had not begun publishing when we began working out our basic ideas, and they do not use intersubjectivity as the central theoretical construct. Nevertheless, their work has profoundly influenced ours, and particularly Lyons-Ruth's (1998, 1999) formulations of implicit relational knowing. Nevertheless, our work is different from theirs. Whereas their work emphasizes a "moment of meeting," ours emphasizes ongoing processes of self- and interactive regulation. Whereas their work assumes a general working understanding of the meaning of the term intersubjectivity, our work pries apart numerous different meanings of this term, as a function of developmental stages, and particularly as a function of differences in presymbolic vs. symbolic meanings.

Lichtenberg, Lachmann, and Fosshage (1992) have also made an important and sustained contribution to articulating the relevance of infant research to adult treatment over the past two decades. They have proposed a system of motivation for psychoanalysis that is rooted in empirical infant research. Their work is particularly valuable for its immersion in the clinical exchange.

We recommend the discussion of various theoretical positions on the nature of intersubjectivity in infancy by Fonagy, Gergely, Jurist and Target (2002), which was published after we had completed our work. We share an interest in the role of early development and the construction of experience, particularly the foundational role of interpersonal contingencies, translated here into "interactive regulation." At the same time, however, we place greater emphasis on the *co*-construction of experience, the nonverbal exchange, and the role of both self- and interactive regulation in this process. Like Fonagy et al., we are impressed with the impact of parental style, history, and distress on children's development as well as the impact of the child's constitution. But our analysis of the moment-by-moment exchange between mother and infant has led us to emphasize a bi-directional co-constructive process in which *both* parent and infant coordinate with each other, and organize each other's behavior and experience. In contrast, they emphasize the parent's influence on the child, a uni-directional process: "the caregiver mirroring the internal experience of the infant comes to organize the child's emotional experience" (Fonagy et al. 2002, p. 8). In addition we place far more emphasis on the contribution of nonverbal communication to the organization of experience across the lifespan, which we integrate with the symbolized representational aspects of experience, as we illustrate in the case in the fourth chapter, "Faces-in-Relation." In contrast, Fonagy et al. make their central contribution in the domain of the symbolized representational aspects of experience, and the role of variations in the capacity to reflect on this experience. Finally, we make a firm distinction between presymbolic and symbolic forms of representation. We stress the importance of presymbolic and nonconscious forms of intersubjectivity, taking the position that linguistic forms of intersubjectivity are built on and influenced by prelinguistic forms. In contrast, Fonagy and colleagues tend to reserve the term intersubjectivity for a linguistically mediated process which involves the capacity to reflect on one's own and the partner's experience. Despite the differences in emphasis, our approaches run in parallel and could be fruitfully integrated.

In this book we do not attempt an extensive review of all current concepts of intersubjectivity, either in psychoanalysis or in infant research. Instead, Chapter 1 sets the stage with definitions of our central concepts, and it illustrates different meanings of intersubjectivity in psychoanalysis with brief comparisons of various key theorists: Theodore Jacobs, Darlene Ehrenberg, Thomas Ogden, Jessica Benjamin, and Robert Stolorow and colleagues George Atwood, Bernard Brandchaft, and Donna Orange. We argue that until recently psychoanalysis has addressed the concept of intersubjectivity primarily in the verbal/explicit mode, in contrast to infant research which has addressed the concept in the nonverbal/implicit mode of action sequences or procedural knowledge. We hold that an integration of explicit and linguistic with implicit and nonverbal theories of intersubjectivity is essential to a deeper understanding of therapeutic action in psychoanalysis today.

Chapter 2 compares three infant theorists of intersubjectivity: Andrew Meltzoff, Colwyn Trevarthen, and Daniel Stern. These three authors generate theories with important differences. Nevertheless, they converge on the concept of nonverbal correspondences as the core definition of intersubjectivity in infancy. Based on these theorists we conclude that communicative competence is far more fundamental than language—and prior to language. Further, the origin of mind is dyadic and dialogic, and forms of adult intersubjectivity are built on infant forms.

Chapter 3 addresses ways in which infant research can contribute to elaborating our concepts of forms of intersubjectivity in psychoanalysis. We first suggest that the work of Meltzoff, Trevarthen, and Stern can enrich the concept of intersubjectivity in psychoanalysis primarily through the dialogic origin of mind and the role of nonverbal, implicit correspondences. These implicit correspondences provide a rich and complex organizing principle of interaction, which can make a powerful contribution to the understanding of intimacy and exuberance as well as distress regulation in psychoanalysis.

As important as the concept of nonverbal correspondence is, in Chapter 3 we make the argument that it is not *sufficient* to help the analyst conceptualize the full range of the nonverbal, implicit interactive processes in intersubjectivity. We build on the work of Meltzoff, Trevarthen, and Stern to define a fourth position. Using a more neutral definition of intersubjectivity as referring to what is occurring between two minds, rather than a more positive definition implying mutuality, we argue that the full range of patterns of self- and interactive regulation provides the broadest definition of the presymbolic origins of intersubjectivity, with correspondence being only one of many critical patterns. In addition we address the place of interactive regulation, problems with the concept of matching, the role of self-regulation, a full dialectic between similarity and difference, and the balance model of self- and interactive regulation. We take the position that all forms of self- and interactive regulation are relevant to the possibility of perceiving and aligning oneself with the moment-by-moment process of the other. A broadened understanding of intersubjectivity in infancy sets the stage for a more fruitful exchange between infant researchers and psychoanalysis.

Chapter 4 presents a clinical case by Beebe, illustrating many of the concepts from Chapter 3. In this treatment the face became the central metaphor for the negotiation of relatedness. This treatment demonstrates the clinical value of attention to the nonverbal and implicit mode of the interaction. Moreover, it illustrates the critical necessity of integrating both implicit and explicit processes. It particularly addresses the issue of *how* implicit and nonverbal forms of intersubjectivity can be transformed, and the importance of the participatory role of the analyst as a new relational partner (Lyons-Ruth 1999).

In this case Beebe made the unusual intervention of taking a series of videotapes, based on her background with video micro-analysis of mother–infant interaction. These videotapes included some sections of Dolores and Beebe together, and some of Beebe's face only.

Because Dolores did not look at her therapist at this time, seeing Beebe's face watching her as she viewed the videotape, and hearing Beebe's sounds responding to her, heightened Dolores's experience of her therapist's response and her own visceral experience: she came to recognize herself in Beebe's face recognizing her. Working with video in an adult treatment is not a usual or in any way a necessary aspect of our approach to forms of inter-subjectivity in adult treatment. However, the video made possible a detailed examination of the nonverbal processes of this treatment, which would not have been possible without it.

Beatrice Beebe was invited by Ted Jacobs to join him and Regina Pally in his study group on nonverbal communication at the American Psychoanalytic meetings in New York City from 2000 to 2005. Segments of our work on forms of intersubjectivity were presented at that study group and were discussed by Jacobs and Pally. Out of this collaboration grew our invitation to Jacobs and Pally to discuss our book more formally. We welcomed the opportunity to extend the discussion of our work from different viewpoints. The original discussions by Carolyn Clement, Judith Edwards, and Michel Heller that appeared in *Psychoanalytic Dialogues* reflected relational and Kleinian psychoanalysis as well as a combination of academic analysis of nonverbal communication and psychotherapy, respectively. These discussions were powerful and creative interpretations of our work, and we recommend them to our readers.

In contrast, Ted Jacobs discusses the papers from the viewpoint of a classical adult and child psychoanalyst trained and teaching at the New York Psychoanalytic Institute. We were excited by the prospect of a dialogue between quite different "stripes" of psychoanalysis that are rarely brought together. Ted Jacobs is quite unusual across the broad spectrum of psychoanalytic schools. He was an early innovator in understanding the role of nonverbal communication in psychoanalysis, and particularly the ways in which transference and countertransference are expressed nonverbally. He was also an innovator in using his own experience as a powerful source of information in the treatment, as we describe in Chapter 1. Through the concept of enactments, Ted Jacobs opened up classical psychoanalysis to the influence of the analyst's subjective experience on the analytic process.

In his discussion Jacobs takes the view that nonverbal communication is a vitally important aspect of psychoanalysis. His review of literature on nonverbal communication covers entirely different territory from that covered by our chapters: Freud, Reich, and Deutsch; nonverbal communication research in psychotherapy such as Scheflen, Birdwhistell, and Kendon; and current psychoanalytic contributions. He calls for more research on the degree to which forms of mother–infant communication may or may not be carried over into childhood and adulthood. In his comments on the case of Dolores, Jacobs is struck with the power and vividness of the role of the face in the treatment, and how carefully Dolores attended to her analyst's face. Jacobs also reminds us that nonverbal behavior, like other behavior, may function as a compromise formation that may be utilized protectively to keep at bay other aspects of experience.

Jacobs illustrates his own approach to nonverbal behavior in the analytic process with Ms. C. He describes how he gradually became aware of a repetitive nonverbal interactive process, which he terms "enactments." Following negative periods of resistance and frustration, Ms. C's postural withdrawals on the couch evoked Jacobs's own postural and emotional withdrawals. Eventually Ms. C would reengage Jacobs, placating or seductive; and gradually Jacobs would return emotionally and join Ms. C's tone. Becoming aware of these nonverbal enactments of disruption, mutual withdrawal, efforts at repair, and covert shared sexuality facilitated the treatment; lack of their awareness at times disturbed the treatment.

Jacobs has been a pioneer in sharing his own struggle to become aware of these enactments, and to use them creatively in the analytic process. In closing, Jacobs cautions us that the neglect of nonverbal phenomena is a major deficiency in psychoanalytic education today.

A practicing psychoanalyst, Regina Pally brings yet another perspective, that of the relevance of neuroscience to psychoanalysis (Pally 2000, 2001). Like Jacobs, but from a very different perspective, Pally is also an unusual voice calling for more attention to the role of nonverbal communication in adult treatment. As she notes, "While most of psychoanalysis has focused on the unconscious symbolic meanings of nonverbal communication (Jacobs 1994), neuroscience emphasizes the unconscious influence that one person's nonverbal communication has on another's biology, emotions, and verbal conversation" (1998, p. 358). Pally argues that much of psychoanalysis is nonconceptual, nonlinguistic, and not accessible by our usual verbal methods. "Emotional nonverbal exchange may play at least as much importance in analytic treatment as does verbal exchange. Analysts and patients may influence one another's body sensations, imagery, thoughts, behaviors, and even words, by unconsciously processed nonverbal cues of emotion. . . . *How* the analyst communicates may be as important as what the analyst says" (1998, p. 360).

Pally discusses our work from the point of view of whether it is consistent with current findings from neuroscience research. She focuses on our broadened view of "forms of intersubjectivity," noting that we use nonverbal and implicit forms of interaction as a bridge from infant research to adult treatment. She highlights some of the new features of our view: our emphasis on interactive regulation, and particularly the importance of varied and flexible forms of interactive regulation; the contingent and predictable nature of interaction; and the optimal mid-range model of interactive regulation. She views these features as consistent with what we know about brain functioning. She notes the survival value of variations of "forms" in all biological and social domains, and the ability flexibly to shift among forms. She emphasizes neuroscience research documenting that prediction is one of the brain's most fundamental functions. Our model of optimal midrange degrees of regulation is consistent in Pally's view with the importance of a balance between stability and change in the brain's functioning. Finally, Pally gives an extensive description of neuroscience research consistent with a two-fold process of therapeutic change, one implicit and nonconscious, the other explicit, conscious, and verbalizable, each with its own unique contribution.

REFERENCES

Aron, L. (1996). *A Meeting of Minds* (2nd ed.). Hillsdale, NJ: Analytic Press.

Beebe, B. (2003). Brief mother–infant treatment using psychoanalytically informed video microanalysis. *Infant Mental Health Journal* 24(1): 24–52.

Beebe, B., Jaffe, J., Buck, K., Chen, H., et al. (2005, in press). Maternal depression at 6 weeks postpartum and mother–infant 4-month self- and interactive regulation. *Infant Mental Health Journal.*

Cohen, P., and Beebe, B. (2002). Video feedback with a depressed mother and her infant: a collaborative individual psychoanalytic and mother–infant treatment. *Journal of Infant, Child, and Adolescent Psychotherapy* 2(3):1–55.

Fonagy, P., Gergely, G., Jurist, E., and Target, M. (2002). *Affect Regulation, Mentalization, and the Development of Self.* New York: Other Press.

Jacobs, T. (1991). *The use of the self: Countertransference and communication in the psychoanalytic situation.* New York: International Universities Press.

——— (1994). Nonverbal communications: some reflections on their role in the psychoanalytic process and psychoanalytic education. *Journal of the American Psychoanalytic Association* 42:741–762.

Jacobs, T. & Rothstein, A. (1997). *On Beginning an Analysis.* New York: International Universities Press.

Jaffe, J., Beebe, B., Feldstein, S., et al. (2001). Rhythms of dialogue in infancy. *Monographs of the Society for Research in Child Development* 66 (2 serial no. 256).

Knoblauch, S. (2000). *The Musical Edge of Therapeutic Dialogue.* Hillsdale: Analytic Press.

Lichtenberg, J., Lachmann, F., and Fosshage, J. (1992). *Self and Motivational Systems*. Hillsdale, NJ: Analytic Press.

Lyons-Ruth, K. (1998). Implicit relational knowing: its role in development and psychoanalytic treatment. *Infant Mental Health Journal* 19:282–291.

——— (1999). The two-person unconscious: intersubjective dialogue, enactive relational representation, and the emergence of new forms of relational organization. *Psychoanalytic Inquiry* 19:576–617.

Mitchell, S. (1997). *Influence and Autonomy in Psychoanalysis*. Hillsdale, NJ: Analytic Press.

Pally, R. (1998). Emotional processing: the mind–body connection. *International Journal of Psycho-Analysis* 79:349–362.

——— (2001). *The Mind-Brain Relationship*. London: Karnac.

——— (2001). A primary role for nonverbal communication in psychoanalysis. *Psychoanalytic Inquiry* 21:71–93.

——— (2005, in press). Non-conscious prediction and a role for consciousness in correcting prediction errors. *Cortex, 41.*

Rustin, J., and Sekaer, C. (2004). From the neuroscience of memory to psychoanalytic interaction: clinical implications. *Psychoanalytic Psychology* 21(1):70–82.

Sorter, D. (1996). Chase and dodge: an organization of experience. *Psychoanalysis and Psychotherapy* 13:68–75.

Stern, D., Sander, L., Nahum, J., et al. (1998). Non-interpretative mechanisms in psychoanalytic therapy. *International Journal of Psycho-Analysis* 79:903–921.

Tronick, E. (1998). Dyadically expanded states of consciousness and the process of therapeutic change. *Infant Mental Health Journal* 19:290–299.

Forms of Intersubjectivity in Infant Research and Adult Treatment: A Systems View*

BEATRICE BEEBE, STEVEN KNOBLAUCH,

JUDITH RUSTIN, DORIENNE SORTER

One of the most pressing questions in psychoanalysis today is the nature of interaction in the therapeutic encounter. Interest in interaction derives in part from a shift from positivist to perspectivist approaches and systems views in late twentieth-century psychoanalysis (Hoffman 1998, Orange et al. 1997, Reese and Overton 1970, Silverman 1994, 1999). Although interactive models and a shift toward systems thinking have been operative in various ways in psychoanalysis throughout the century, what is new is the increasing centrality of the interactive process itself. "Intersubjectivity" has emerged as the leading concept among psychoanalytic approaches to interaction.

Our goal in this series of chapters is a further refinement of a theory of interaction for psychoanalysis, with specific focus on the concept of intersubjectivity. Psychoanalysis has addressed the

*We acknowledge the contributions of Joseph Jaffe, Mary Sue Moore, Carolyn Clement, Lin Reicher, Karlen Lyons-Ruth, Bob Stolorow, Jessica Benjamin, Julie Gerhardt, Sara Markese, Marina Tasopoulos, and Lauren Cooper.

concept of intersubjectivity primarily in the verbal, explicit mode (for important exceptions see Jacobs 1991a,b, Knoblauch 1997, 2000, McLaughlin 1991, Ogden 1994, Pally 2000). In contrast, infant research has addressed the concept of intersubjectivity in the nonverbal, implicit mode of action-sequences, or procedural knowledge. We propose that an integration of explicit, linguistic and implicit, nonverbal theories of intersubjectivity is essential to a deeper understanding of therapeutic action in psychoanalysis today. To shed light on an implicit, nonverbal dimension of intersubjectivity in psychoanalysis, we include concepts from adult psychoanalysis, infant research, developmental systems theories, and nonverbal communication, particularly the distinction between implicit processing out of awareness vs. explicit processing at the declarative, verbal level.

Psychoanalytic concepts of interaction have included, for example, transference-countertransference (Freud 1911, 1914, Gill 1982), holding environment (Modell 1984, Winnicott 1965), a two-person view (Modell 1984), interactive matrix (Loewald 1980), the selfobject transference (Kohut 1984), empathic immersion (Ornstein and Ornstein 1984), optimal responsiveness (Bacal 1985), projective identification (Ogden 1982), role-responsiveness (Sandler 1987), social construction (Hoffman 1998), enactment (Jacobs, 1991a,b), procedural knowledge (Clyman 1991), surrender (Ghent 1989), the clinical exchange (Lichtenberg et al. 1992, Fosshage 2000), reflective function (Fonagy 1991, 1994, 1995), the intimate edge (Ehrenberg 1992), a dyadic systems view (Beebe et al. 1992), affect regulation (Schore 1994), mutual regulation (Beebe and Lachmann 1988, 1998, Lachmann and Beebe 1996, Tronick 1998), mutuality (Aron 1996), implicit relational knowing (Lyons-Ruth 1998, Stern et al. 1998), relational matrix (Mitchell 1997, 2000), intimate attachment (Shane et al. 1998), emotional nonverbal exchange (Pally 2000), resonance (Knoblauch 2000), and moving and being moved (LaBarre 1995, 2001). Especially in the past decade, the concept of intersubjectivity has become increasingly central in discussions of interaction in psychoanalysis, as we detail below. But, despite the importance of the concept of intersubjectivity, we are impressed by the multiple uses of the term in current discourse and a striking lack of consensus on its meaning.

Empirical infant research on mother–infant face-to-face "play" has been preoccupied for three decades with the problem of defining the nature of interaction. Concepts of interaction in infant research have included, for example, mutual regulation or mutual influence (Beebe and Stern 1977, Jaffe et al. 1973, Sander 1977, Stern 1985, Tronick 1989, Tronick et al. 1980), synchronization (Stern 1977), reciprocity (Brazelton et al. 1975), behavioral dialogues (Bakeman and Brown 1977), reciprocal and compensatory mutual influence (Capella 1981), accommodation (Crown 1991, Jasnow and Feldstein 1986), coordination (Sander 1977), rhythms of dialogue (Jaffe et al. 2001), attunement (Stern et al. 1985), protoconversation (Beebe et al. 1979), the moment of meeting (Sander 1995, Stern et al. 1998), and, especially in the past decade, intersubjectivity (Meltzoff 1985, Meltzoff and Moore 1998, Stern 1985, Trevarthen 1980, Tronick 1998, Tronick et al. 1980).

We are intrigued by parallel developments in theories of intersubjectivity in the last decade by leading theorists in both infant research and psychoanalysis, yet with little dialogue between them. We are perplexed that the very same term is used by psychoanalytic theorists to describe a symbolic mind and by infant researchers to describe a presymbolic mind. We find it remarkable that the term is used with a wide range of meanings within both psychoanalytic and infant theorists: the adult theorists themselves do not agree on the meaning of intersubjectivity, nor do the infancy theorists. Given the widespread usage and appeal of the concept of intersubjectivity and the multiple uses of the term, the resulting difficulties of communication are currently an important problem in psychoanalysis. Based on our reviews of both adult and infant theorists, we develop the argument that the term intersubjectivity has no one, coherent meaning either in psychoanalysis or infant research. As a solution to this problem, we recommend adoption of the concept of *forms of intersubjectivity*.

Three orienting proposals guide our thinking:

1. We begin with the premise that all theories of intersubjectivity are theories of interaction. Any theory of intersubjectivity can be evaluated in terms of the degree to which it articulates a systems view of interaction, a broader concept that can integrate the various forms of intersubjectivity described in both infant research and psychoanalysis.

2. Insofar as psychoanalysis is interested in integrating concepts of intersubjectivity from infant research, it is necessary to consider how different levels of cognitive development affect the possible ranges of different forms of intersubjectivity. To this end, it is essential to draw distinctions between presymbolic and symbolic forms of intelligence, as well as among different levels of "theory of mind."

3. For a theory of intersubjectivity to be most generally useful for psychoanalysis, it must address both verbal and nonverbal, more recently conceptualized as explicit and implicit, forms of intersubjectivity.

To set the stage, we briefly review here the distinction between implicit and explicit processing and our use of a dyadic systems model of interaction. We then use a systems model to compare several different psychoanalytic theories of intersubjectivity: Jacobs, Ehrenberg, Ogden, Benjamin, and Stolorow and colleagues. Finally, to prepare for the review of infant theorists of intersubjectivity in Chapter 2, we describe the difference between presymbolic and symbolic forms of mind, and distinctions in theories of mind in the young child's emerging symbolic development.

IMPLICIT VS. EXPLICIT PROCESSING

The most obvious difference between adult vs. infant forms of intersubjectivity might be described as verbal vs. nonverbal forms of communication. However, the distinction between verbal and nonverbal communication has been refined, and made more complex, by recent distinctions between implicit and explicit forms of information processing, subcortical and cortical, respectively. Although a review of this literature is beyond the scope of this work, we briefly clarify our terminology.

Implicit refers to things that we know or do automatically without the conscious experience of doing them or remembering them, such as ice-skating, or the feel of cat fur on one's skin, or knowing how to joke around (Clyman 1991, Grigsby and Hartlaub 1994, Lyons-Ruth 1998, 1999, Rustin and Sekaer 2001, Squire and Cohen 1985). Explicit processing or memory refers to things that we do or remember that can be brought to consciousness as symbolically organized recall for information and events, such as facts and concepts ("semantic") or personal history ("episodic") (Pally 1997a,b).

Three distinctions are made within implicit processing: cued/associative, procedural, and emotional (Pally 2000). Implicit processing that is "cued" or "associative" involves associations among words and verbalized images that are entirely out of awareness. The method of free association in psychoanalysis utilizes this form of processing. When we use the term "implicit" in these papers, we are not referring to this meaning. "Procedural" refers to skills or goal-directed action sequences that are encoded nonsymbolically, become automatic with repeated practice, and influence the organizational processes that guide behavior; this meaning of implicit is central to our use (Emde et al. 1991, Grigsby and Hartlaub 1994). Our use of the concept of infant "expectancies" illustrates one definition of implicit, procedural knowledge (Beebe and Lachmann 2002). Although various controversies exist around the meaning of "procedural" (Mandler 1988, Mounoud 1995, Muller and Overton 1998), our use of the term includes both conscious and nonconscious processing, and a view of the infant as well as adult as an active agent in the construction of procedural knowledge.

Implicit "emotional" processing refers to primitive emotional perceptions and memories that utilize the amygdala and limbic systems (Pally 1997a,b). As an example of implicit emotional knowlege, Dimberg and colleagues (2000) showed that adults can process a facial expression, and match it, within 30 milliseconds, entirely out of awareness. These results show that both positive and negative emotional reactions can be evoked out of awareness, so that important aspects of face-to-face communication occur on a nonconscious level. This meaning is included in our use of the term "implicit."

Heller and Haynal (1997) illustrate both procedural and emotional implicit knowledge in a paper entitled "The Doctor's Face: A Mirror of His Patient's Suicidal Projects." Fifty-nine patients who had attempted suicide in the previous three days were given an initial interview by the same psychiatrist. Two videotape cameras recorded the faces of both doctor and patient. One year later, 10 of these 59 patients had made another suicide attempt: the "re-attempter" group. Whereas the psychiatrist's own written predictions were random, fine-grained microanalyses of the videotapes of the psychiatrist's face identified 81 percent of the re-attempters. With her patients who would later try another suicide attempt, the psychiatrist frowned more, showed more head and eye orientation, and showed more overall facial activation and increased speech. This greater activation and negative expressiveness of the psychiatrist can be seen as both regulating her own inner state and communicating with her patient, both out of her awareness (Beebe and Lachmann 1998, 2002). Thus the psychiatrist "knew" something through her nonverbal behavior (both implicit procedural action-sequences of head, eye, face, and voice, and implicit emotional reactions) that she did not "know" at an explicit, linguistic level. The re-attempter group was also discriminated by patient behaviors: self-regulatory movements (excluding smiles) with no apparent communicative intent, such as pinched or pursed lips, opening and closing the jaw while lips remain closed, and elongating a mouth corner.

Various terminologies, such as verbal-nonverbal, explicit-implicit, or continuous process-discrete state (Fogel 1993, Knoblauch 2000), do not have identical meanings, and they do not map onto each other in any neat fashion. For example, words can be used in an explicit fashion, that is, consciously and intentionally, or in an implicit fashion, such as cued through associations out of awareness. Likewise, words can, and usually do, have "discrete" meanings, but they also have a "process" dimension, conveyed through the rhythm and intonation, for example, which is implicit or "affective." The nonverbal dimension of communication, conveyed through face, gesture, vocal tone, and rhythm, is usually implicit, out of awareness, not consciously "intentional" (although it is goal-oriented action), and conveying a moving "process" rather than a discrete moment. But certain nonverbal gestures, such as putting out one's hand to indicate "stop," or waving "goodbye," have a discrete, explicit meaning. Compared to words, which are slower, with a distinct turn-taking format due to the impossibility of speaking and listening at the same time (Jaffe and Feldstein 1970), nonverbal communication tends to be extremely rapid, and frequently simultaneous between partners, without an alternating turn-taking constraint. Furthermore the language of the body can be entirely out of awareness, but it can in some instances be readily brought into awareness. Lyons-Ruth (personal communication 2002) suggests that we distinguish *how words are used*: the enactive, action-potential of words that directly engage the partner, which is an *implicit* use of language; vs. the symbolic, interpretive, reflection-potential of words, which is *explicit*. While acknowledging these complexities, in these chapters we nevertheless retain the term "nonverbal" because of its importance in the history of ideas. We *roughly* equate implicit with nonverbal, or the "affective" dimension of relating, noting that words can also be used in enactive, affective fashion following Lyons-Ruth; and explicit with verbal processes used in a symbolic, reflective fashion.

Bucci (1997)[1] suggests that there are three levels of organization in the adult: (1) organization within the nonverbal realm, such

---

1. Bucci distinguishes a nonsymbolic or "subsymbolic" form of processing from two different types of symbolic processing: nonverbal vs. verbal symbolic: (1) a "continuous processing" format, or "subsymbolic," such as many

as procedural action sequences, and somatic sensations; (2) organization within the verbal realm; and (3) a referential process between the verbal and nonverbal (similar to Loewald's [1980] concept of "linking" between verbal and nonverbal; see also Mitchell 2000), which makes connections between the words and the visceral bodily experience, through metaphor and imagery for example. Based on a study of adult attachment interviews, Appelman (2000) found that Bucci's measure of referential activity was higher in secure as compared to insecure mothers.

Lyons-Ruth (1998, 1999) argues that much of our relational experience is represented in an implicit format, which she terms "implicit relational knowing," such as knowing how to participate in greetings and partings, or how to joke around. The organization of meaning is implicit in the organization of the action-sequences of the relational dialogue and does not require reflective thought or verbalization to be known. The various procedural action patterns of mother–infant interaction constitute the first form of implicit relational knowing. Procedural forms of knowing are intrinsic to many forms of skilled action, including intimate relating. Echoing Bucci (1985), Lyons-Ruth (personal communication, August 17, 1999) suggests that we conceptualize the implicit and the explicit (*roughly* the verbal and the nonverbal) as organized in parallel, as separate organizing principles that can nevertheless influence each other. Consistent with other authors such as Schore (1994), Pally (2000), and Grigsby and Hartlaub (1994), Lyons-Ruth (1999) declares that ". . . development does not proceed only or primarily by moving from procedural coding to symbolic coding" (p. 579). Instead, Lyons-Ruth conceptualizes development, and developmental change in psychoanalysis, as an increasing differentiation and integration of implicit relational procedures for being with others,

---

different shades of facial expression within the same affect, which cannot be made discrete or categorical; (2) presymbolic categories or prototypes that are "chunked" or discrete but are nevertheless concrete and visceral, not yet symbolized, such as an infant's discrimination of gender, or action-sequences of intrusion and withdrawal; and (3) discrete, symbolized, verbalizable categories, and a verbal organization that can differentiate, negate, generalize, and reorganize categories.

in a wide range of emotionally charged contexts. A parallel development takes place in the explicit mode. Lyons-Ruth (1999) notes that the nature of the organization of implicit relational knowing is extremely sensitive to the quality of participation by the relational partner. Yet there is very little literature on *how* implicit relational procedures become reworked, or increasingly articulated and complex in adult treatment (but as exceptions see Grigsby and Hartlaub 1994, Sorter 1994). Our goal in the illustration of an adult treatment in Chapter 4 is just such a description.

Implicit forms of knowing begin in infancy, through the development of expectations of action-sequences. A considerable literature describes the infant's capacity to construct expectations of action-sequences, which are then represented in a presymbolic, procedural format (Emde et al. 1991, Fagen et al. 1984, Haith et al. 1988, Shields and Rovee-Collier 1992, Stern 1985, 1995). This view of representation uses a constructivist and transformational model (Lewis and Brooks 1975, Reese and Overton 1970, Sameroff 1983).

In previous work we used the concept of patterns of expectation —the anticipation of the partner's pattern in relation to one's own— to define presymbolic representation in the first year (Beebe and Lachmann 1988, 1994, 2002, Beebe and Stern 1977, Beebe et al. 1997, Stern 1977, 1985, 1995). Both infant and adult partner generate patterns of expectation, constructed through the *sequence* of one's own actions in relation to that of the partner (patterns of coordination), and an associated self-regulatory range and style. For example, learning the regulation of dialogic timing patterns (Jaffe et al. 2001) involves learning when to vocalize, when to pause and for how long, whose turn it is, when to join in simultaneously (coactive speech), and how to exchange turns. Furthermore, it involves coming to expect *how the dyad* coordinates these rhythmic patterns. Variations in the coordination of these timing patterns between mother and infant at 4 months predict infant attachment and cognition at one year. These are lifelong forms of procedural knowing that begin in infancy, but eventually operate parallel to, and intersect with, linguistic forms of knowing.

DYADIC SYSTEMS MODEL OF INTERACTION

We use a systems approach most generally to refer to a view that construes the (dyadic) system to be the most basic unit of interest, within which both interactive regulation and self-regulation can be defined, each affecting the other (Beebe and Lachmann 2002, Beebe et al. 1992, 2000, Jaffe et al. 2001, Sander 1977, 1995, Tronick 1989). This view links the individual to the dyad, emphasizing what Beebe and Lachmann (1998) have called the "co-construction" of inner and relational processes. In a dyadic systems view of communication, each person's behavior is created in the process of joint coordination.

To address the central issue of documenting that each person does indeed "affect" the other, or "communicate" with the other, we use the concept of bidirectional (or "mutual") regulation. Bidirectional regulation refers to a two-way, reciprocal process in which each person's behavior can be statistically *predicted from* (and in this sense is "influenced" by) the behavior of the partner. We use the term coordination as a synonym to regulation. We prefer the term "bidirectional" to "mutual" to avoid any implication of positive mutuality, since bidirectional regulation occurs equally in aversive as well as positive interactions. The concept of bidirectional regulation carries no causal implication, but rather is probabilistic. Such regulation can, and often does, occur entirely out of awareness. At the nonverbal level of action-sequences, at every instant, any action in a dyadic relationship is jointly defined by the behavior of both partners (Jaffe et al. 2001). Thus, psychologically, "individuals" do not exist apart from the totality of their interpersonal relationships (see also Sullivan 1940, Winnicott 1965).

Winnicott's (1965) famous remark, "There is no such thing as an infant" (p. 39), is analogous to Sullivan's similarly famous phrase, "the myth of personal identity." Winnicott and Sullivan, among many authors both within and outside of psychoanalysis, participated in building a relational systems approach to the understanding of the person, in which "individuals" do not exist apart from the totality of their interpersonal relationships (for example

Bowlby 1969, Fairbairn 1952, Kohlberg 1969, Lewin 1935, Piaget 1954, Reese and Overton 1970, Sander 1977, Spitz 1963, Werner and Kaplan 1963; and recently Aron 1996, Bromberg 1998, Ghent 1989, Harris 1992, Mitchell 1997, 2000, Stolorow 1997, Stolorow and Atwood 1992). This relational systems approach contrasts sharply with an alternative view, also very influential in the twentieth century, that the individual is fundamentally alone, and is drawn into interactions and relationships, a position that Stolorow and Atwood (1992) term the "myth of the isolated mind." Overton (1994) suggests that the latter view splits the relational matrix into separate independent individuals, and then searches for the glue that puts them together; the former begins with the relational matrix as a system, in which each component affects and is affected by the other.

Figure1–1 illustrates the core of our theory of interaction. Moment-by-moment each person "influences" or coordinates with the other. And moment-by-moment each partner regulates arousal and inner state: threshold, intensity, activation, dampening, self-soothing. In the adult, self-regulation also refers to defenses and fantasies and unconscious fantasies. The arrows refer to "predictability" or "regulation," indicating recurrent nonrandom patterns, within the individual and between the partners (Beebe and Lachmann 1994, 1998, 2002, Tronick 1989). The dotted lines represent the *history* of the interactive- or self-regulation patterns. How each person self-regulates affects the process of how the interaction goes, and vice-versa. Each process is "emergent" from the other: inner and relational processes are co-created in tandem. In Fogel's (1993) description of a systems model, all behavior is simultaneously unfolding in the individual, while at the same time each is modifying and being modified by the changing behavior of the partner.

Figure 1–2 illustrates the application of our systems view of interaction to adult psychoanalysis. The top half of the drawing at the level of "explicit" processing illustrates the usual verbalizable symbolic narrative, from which both conscious and dynamically unconscious processes are inferred. On a parallel track, the bottom

- Infant   Interactive   Mother
- Self-Regulation   Regulation   Self-Regulation

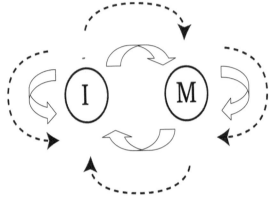

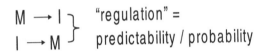

$M \rightarrow I$
$I \rightarrow M$ $\bigg\}$ "regulation" = predictability / probability

FIGURE 1-1. A Systems Model of Interaction.

Arrows indicate predictability ("coordination," "regulation" or "influence") between partners. Dotted arrows represent the history of the pattern of predictability.

M $\longrightarrow$ I indicates that mother behavior in the previous few seconds predicts infant behavior in the current second;

I $\longrightarrow$ M indicates that infant behavior in the previous few seconds predicts mother behavior in the current second.

$\longrightarrow$ Regulation is present

- - - -▶ History of the regulation process

Reprinted with permission from Beebe, B., and Lachmann, F. (2002). *Infant Research and Adult Treatment: Co-constructing Interactions.* Hillsdale, NJ: Analytic Press. p. 27.

half illustrates the level of "implicit" processing which is nonconscious or out of awareness. These are the interactions of looking, facial mirroring, vocal rhythm, spatial orientation, touching, self-touching, and so on. Although both explicit and implicit processing affect the psychoanalytic encounter at every instant, psychoanalysis

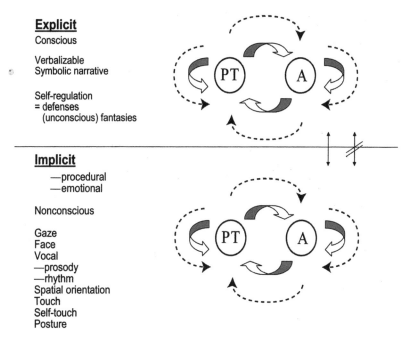

FIGURE 1–2. Interaction in Adult Treatment Illustrating Explicit and Implicit Processing.

Arrows indicate predictability ("coordination" or "influence") between partners. Dotted arrows represent the history of the pattern of predictability. The arrow between the explicit and implicit realms indicates that, when necessary, the implicit and explicit systems can be translated back and forth; the broken arrow between the two realms indicates that, in some difficulties of communication, this translation is disrupted.

⟶ Regulation is present

- - - → History of the regulation process

Reprinted with permission from Beebe, B., and Lachmann, F. (2002). *Infant Research and Adult Treatment: Co-constructing Interactions.* Hillsdale, NJ: Analytic Press. p. 35.

has primarily conceptualized the former and not the latter. An integration of the two kinds of processing within psychoanalysis requires an integration of two very different theories. The explicit level refers most generally to the idea that conscious and unconscious symbolic representations of self and object organize experience. The implicit level refers to the idea that the control or regulation of behavior is in the moment-to-moment interaction itself, through self- and interactive regulation (Beebe and Lachmann 1998, 2002, Lyons-Ruth 1998, 1999).

This systems model of interaction can be used as a lens for comparative analysis of recent theories of adult intersubjectivity. This way of viewing a particular theory facilitates a comparative examination of the key routes of influence and central moments of regulation that are emphasized as mutative. This schematic approach articulates only the bold strokes of a theory, and of necessity loses finer-grained distinctions. Nevertheless it is useful in clarifying where each of the theorists may differ. Although all of the theorists reviewed below appreciate the contribution of both partners to the psychoanalytic exchange, as well as the contribution of each partner's self-regulation, which aspects of the process are *relatively more emphasized* as central to therapeutic action? We pull out these relative emphases as points of distinction for purposes of comparison only, without any implication that other dimensions of these theories are not also important or even central. The points of difference in these adult theorists, when taken together, can expand and enrich the meaning of intersubjectivity in psychoanalysis. We endorse Ogden's (1994) suggestion that "Our goal is . . . to escape the pitfalls of ideology and to learn from our . . . efforts at thinking within the context of different systems of ideas that together, constitute psychoanalysis" (p. 103).

ILLUSTRATIONS OF INTERACTION AND FORMS OF INTERSUBJECTIVITY IN THE PSYCHOANALYTIC THEORIES OF JACOBS, EHRENBERG, AND OGDEN, BASED ON MITCHELL'S (1997) DESCRIPTION

To illustrate different theories of interaction underlying varying current views of intersubjectivity in psychoanalysis, we draw on Mitchell's (1997) comparative analysis of varieties of theories of interaction, in which he emphasized that there are many authentic modes. He described "prototypical features" of the "clinical tales" (p. 145) of Theodore Jacobs, Darlene Ehrenberg and Thomas Ogden to characterize the different kinds of interaction and self-experience that each brings to the analytic process. We use Mitchell's descriptions here without attempting to evaluate or comment on their relative accuracy.

<u>Jacobs.</u> Mitchell (1997) suggests that Jacobs (1991a,b), working primarily within the Freudian perspective, uses enactments as the point of entry and "illustrates the ways in which the analyst comes to know and understand the patient's childhood conflicts through the evocation of parallel childhood conflicts in the analyst" (p. 147). Features of the patient's dynamics are mirrored in the analyst's dynamics, a parallel process captured in Jacobs's image of interaction as two swimmers. The analyst thus enters the patient's experience most powerfully through the affects, conflicts, and self states from the analyst's past. He uses his own experience to reach the patient, but for the most part he does not share his countertransference. Jacobs (personal communication, May 5, 2002) notes that, although Mitchell's description is accurate for the material Mitchell had available, in his current approach Jacobs does at times reveal and discuss countertransference.

We illustrate Jacobs's view of interaction in Figure 1–3. The line representing the patient's impact on the analyst is darkened far more than the reciprocal route of the analyst's impact on the patient. Thus the greater relative emphasis in Jacobs's model is the impact of the patient on the analyst. The dotted line depicts the history of the patient's impact on the analyst. The line representing the analyst's own self-regulation process, and particularly the dotted line representing the *history* of the analyst's own past modes of inner regulation, are darkened far more than the patient's own self-regulation process.

<u>Ehrenberg.</u> Mitchell (1997) suggests that Ehrenberg (1992), working from the interpersonal perspective, "seems very much grounded in the present. . . . In reading Ehrenberg, we learn nothing about her childhood and family, but a great deal about her personal reactions to her patients, what it feels like to be her in their presence" (pp. 148–149). Mitchell (1997) describes Ehrenberg as seeking intense engagement, a heat or intensity, in the here-and-now.

MODELS OF INTERACTION IN PSYCHOANALYSIS

Jacobs

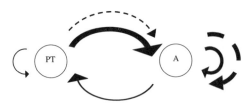

Enactments as point of entry. Patient evokes in analyst memories, affects, conflicts from analyst's past. Analyst does not share countertransference.

Ehrenberg

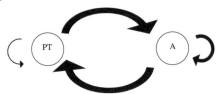

Analyst seeking intense engagement in present. Analyst uses her own feelings about the patient, and her own reactions (desire, threat, burdened, deadened, punished), and shares her reactions with the patient. Present emphasized over past.

Ogden

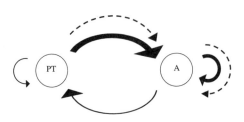

Patient initiates projective identification. Analyst recipient and container of patient's deepest pathology (especially deadness). Analyst's own inner states (associations, somatic sensations) are key. Analyst struggles to symbolize own inner states, communicate to patient in words.

—Verbal descriptions from Mitchell 1997,
Influence and Autonomy

FIGURE 1–3. Models of Interaction in Psychoanalysis: Jacobs, Ehrenberg, and Ogden.

Note: ⟶ Regulation is present

⟹ Regulation is emphasized

- - -▶ History of the regulation process is emphasized

▬ ▶ History of the regulation process is emphasized to a greater degree

Reprinted with permission from Beebe, B., Knoblauch, S., Rustin, J., and Sorter, D. (2003). Introduction: A Systems View. *Psychoanalytic Dialogues* 13(6): 743–775.

Her image of interaction is one of boundaries and edges, particularly her metaphor of the "intimate edge." She is concerned with
what the partners expect of each other, the awakening of desire,
longing, and threat. She uses, and at times discloses, her own reactions of feeling ignored, burdened, punished, deadened, humored,
or distracted, to reach and to understand the patient. Figure 1–3
depicts equal darkened lines representing the patient's impact on
the analyst, and the analyst's on the patient, in Ehrenberg's model.
In addition, the line representing the analyst's own self-regulation
process is darkened, but not that of the patient. The dotted lines
representing the history of these patterns are not depicted.[2]

Ogden. Mitchell (1997) suggests that Ogden (1994, 1995),
working from an object relations perspective, describes ". . . a form
of analytic participation entailing an exquisite emotional presence
and reactivity that, for extended periods of time, is largely silent. . . .
The patient . . . has (dissociated, presymbolic) thoughts but no
voice with which to speak them; has experiences, but no subjectivity to know them in. The analyst . . . surrenders his subjectivity
to the process, emptying it to some extent, so that it can receive,
process, and bring to life the voiceless experience of the author"
(pp. 152–153). The analyst surrenders himself to the patient's deepest pathology: rage, isolation, and especially deadness. Ogden's
image of interaction is one of interpenetrating permeability. In
Ogden's (1994) words, "You . . . must allow me to occupy your
thoughts . . . I must allow myself to become your thoughts . . ."
(p. 1). In this process, the two partners jointly create something
new, emergent: "the intersubjective third." The analyst's own ability
to evoke, contain, and transform the patient's nonsymbolized and
dissociated states into symbolized communications is a central form
of therapeutic action relatively more emphasized by Ogden. In this
way Ogden emphasizes the analyst's own self-regulation process:
his inner states, associations, somatic sensations, and reveries.

---

2. Ehrenberg (personal communication, April 14, 1999) notes that she uses
the history of her own experience, as well as that of the patient, more than Mitchell
(1997) suggests in his description of her theory.

We note that Aron (1996) also describes Ogden (1982, 1986, 1989, 1994) as emphasizing the dialectical nature of intersubjectivity, but critiques Ogden for not holding a view of analytic participation as mutually influenced from the beginning. Aron notes that Ogden gives the impression that his own subjectivity is reactive to the patient.

Figure 1–3 depicts Ogden's model of interaction with a darkened line representing the patient's impact on the analyst, but the reciprocal line of influence from analyst to patient is not darkened. It is present, but does not carry as much emphasis. The history of the patient's influence on the analyst is also represented in the dotted line from patient to analyst. Similar to the drawing for Jacobs, the line representing the analyst's own self-regulation process is darkened far more than the patient's own self-regulation process. However, for Ogden, the analyst's current self-regulation process is more darkened than the dotted line representing the *history* of the analyst's past modes of inner regulation; whereas for Jacobs, the history of the analyst's self-regulation carries just as much weight as the current process of self-regulation.

ILLUSTRATIONS OF INTERACTION AND FORMS OF INTERSUBJECTIVITY IN THE PSYCHOANALYTIC THEORIES OF BENJAMIN AND STOLOROW AND COLLEAGUES

To continue our illustration of different theories of interaction underlying varying current views of intersubjectivity in psychoanalysis, in Mitchell's (1997) spirit of arguing that there are many authentic modes, we draw on comparative analysis of Jessica Benjamin (1988, 1992, 1995, personal communication, July 20, 1998) and Robert Stolorow and colleagues (Stolorow 1997, Stolorow and Atwood 1992, Stolorow et al. 1987, personal communication, April 10, 2001) by Knoblauch and colleagues (1999). Although both Benjamin and Stolorow and colleagues work with a theory of interaction, they differ in their use of a systems approach and in their

MODELS OF INTERACTION IN PSYCHOANALYSIS

Benjamin

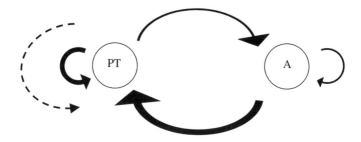

Mutual recognition is a dialectical process of negation and recognition of the other, expanding the sense of self for both. The patient's recognition of the analyst's subjectivity as separate and different is relatively more emphasized in the therapeutic action.

Stolorow et al.

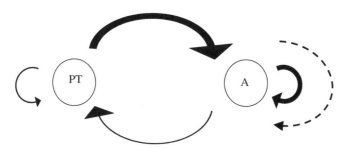

Continual process of mutual influence between two differently organized subjectivities. Analyst's experience of patient's subjectivity is central. Analyst resonates with patient's experience; patient comes to feel deeply understood.

FIGURE 1–4. Models of Interaction in Psychoanalysis: Benjamin and Stolorow et al.

Note: ⟶ Regulation is present
         ⟹ Regulation is emphasized
         - - -▶ History of the regulation process is emphasized

Reprinted with permission from Beebe, B., Knoblauch, S., Rustin, J., and Sorter, D. (2003). Introduction: A Systems View. *Psychoanalytic Dialogues* 13(6): 743–775.

definitions of interaction. Viewing each theorist within the lens of our systems model of interaction, the darkened lines show which routes of influence are relatively more emphasized by each theorist. Again we note that we pull out these relative emphases as points of distinction for purposes of comparison only, without any implication that other dimensions of these theories are not also important or even central.

Aron (1996) has also compared Benjamin and Stolorow and colleagues in their use of the concept of intersubjectivity. Aron sees Benjamin (1988, 1992, 1995) as using the term to describe a developmental achievement in which analyst and analysand mutually recognize the other's subjectivity. In Aron's view, Stolorow and colleagues (1987) use the term as synonymous with the principle of mutual regulation and unconscious influence. Although both Aron and Mitchell have made important comparative analyses (see also, for example, Frie and Reiss 2001, Gerhardt et al. 2000, Teicholz 1999), here we focus on the different uses of a systems approach and the different aspects of interactive experience emphasized by these two theorists of intersubjectivity.

Benjamin. Influenced by Winnicott, Hegel, and Mahler, Benjamin (1995) defines for psychoanalysis the task of mutual recognition: "both analyst and patient make known their own subjectivity and recognize the other's" (p. xii). The developmental process of *mutual recognition of self by other and other by self* defines Benjamin's interactive focus. Analyst and analysand construct a sense of being a subject through the dialectical process of identifying with and differentiating from the other, resulting in an expanded sense of self for both. When the patient recognizes the analyst's identification with her, that is an important step in differentiating the analyst from internal objects, the "new" from the "old" self–other experience. Working with developmental levels in the recognition process, in the earlier stages of the treatment Benjamin holds that the analyst's recognition of the patient's subjectivity is essential. But in the key mutative moment of therapeutic action, Benjamin places a greater relative emphasis on the patient's recognition of the analyst as an outside other with her own separate center of emotion and subjectivity, not under the patient's control, although both analyst and patient must struggle to do this. The recognition and acceptance of the other as a subject with his or her own independent center, goals, and desires, is quite different from simply accepting that other disappoints, or wins. The goal is the restoration of recognition after its breakdown, which includes re-establishing the tension between differences and sameness, negation and recognition. Such restoration increases the patient's sense of agency and ability to contain pain and loss. Although theoretically both the patient and the analyst participate in a recognition of the other in Benjamin's model, the patient's reorganization of recognition is relatively more emphasized than the reciprocal reorganization of the analyst's recognition.

Figure 1–4 depicts Benjamin's model of interaction with a darkened line representing the analyst's impact on the patient in the therapeutic action. The reciprocal line of influence from patient to analyst is present but not darkened: it does not carry as much emphasis (although in the developmental process of the treatment, this line of influence was initially central; see above). The recognition process can be conceptualized as a self-regulation process, as well as an interactive one, and the patient's reorganization of subjectivity in the recognition process is represented by a darkened line representing the patient's self-regulation. The dotted line, representing the history of the patient's self-regulation, is also depicted, to represent Benjamin's work with the history of the patient's difficulties in recognition. The line representing the analyst's self regulation is present but not darkened. Benjamin's model stands in contrast to the emphasis on the analyst's experience of his/her own subjectivity, and the emphasis on the patient's influence on the analyst, as described by Mitchell in Jacobs, Ehrenberg, and Ogden, noted above.

Stolorow and Colleagues. Influenced by Gadamer (1979), Murray's (1938) personology, and Tomkins's (1962, 1963) work on affect, Stolorow and his colleagues George Atwood, Bernard Brandchaft, and Donna Orange argue that the organization of experience is always embedded in, or contextualized, by a larger system, the "field." Their approach to interaction is the field, created by a continuous process of mutual influence between analyst and patient. Intersubjectivity is defined as the psychological field formed by an infinite variety of forms of interaction as two differently organized subjectivities collide, interface and impact the other (Stolorow 1997). In describing the key mutative process, Stolorow and colleagues (Stolorow and Atwood 1992, Stolorow, Atwood, and Brandchaft 1994), place greater relative emphasis on the analyst's experience of the patient's subjectivity, rather than the analyst's experience of his or her own subjectivity, or the patient's experience of the analyst's subjectivity. As the analyst conveys his experience of the patient's subjectivity, the patient comes to feel deeply understood. The analyst is influenced by the patient in grasping the patient's experience. The analyst then attunes or resonates with the patient's experience, which we draw as both a self-regulation function of the analyst and an interactive process. The analyst then communicates this resonance to the patient, a second mutative moment.

Figure 1–4 depicts Stolorow and colleagues' model of interaction with a darkened line representing the patient's impact on the analyst, but the reciprocal line of influence from analyst to patient is not darkened. It is present, but does not carry as much emphasis. The line representing the analyst's own self-regulation process in the present is also darkened (but not the history of this process). Figure 1–4 depicts the patient's reciprocal self-regulation process as present but not darkened.

Comparison of the theorists. Like Atwood and Stolorow's (1974) argument in their book *Faces in a Cloud*, each of these theorists brings a different history and lens to a conceptualization of the central dynamic of therapeutic action. Through mutual recognition, to be separate and recognized as different (Benjamin); through a mutual influence process and affect attunement, to be deeply understood (Stolorow et al.); to be understood through the parallel conflicts of analyst and patient (Jacobs); to be more fully alive through a new, mutually generated experience (Ogden); or to be able to be intensely reciprocally engaged in the present moment (Ehrenberg), are different themes of these theories of intersubjectivity. We suggest that they describe *different forms of intersubjectivity*. In addition, all emphasize different aspects of a theory of interaction. The advantage of working with a systems view of interaction is that all routes of self- and interactive regulation can be seen and held in mind. The broadest view is one in which all routes are potential routes of therapeutic action, at different times, with different patient–therapist dyads.

While all theorists described above conceptualize the significance of two subjectivities in interaction and the key importance of the dyad in relation to the individual, each emphasizes a different focus as central to therapeutic action. Benjamin emphasizes the patient's experience of the analyst's subjectivity. Stolorow and Jacobs emphasize the analyst's experience of the patient's subjectivity. Ogden emphasizes the analyst's experience of her/his own subjectivity. Ehrenberg emphasizes the analyst's and patient's experience at the "intimate edge" of intense engagement. We need an integration of all views for the broadest vision of forms of intersubjectivity in psychoanalysis.

On the basis of this brief review of various theories of adult intersubjectivity in psychoanalysis, we conclude that from theorist to theorist, different relational themes are emphasized and different routes of the dyadic systems view of interaction are accentuated. However, each theorist cited above works primarily with the analyst's and patient's capacity to symbolize and verbalize experience. The one exception may be Ogden, who also accords a central role to the sensation-based "autistic-contiguous" mode (but who does not work with any of the data of empirical infant research on the face-to-face exchange). Thus adult theories of intersubjectivity in general assume a symbolic mind and the dominance of explicit processing.

In contrast, theories of intersubjectivity in infant research work with an implicit, procedural dimension of communication, including gaze, facial configurations, spatial orientations, touch, posture, and the prosodic and rhythmic dimensions of vocalization. Furthermore, infant theories of intersubjectivity work with a presymbolic mind and implicit processing. We turn to this topic in Chapter 2.

Returning to a central theme of these four chapters, the complex, elusive, and potentially confusing meanings of the term "intersubjectivity" in psychoanalysis, we propose that there are three major sources of this confusion. First, this confusion stems from the varied definitions that each theorist (of infancy or adulthood) accords the term. Second, different theorists of adulthood and infancy use different aspects of the systems view of interaction. We have briefly illustrated varied definitions of the term intersubjectivity and different uses of the systems view of interaction in adult psychoanalytic theorists; Chapter 2 will review the same issues in the infant theorists. Third, this confusion has been confounded by the use of the identical term, intersubjectivity, to describe both the presymbolic and the symbolic mind, and different levels of symbolic development or "theory of mind" in the young child, to which we now turn.

LEVELS OF COGNITIVE DEVELOPMENT AND INTERSUBJECTIVITY

Presymbolic and Symbolic Forms of Mind

Forms of intersubjectivity are dependent on levels of cognitive development (see Lewis 1995, 1999). One fundamental difference in the meaning of the term intersubjectivity as used by adult as compared to infant theorists is the level of cognitive development assumed. A symbol has an arbitrary relation to its referent (Werner and Kaplan 1963). Symbolic forms of cognition begin toward the end of the first year (Mandler 1988, 1991, Piaget 1954). However, the rudimentary achievement of a symbolic intelligence is not completed until approximately age three, and many other transformations occur prior to adult forms of symbolic intelligence. An infant's presymbolic intelligence is organized around action schemes, and expectancies of how action and "inter-action" sequences unfold in time and space from moment-to-moment, with accompanying affect and arousal patterns (Beebe and Lachmann 1994, Mandler

1988, Stern 1985). Thus the perception of correspondences and behavioral matching described by the infant theorists in Chapter 2 is made possible by the mind of an infant who detects temporal and spatial features of stimuli, creates expectancies of how action sequences proceed from moment to moment, and has a rudimentary memory of these sequences.

In contrast, the adult theorists of intersubjectivity assume a symbolic mind capable of perceiving that the partner's mind is potentially organized differently from one's own. Whereas the infancy theorists focus on correspondences, as described in Chapter 2, for the adult theorists the perception and negotiation of the differently organized mind of the other is central, as we have seen above, and the role of correspondences is to varying degrees in the background.

Theory of Mind in Early Childhood

Although the above distinctions between presymbolic and symbolic forms of mind are critical to further distinctions in the way we use the term intersubjectivity, a further set of distinctions in early childhood "theory of mind" are equally essential. Research on theory of mind provides further distinctions in the child's developing symbolic capacity.

Research on the child's developing *theory of mind* shows that the capacity to appreciate the differently organized mind of the other develops only gradually over the first 4 to 5 years of age. As early as age 2, the child begins to have "inner state words" that refer to emotions (Bretherton and Beeghly 1982), indicating the initial capacity to reflect on the self. There is a growing consensus that children as young as 3 begin to develop a "theory of mind," where they distinguish between internal mental phenomena and external physical and behavioral phenomena, and use theories to explore and predict people's actions and mental states (Flavell 1988, Flavell et al. 1991, Gopnik 1990, Gopnik and Meltzoff 1997, Wellman 1990). However, 3-year-olds have difficulty in understanding that beliefs can misrepresent reality. Wellman (1990; see also Flavell et al. 1991) describes the 3-year-old's model of mind as a "copy-container model" that passively copies reality. In contrast, children of ages 4 to 5 have a more "constructivist" model of mind, in which the mind is seen as actively and sometimes inaccurately interpreting or constructing reality.

In a typical experiment, the child is presented with what looks like a box of candy. But inside there are crayons. The child is asked, What will the next child think? Whereas a 5-year-old answers, "Candy," a 3-year-old answers, "Crayons." Goldman (1989) suggests that 3-year-olds have trouble imagining mental states that contradict their own current mental states, and thus exhibit difficulty with the false belief tests. By contrast, 5-year-olds can imagine having the beliefs and desires of another person, and they can mentally simulate that person's feelings and behaviors. Five-year-olds understand that individuals may perceive an object in different ways, depending on their line of sight (Piaget 1954). They also recognize that beliefs dictate a person's emotional reactions to particular situations, such as expressions of surprise at discovering crayons in a candy box (Gopnik 1990). Different explanations of these evolving capacities have been proposed (Baron-Cohen 1991, Gopnik and Meltzoff 1997). For example, one viewpoint is that 4- and 5-year-olds change their theory of mind due to the emergence of the ability to reason first from one perspective, and then from another incompatible perspective, thus recognizing the possibility of different organizations, or multiple perspectives that do not easily resolve (Flavell 1988, Flavell et al. 1991, Frye et al. 1995, 1998). Despite differences in experimental design and views on exactly which capacities emerge at which age, there is extensive evidence and agreement that not until a period distinctly later than infancy do children develop the capacities necessary for grasping that minds are perspectival and subject to error.

If the child's theory of mind does not become sufficiently "constructivist" to be able to reason about incompatible perspectives on the same object until approximately age 5, then the recognition of differently organized minds is not possible until this point.

Thus forms of intersubjectivity that could be constructed in the mind of a neonate, as described by Meltzoff or Trevarthen, or toward the end of the first year, as described by Stern, presented below in Chapter 2, are profoundly different from the forms of intersubjectivity that might be possible for a 5-year-old, or an adult. Presumably many other transformations of the symbolic mind, most notably the logical operations of adolescence described by Piaget (1954), contribute to the adult's capacities to perceive and appreciate a differently organized mind. Lewis (1995, 1999; see also Ruesch and Bateson 1951) suggests the following distinctions: in the first year the infant is capable of "knowing"; in the second year, the toddler is capable of conceptualizing that "I know that I know"; by approximately age 5, the child can conceptualize "I know that you know (or I know that you do not know)"; and the adult can conceptualize "I know that you know that I know" (although perhaps this conceptualization is achieved in childhood; see Harrison 1998).

Thus, it is essential to define forms of intersubjectivity in relation to levels of cognitive development. Forms of intersubjectivity in the first year cannot make a contribution to one central issue of adult forms of intersubjectivity, that is, the perception of a differently organized mind at the symbolic level. This is a fundamental difference in the meaning of forms of intersubjectivity in infant research and adult psychoanalysis. However, as we will see in Chapter 3, infant research certainly can address a range of other issues in forms of intersubjectivity relevant to psychoanalysis. In the treatment case described in Chapter 4 we revisit the distinction between a "copy-container" vs. "constructivist" theory of mind.

In conclusion, as we have seen within adult theorists of intersubjectivity, and as we will next see within infant theorists, there is no one meaning for this complex yet central term. Due to the vast differences between a symbolic and a presymbolic mind, we discourage the use of the same term across infancy and adulthood, and instead we recommend the term *forms of intersubjectivity* within each realm. Psychoanalysis needs to conceptualize *forms* of intersubjectivity that distinguish between a presymbolic and symbolic mind, that distinguish between a "copy-container" vs. "constructivist" theory of mind in the child's emerging symbolic development, and that encompass both an explicit, symbolized verbal mode of processing and an implicit, procedural, and emotional mode. A broader conceptualization of intersubjectivity in psychoanalysis can be built on a dyadic systems view of interaction, where all potential routes of self- and interactive regulation can be seen and held in mind. The broadest view is one in which all routes are potential routes of therapeutic action, at different times, with different patient–therapist dyads.

Forms of Intersubjectivity in Infant Research: A Comparison of Meltzoff, Trevarthen, and Stern*

BEATRICE BEEBE, DORIENNE SORTER,

JUDITH RUSTIN, STEVEN KNOBLAUCH

In this second chapter we compare three theorists of intersubjectivity in infant research, Andrew Meltzoff, Colwyn Trevarthen, and Daniel Stern. We chose these three infancy theorists because they explicitly use the term "intersubjectivity" to describe their theories. Other infant researchers who have also used this term at times, but who do not use it as the central metaphor of their theories, such as Sander (1977, 1995) and Tronick (Tronick et al. 1977, 1980) are omitted from this review. Because we focus specifically on the concept of intersubjectivity, we also do not include more recent work by Stern in the context of the Boston Study Group on Change (Stern et al. 1998). By evaluating where Meltzoff, Trevarthen, and Stern concur and differ, our goal is to clarify the meanings or "forms" of intersubjectivity in infancy. In Chapter 3 we consider the relevance of these infant forms of intersubjectivity for adult forms of intersubjectivity in psychoanalysis.

---

*We acknowledge the contributions of George Downing and Regina Pally.

Trevarthen and Stern have been key figures in the tradition of microanalysis of film and videotape of mother–infant face-to-face interaction, with which they have addressed infant representation and an infant "theory of mind." Coming from an experimental tradition, Meltzoff has studied infant imitation behavior as a basis for inferences about the origins of representation and "self." All three have addressed the question of how the infant could sense the state of the other, and all have used the concept of crossmodal correspondences as a central aspect of the answer. Nevertheless each has a distinctly different theory of intersubjectivity in infancy.

MELTZOFF'S THEORY OF INTERSUBJECTIVITY IN INFANCY

Meltzoff has used imitation experiments in the first weeks of life to argue that infants are biologically prepared to perceive crossmodal correspondences between what they see on the face of the partner and what they sense proprioceptively on their own faces. The infant's perception of correspondences between his own behavior and that of his partner provides the infant with a fundamental relatedness between self and other (Meltzoff 1985, 1990, Meltzoff and Gopnik 1993). In Meltzoff's view, the perception and production of similarity has a privileged position in the experience and representation of relatedness.

Meltzoff begins with the question of how the infant could develop a sense of self. Whereas self recognition is usually referred to static featural information, another key source of information about the self is spatio-temporal movement patterns. "The first, psychologically primary notion of self concerns not one's featural peculiarities but rather one's movements, body postures and powers" (Meltzoff 1990, p. 142). Adults are potentially social mirrors: they can see themselves in the actions of others. Infants similarly have the capacity to recognize that movements in the other are "like me."

Meltzoff has done a series of experiments at varying infant ages to test this thesis. For example, at 14 months the infant looks more, smiles more, and shows more test-explore behavior toward the adult who imitates, compared to another adult who is making child-like gestures but not imitating. The idea that imitation of others is critical to the development of the self has a long history (Baldwin 1902, Mead 1934). In Meltzoff's view, imitation is a process by which something of the other is taken on by the self. The infant's ability to imitate novel as well as familiar behaviors, after a lengthy delay, was termed "deferred imitation" by Piaget (1954), who used this behavior as an index of the infant's representational capacity. Whereas Piaget argued that this ability was not available until 16 months, Meltzoff has documented the capacity for deferred imitation at 9 months, and even as early as 6 weeks (Meltzoff and Moore 1994, 1998). Like Piaget, Meltzoff is interested in the implications of imitation for representation. Unlike Piaget, Meltzoff believes that neonatal imitation proves that (presymbolic) representation begins at birth.

The younger the age at which Meltzoff has been able to demonstrate some rudimentary form of imitation, the more remarkable. The earliest age that he has tested is 42 minutes after birth. At 42 minutes the infant watches a model while he sucks on a nonnutritive nipple, so he could not possibly imitate while he watches. The model poses a gesture, such as opening the mouth or sticking out the tongue. The nipple is now taken out of the infant's mouth. Over the next 2½ minutes the infant progressively makes gestures increasingly similar to that of the model.

Meltzoff has used his imitation studies to argue that the infant has the capacity to detect correspondences between his own actions and those of a model. How is this possible? The mechanism is crossmodal matching: the infant maps what he sees onto what he feels proprioceptively with his face. The infant can translate between environmental stimuli and inner states, detecting matches, from the beginning of life. The infant can use the adult as a target against which to match an ongoing movement pattern. Meltzoff believes that this capacity yields the first sense in the infant that "you are like me." In Meltzoff's terms, this is the first origin of presymbolic intersubjectivity: the state of being while intentionally trying to match. The apprehension that the other is similar to the self constitutes the origins of a theory of mind, in Meltzoff's view: other persons have states similar to one's own.

In the imitation experiment at 42 minutes after birth, during the 2½ minutes that the infant is given to respond, there is a gradual increase in the success of the matching. Meltzoff uses this gradual increase in matching to argue that the imitation is far from reflexive. Instead the imitation is intentional, goal-corrected, and mediated by memory. If so, the infant is comparing a motor action against an internal memory, schema, or *representation* of what was previously seen. The infant monitors and modifies her own actions so as to match the model increasingly well.

In pursuing the argument that the infant *represents* what she sees, Meltzoff and Moore (1994) tested 6-week infants in the same experiment, where an experimenter exposed them to several facial displays, but now required them to imitate after a 24-hour delay. When the infants returned one day later, the experimenter sat in front of them with a neutral face. The infants first stared at the experimenter, and then gradually made successive efforts to make the same facial displays as they had seen the day before. "These studies suggested that imitation can be mediated by a representation of the now-absent acts" (Meltzoff and Moore 1998, p. 56).

Meltzoff suggests that in forming these presymbolic representations, the infant encodes the visual-spatial-temporal events of human actions of self and other in a nonmodality-specific representational code. All modalities speak the same language from birth. The social partner may be processed through one modality (for example visual image of experimenter's face), but is accessible to the self in another modality (proprioceptive sensations of one's own facial movements). The *perception* as well as the *production* of human action are both represented within the same framework. The infant maps the visually perceived behavior of the partner onto his own motor plans. *Thus the other is accessible to the self through crossmodal correspondences. The infant appreciates self–other correspondences from birth.* This is the core of Meltzoff's theory of the origins of intersubjectivity and representation. Meltzoff's concept that the infant maps the visually perceived behavior of the partner onto his own motor plans may well be validated by the discovery of "mirror neurons," described below in the discussion section.

Since both parent and infant recognize these correspondences, they provide a common language, and special moments of connection. Correspondences have their own motivational significance: both partners enjoy these moments. Meltzoff describes the parent's intention to participate in these exchanges as selective, interpretive, and creative. They are an essential aspect of parental "scaffolding" (Bruner 1977, 1986, Vygotsky 1962).

One critical aspect of Meltzoff's argument is that the perception of correspondence has a privileged status in the experience of human relatedness, providing a fundamental relatedness between self and other (Meltzoff 1985, 1990). It provides the first sense that "you are like me" in form, and in timing. The other is thus *directly accessible* to the self through proprioceptive perception of crossmodal correspondences. Self and other can be related because their bodily actions can be compared in commensurate terms: I can act like the partner and the partner can act like me (Meltzoff and Moore 1998). Thus Meltzoff's work provides a way of conceptualizing how both infant and partner can sense the state of the other, through the perception of correspondences.

Meltzoff's work is important in another way as well. His explication of mechanisms of matching is relevant to all the studies of face-to-face interaction in the first half of the first year, the lionshare of which are involved in demonstrating some form of correspondence in timing or spatial format. Although many analyses are uni-modal, for example vocal rhythm coordination or facial-visual engagement, in the actual interaction all modalities operate at once as a "package," and thus all information is potentially crossmodal. His mechanism of crossmodal mapping of correspondences can help explain the intense affective involvement that matching interactions such as facial mirroring and vocal-rhythm matching generate, since both mother and infant receive both modalities of information at once.

Finally, Meltzoff has played a central role in the documentation and conceptualization of a neonatal form of presymbolic representation. His work builds on Piaget, but also provides a radical critique: rudimentary representational formats are available at birth, rather than at the end of the first year. Meltzoff's experiments have changed our concepts of the origin of mind.

TREVARTHEN'S THEORY OF INTERSUBJECTIVITY IN INFANCY: A "PSYCHOLOGY OF MUTUALLY SENSITIVE MINDS"

Trevarthen is as interested in neonatal imitation as Meltzoff is. He cites many authors working in the area of neonatal imitation (for example, Field 1981, Heimann 1989, Kugiumutzakis 1985, 1993, Maratos 1982, Meltzoff and Moore 1977, Nagy and Molnar 1994, Uzgiris 1981). Trevarthen (1998) describes in detail the work of Nagy & Molnar (1994) who found that newborns a few hours old may readily imitate tongue protrusion, mouth opening, lip protrusion, smiles, a surprise expression, and hand and finger movements. If the partner waits after eliciting tongue protrusion, the baby will, after 2 or 3 minutes, poke out his tongue, or "provoke" (Nagy and Molnar 1994, Trevarthen 1998, Trevarthen, Kokkinaki and Fiamenghi 1999).

Trevarthen (1998) has argued that the work on neonatal imitation can provide the basis for a *"psychology of mutually sensitive minds,"* based on an "effective interpersonal intelligence" in the newborn. "It has generally been assumed . . . that human sympathetic consciousness is . . . an acquired skill. The new evidence from infancy [is] incompatible with this belief" (p. 15). On this basis, his "theory of innate intersubjectivity" was formulated: ". . . the child is born with the motives [capacity] to use the motives [behaviors] of the partner in 'conversational' negotiation of purposes, emotions, experiences and meaning " (p. 16; brackets added). Each partner can mirror the motivations and purposes of companions, immediately. Infants and their partners are thus in *immediate sym-*

pathetic contact" (p. 35). Thus, from a different route, Trevarthen came to the same conclusion as Meltzoff, that of an innate "intersubjectivity," with neonatal imitation the key form of evidence. But in Trevarthen's hands, this theory is more dyadic, having to do with communication between partners.

Trevarthen (1998) proposed, "The idea of infant intersubjectivity is no less than a theory of how human minds, in human bodies, can recognize one another's impulses, intuitively, with or without cognitive or symbolic elaborations" (p. 17). ". . . since the infant demonstrates the essential cooperative motives before speaking, the crucial awareness of the other's feelings and purposes regarding objects . . . comes without the intervention of words and language" (p. 1). He has argued that the core of human consciousness is the potential for rapport of the self with an other's mind. This potential is immediate, unrational, unverbalized, conceptless, and atheoretical: "A delicate and immediate with-the-other awareness" (Trevarthen 1993b, p. 122).

Trevarthen's ideas about innate human intersubjectivity as the foundation for the development of language are influenced by Ryan and Habermas. Ryan (1974) argued that children begin to speak by communicating states of mind and shared interests with familiar people. Impressed by "how mothers succeed in questioning, prohibiting, informing, encouraging or rejecting their infants before the latter can speak" (Ryan quoted by Trevarthen 1998, p. 35), Ryan proposed that *communicative competence is more fundamental and prior to language* (italics added).

Ryan was also influenced by Habermas, and Trevarthen (1998, p. 35) quotes Ryan (1974, p. 187) at length:

> Habermas (1970) argues that verbal communication cannot be understood only as an application of linguistic competence, limited by prevailing empirical conditions, but instead that the "structure of intersubjectivity" that makes such application possible has to be explained. Intersubjectivity between any speakers capable of mutual understanding is made possible by what he calls "dialogue constituent universals". . . . Whilst one

might query the explicitly linguistic nature of Habermas' dialogue universals, *his emphasis on the structure of intersubjectivity presupposed by successful speech is extremely important.* [italics added by Beebe]

Thus Trevarthen takes the position that intersubjectivity in infancy is initially preverbal. One implication is that linguistic forms of intersubjectivity are built on, and are influenced by, preverbal forms.

Trevarthen's research began around the same time as Stern's, and both initially used the same method, frame-by-frame analysis of 16 mm film of split-screen face-to-face interaction, where both partners are simultaneously visible. Numbers are printed on the top of each frame (24 frames = one second). This method allows the researcher to rock the reels of film back and forth over a small number of frames, across a second or two of time, to see exactly how the behavior of each partner unfolds in time, its precise onset and offset frame, as well as to see patterns of synchronization. Trevarthen began his research in 1967–1968 with Martin Richards at Jerome Bruner's Research Program on Intellectual Development at Harvard University, examining 16 infants from birth to 3 months. In 1968 he also worked with T. Berry Brazelton on the infant's differential response to persons vs. objects. In 1972 he presented microanalyses of film (see Trevarthen 1974, 1977, 1979) and argued that newborns were coherent in their behavior. He observed a precise coordination in time, synchronized to within 0.10 seconds, of lip and tongue movements, expressive head movements, eye movements, hand gestures, finger movements, and pointing. He suggested that "intrinsic rhythmicity is essential to the intercoordination observed in protoconversations" (Trevarthen 1998, p. 23).

Around the same time, 1969–1972, Catherine Bateson studied mother–infant vocal exchanges from films made by Margaret Bullowa. Bateson's first publication was in 1971, the same year as Stern's. Bateson described a pattern of alternating vocal exchanges and termed it "protoconversation." Trevarthen concurred with Bateson's argument that the infant's behavior was an innate emotional foundation for learning language, culture, and for making emotional bonds (see Dissanyake 1992, for an elaboration). Stern and colleagues (1975) argued that these vocal exchanges were coactive as well as alternating, providing the basis for two different functions, one organized through simultaneous exchanges (bonding, emotion, oneness) and the other through sequential, alternating exchanges (logic, language).

In what follows, the key mechanisms of interpersonal coordination proposed by Trevarthen are summarized:

1. *Infants possess an emotional and communicative brain at birth.* The capacity for communication is innate in the human brain: we possess an inherently dyadic "conversational" mind. Trevarthen (1998) holds that within a few weeks after birth, infants take up "direct face-to-face exchanges and effectively coordinate vocal, oral and gestural expressions" (p. 15). Influenced by the work of Holstege and colleagues (1997) and Damasio (1994) on the "emotional brain," Trevarthen (1993a,b; 1998) concluded that neonatal imitation and protoconversation prove that the human brain is formed to integrate expressive movements of eye, face, mouth, vocal apparatus, hand, and posture. The neonate brain is sensitive to corresponding movements and expression in a human conversational partner through temporal and morphological markers (Trevarthen 1998), a position very similar to that of Meltzoff.

An infant who is only a few months old has a remarkable range of perceptual capacities that allows for "imitative identification, emotional empathy and reciprocal communication that all humans possess" (Trevarthen 1993b, pp. 127–128). These capacities include binocular acuity; selective attention (Fantz et al. 1975); categories of objects (Bornstein 1985, Mandler 1988, Younger and Cohen 1985); memory of contexts for object recognition (Fagen et al. 1984, Shields and Rovee-Collier 1992); physical laws of objects with mass, such as above/below, container, or barrier (Mandler 1988); discrimination of face patterns (Field et al. 1982, Meltzoff 1990, Meltzoff and Moore 1977); and discrimination of musical and phonological parameters of sounds (Trehub 1990). By 6 months infants discriminate features of tempo, rhythm, melody, and key, and they can isolate musical invariants. In addition, Mandler (1988) has shown that infants perceive animacy, providing the infant with a primitive perception of agency, causality, and intentionality. Infants detect the "effort" or "vitality" of action (see also Werner 1948 who described "physiognomic perception" of the directedness, shape, and velocity of action).

2. *The basic dimensions through which intersubjective coordination occurs are time, form, and intensity*, which the neonate can perceive. Fundamental carriers of information about changes in the emotional and motivational state of the partner include "fine and rapid glides and leaps of pitch or volume of voice, eyebrow flashes, pre-beat syllables, suffix morphemes, rhythmic details and embellishments, rapid hand gestures, quick head moves, shifts of gaze . . . that appear in abundance in all spontaneous conversational communciation" (Trevarthen 1993b, p. 151). As evidence, Trevarthen (1993) cites Buck (1984), Duncan and Fiske (1977), Eibl-Eibesfeldt (1989), Kendon (1980), and Stern (1985).

Young infants are not conversational unless appropriate receptive invitations are given by the partner. Mother's expressive behavior is adapted to the multimodal perceptual readiness of the infant and conveys animacy, vitality, and energy. The movements of the mother "include the fundamental beat of repeating movement, short bursts of expression, repetition of rhythmic groups of movement, exaggerated dynamic expressive 'sentic' forms, and precise modulation of the intensity or force of expression in a moderate to weak range" (Trevarthen 1993b, p. 135). Predictable cycles of behavior become entrained on an adaggio beat, one per 700–800 milliseconds.

3. *The infant is aware of, and shows a preference for, contingent effects. The human brain is specialized for mutual regulation of joint action* (based on contingent effects). In a "dual prospective motor control," both partners anticipate in detail what the other will do. One translation of this concept is that the infant experiences being experienced. Here Trevarthen is very similar to Stern, as described below. An experimental confirmation of the mutual regulation model (see also Tronick 1989) was conducted with Trevarthen's

colleague Lynne Murray in her "re-play" experiment (Murray and Trevarthen 1985). Murray and Trevarthen first showed that normal 2-month-old infants and their mothers could communicate successfully in two separate rooms via closed-circuit TV of the other's live interacting face. Then both mother and infant were subjected to a "replay" of the partner from the normal interaction a few minutes before. In the replay condition both partners thus lost the normal moment-by-moment contingent responsiveness of the other, although each "seemed" to be interacting normally. In the replay condition, infants became distressed and avoidant, and mothers lost their usual empathic mode, becoming controlled, critical, and self-focused. Trevarthen (1998, p. 34) commented that *"normal happy protoconversational games need mutual awareness and purposeful replies, with both parties in immediate sympathetic contact"* (see also Tronick 1989, for a description of the "still-face" experiment). Emotions are regulators of interpersonal contact and relationships, not just state-regulators of the infant's self.

4. *The infant coordinates perception and action through a single time base*, a "neural conductor," mapped in the neurons, probably operating through the coupling of coordinated rhythmic oscillators. The pacemakers of motor systems are already coupled at birth, and all movements are played out in one time frame, "intersynchronized" (Poppel 1994). This coupling provides a physiological basis for endogenous coordination of perception and action in time, guided by environmental input, producing motor schemes and selection of sequences. The infant seeks information to direct and control actions and their effects. From birth the human brain is able to coordinate movements of trunk and limb with receptors capable of aiming the pickup of detailed information about objects (Trevarthen 1989). To illustrate this intercoordination of infant movements within a single time-base, Trevarthen (1998) described "prespeech" in a 7-week infant, "lip and tongue movements resembling adult articulation movements and coupled with expressive head movements, eye movements, and hand gestures . . ." (p. 27).

5. *The most basic mechanism of intersubjective coordination is matching of communicative expressions through time, form, and intensity,* across modalities. Patterns are entrained in time, imitated in form, and brought into register in intensity range. This intercoordination of inner states between subjects enables each to resonate with or reflect the other. The particular temporal-spatial-intensity patterns formed by the dyad will guide actions, tune each to notice and remember them, and affect learning and memory. "Reciprocity in rhythmic timing" and "equivalence of movement or mimetic sympathy" (matching of form) characterize protoconversation (Trevarthen 1998, p. 36).

6. *How does this "intersubjective matching" occur?* Trevarthen uses a theory of coupled rhythms to explain not only coordination within the infant, but also the infant's coordination with the partner. Just as timing is central to intrapersonal coordination, timing is fundamental to interpersonal coordination. Infants and adults share a common time base. They demonstrate similar autonomous periodicities, for example those of oculomotor saccades, or prereaching and reaching.

Trevarthen hypothesized that infant and adult coordinate behaviors through coupled pacemakers or neural clocks. Expressions become manifestations of an empathic awareness and mutual control. This awareness is based on a sensitivity to rhythmic patterns by some process that couples inherent pacemakers in each partner. Intercoordination depends on a common beat, assisted by mutual imitation and matching/complementarity. For short intervals, infants and adults can achieve mutually "entrained" close intercoordinations. (For a discussion of other modes of rhythmic coupling in infancy, see Jaffe et al. 2001.)

Influenced by Sperry (1952), von Holst and Mittelstaedt (1950), and Bernstein (1967), Trevarthen formulated the theory of intersubjectivity in terms of "intersubjective motor control by rhythmic expression, and the infant's innate sensitivity to kinematic, energetic, and physiognomic parameters of others' movements" (Trevarthen 1993b, p. 123). These parameters of movement are "transmodal features of motivation, coded as emotions." They are transferred from subject to subject via timing, intensity, and spatial configuration. This "permit[s] the intercoordination of inner psychological states between subjects" (Trevarthen 1993b, p. 126). Corresponding parameters (in timing, intensity, and form) in the two subjects "enables them to 'resonate with' or 'reflect' one another." Their patterns can become "entrained," brought into register, imitated. "These are the features that make possible . . . empathic communication . . . between infants and mothers" (Trevarthen 1993b, p. 126).

7. *Cerebral representation of self and other.* The process of matching in neonatal imitation "does not necessarily depend on body sensations caused by movement of the limbs or face, or comparison of seen and felt movement, but some kind of adjustment of the 'image' of a movement to be made, to that of a movement seen, must be taking place in the brain. In order to imitate, the infant must have a cerebral representation of persons" (Trevarthen 1998, pp. 28–29). Trevarthen (1984, 1998) hypothesizes a neural image of the expressive apparatus that can detect the species of affect in the other, while transmitting it to the perceiver's own motor system. Here Trevarthen is very close to Meltzoff.

Influenced by Braten's (1988) theory of the "virtual other," Trevarthen argues that the mapping of the infant's body into the infant's brain must also be able to reflect the action of the other person's body. "Now I would say that the cerebral 'representation' of the 'other' is rooted in a motor image (Sperry 1952, Di Pelligrino et al. 1992, Jeannerod 1994) sensitive to both the body-related form and the timing of the movement imitated, and in these respects indifferent to the sensory modality . . . A formal theory of *how intrinsic pacemakers coordinate* body part with body part prospectively, by reference to any or all forms of proprioceptive information . . . may offer a key to *the problem of what information is critical in intersubjective coordination*" (Trevarthen 1998, p. 29). Trevarthen's concept that the cerebral representation of the other is rooted in a motor image may well be validated by the discovery of "mirror neurons," described below in the discussion section.

8. *Primary and secondary intersubjectivity.* Trevarthen conceptualizes progressive levels of intersubjectivity, specifically defining "primary" and "secondary" intersubjectivity. The three fundamental facets of motives and emotions are self, other, and object. Whereas "primary intersubjectivity" refers to the coordination of self and other based on correspondences of form, timing, and intensity, "secondary intersubjectivity" includes an object, and refers to the intercoordination of self, other, and object based on the cooperative exchange of referential gestures. Secondary intersubjectivity develops at 9–12 months with the beginning of symbolic functioning (Hubley and Trevarthen 1979, Trevarthen and Hubley 1978). Trevarthen defines a developmental sequence from (1) protoconversation (primary intersubjectivity), to (2) games, to (3) cooperative awareness of persons and objects (secondary intersubjectivity). A critical shift occurs at 9–10 months, from game-playing to increased initiative-taking, to systematic combining of purposes to partner and object. Symbols are motivated by a co-orientation to people and to objective referents of potential joint interest, generating acts of meaning, rudimental demands, refusals, and inquiries. By 9–10 months, objects have permanence, self-awareness begins, and a theory of mind that includes other people emerges, accompanied by proto-language and specific attachment patterns. Like Meltzoff, for Trevarthen intersubjectivity begins at birth. Like Stern, Trevarthen reserves the origin of a theory of mind for the point at which a symbolic intelligence begins to emerge, toward the end of the first year.

STERN'S THEORY OF INTERSUBJECTIVITY IN INFANCY

Stern reserves the term intersubjectivity for a later point than Meltzoff and Trevarthen, toward the end of the first year. At approximately 9–12 months, Stern proposed that the infant discovers he has a mind, that other people have minds (see Bretherton and Bates 1979, Bretherton et al. 1981), and that inner subjective experiences are potentially shareable. This view of intersubjectivity is a theory of mind in an infant at the beginning of the transition to symbolic intellegence, and it contributes to our understanding of how symbols evolve out of presymbolic mentation. Intersubjectivity occurs at the point of a "quantum leap" (Stern 1985, p. 124) in development, when the infant can point, use gestures to refer to objects, begin to use words, and have the intention to communicate. The infant discovers that the focus of attention (look at that toy), feeling state (this is exciting), and intention (I want that cookie), can be *shared*. In Stern's view, this discovery constitutes a new organizing principle, a new subjective perspective that can be aligned with that of another to become "intersubjective."

Stern's theory of intersubjectivity is thus a view of how inner subjective states can be shared. Very different from Meltzoff and Trevarthen, in Stern's hands the domain shifts from overt behaviors to inner states. The infant perceives his own attentional focus, and that of the partner; these can be similar, or different. Building on the infant's previous ability to perceive a distinct, separate self and other, now a mental self and a mental other can be interfaced, aligned, or misaligned. The partner's alignment is now a direct subject in its own right. "What is at stake . . . is nothing less than the shape and . . . extent of the shareable inner universe" (Stern 1985, p. 151), what may become the subject matter of intimacy, and what may become linguistically encodable. In fact, psychic intimacy is first made possible by this developmental leap. What is not shareable may come to define "not-me" experiences.

Similar to Meltzoff, Stern argues that the infant's capacity to recognize crossmodal correspondences is the central mechanism allowing the infant to capture the quality of another's inner feeling state. However, very different from Meltzoff, Stern is interested in correspondences as a reciprocal dyadic process across time: *each is changing with the other*. This emphasis on the bi-directional influence process is similar to Trevarthen's and defines a critical point of difference with Meltzoff. Whereas Meltzoff privileges "form" information over that of timing, both Stern and Trevarthen consider time, as well as form, absolutely critical.

Stern, similar to Trevarthen, uses timing, form, and intensity to define the dimensions of correspondences. Stern is interested in the *how* of behavior, the dynamic, shifting patterns of rhythms, shapes, and activation. "Dynamic micro-momentary shifts in intensity over time that are perceived as patterned changes within ourselves and others" allow us, rather automatically and without awareness, to "change with" the other, to "feel-what-has-been-perceived-in-the-other" (Stern et al. 1985, p. 263). This view is very similar to that of Werner (1948) who used the term "dynamic-vectorial" to describe the quality of feeling conveyed by action patterns changing over time. Stern's concept of the infant's capacity to "feel-what-has-been-perceived-in-the-other" may well be validated by the discovery of "mirror neurons," described below in the discussion section.

Why does the infant take a quantum leap into intersubjective relatedness? Stern endorses three different viewpoints, all necessary. First, following Bates (1976), the infant discovers generative rules and procedures for interactions that lead to the discovery of intersubjectivity as an acquired social skill. Second, following Vygotsky (1962) and Newson (1977), the mother attributes meaning and interprets the infant's behaviors. Third, following Trevarthen and Meltzoff, intersubjectivity is an innate, emergent human capacity, based on a very highly developed special awareness of other humans. However, Stern quickly adds the caveat that not until 9–12 months can "true" intersubjectivity be said to exist. Here is Stern's most essential point of disagreement with Meltzoff and Trevarthen.

Stern defines three forms of intersubjectivity: joint attention, joint intention, and joint affect ("interaffectivity"). In describing joint *attention*, Stern notes that the infant's capacity to point and to follow the other's line of regard has been suggested by Bruner (1977) to constitute a critical means by which the infant can transcend egocentrism. In Emde's social referencing experiments, the infant is enticed by interesting toys to cross a glass table that is made to look like a "visual cliff." Infants hesitate, look back to mother, and cross only if mother's face indicates that it is safe. Stern suggests that this experiment portrays the infant's deliberate attempt to make sure that the focus of attention is being shared.

In describing joint *intention*, Stern is influenced by the work of Bates (1979, p. 36) who defined intentional communication as "signaling behavior in which the sender is aware, a priori, of the effect that the signal will have on his listener, and he persists in that behavior until the effect is obtained or failure is clearly indicated" (quoted by Stern 1985, p. 130). For example, the infant requests a cookie with an imperative prosody, and the infant attributes to the partner the capacity to understand the infant's intention: "inter-intentionality."

STERN'S THEORY OF AFFECT ATTUNEMENT

Stern suggests that the term intersubjectivity is too broad, covering interattentionality, interintentionality, and interaffectivity. He wants to specify affect attunement as a particular kind of intersubjectivity, specifically about interaffectivity. Of the three forms of intersubjectivity, joint affect, or "affect attunement," is the first and most important mode of sharing subjective experiences. Throughout the first year, affects are both the "primary medium and the primary subject of communication" (Stern 1985, p. 133). Not only interpersonal exchanges, but exchanges involving objects and intentions, are affective as well.

As an example of interaffectivity, Stern cites an experiment of MacKain and colleagues (1985) in which 9-month-old infants were briefly separated from their mothers, and then reunited. Right after the reunion, the infants were no longer upset, but they remained solemn. At this moment they preferred to look at a sad face than a happy face. They seemed to notice the congruence between their own affective state and the expression on the other's face. "One conclusion is that the infant somehow makes a match between the feeling state as experienced within and as seen 'on' or 'in' another, a match that we can call *interaffectivity*" (Stern 1985, p. 132). This position is the same as that of Meltzoff, with the exception that Meltzoff describes this capacity at birth.

What is Stern's evidence for affect attunement? Nine to 12-month infants were videotaped in the lab during a free-play session with their mothers. Coders first noted moments whenever the infant made some affect expression—facial, vocal, gestural, or postural. Coders then evaluated the mother's observable response, for verbal comments, imitations (defined as matching within the same modality), and attunements (defined as matching across modalities). Attunements were coded along the dimensions of matching: intensity, timing, and shape of the infant's behavior. Note that these dimensions are identical to those of interest to Trevarthen. Intensity was subdivided into absolute intensity and intensity contour (acceleration/deceleration). Timing was subdivided into beat (a regular pulsation is matched), rhythm (a pattern of pulsations of unequal stress is matched), and duration. Shape was illustrated by the infant's up-down movement of the arm matched by mother's up-down movement of the head.

The first finding was that, of all mother's responses, 33 percent were verbal comments, 19 percent were exact imitations of the infant's behavior, and 48 percent were considered attunements (occurring on average approximately once per minute). Second, in most attunements, more than one dimension of behavior was matched. Third, the dimension of intensity contour (profile of change in intensity over time) was the most frequent dimension of matching, occurring in 97 percent of attunements, and the dimension of timing the next most frequent, occurring in 76 percent. Stern coined the term "vitality affects" or "activation contours" to describe the feeling quality of *how* a behavior is performed. To illustrate an attunement, Stern described a 9-month-old girl excited about a toy. She reached for it, and as she grabbed it, she let out an "ahhhhh." Simultaneously with the "ahhhhh," mother did a shimmy, wiggling her body with the same activation as the infant's sound.

These data, together with his earlier work on younger infants (Stern 1971, 1977), consolidated one of Stern's most central contributions, that is, his emphasis on the micromomentary dynamic shifts in each person's behavior that allow the partner to *change with* the other. Affect attunement is thus defined as the crossmodal matching of intensity, timing, and "shape" (contour) of behavior, based on dynamic micromomentary shifts over time, perceived as patterns of change that are similar in self and other. The infant perceives a mental state in the other, based on the intensity, timing, and shape of the partner's behavior. Stern argued that the infant's capacity to recognize crossmodal correspondences is the perceptual underpinning of affect attunement, enabling the infant to capture the quality of another's inner feeling state, and to discriminate whether it is shared.

Stern's description of affect attunements as "automatic," with relative lack of awareness, places them clearly within implicit, procedural processing. Following the interaction, mothers were interviewed about their responses, while watching the videotape with the experimenter. Mothers judging themselves to be entirely unaware of their attunement behavior were 24 percent; only partly aware 43 percent; fully aware 32 percent. Even so, Stern argued that mothers were more aware of the desired consequences of their behavior than the behavior itself, and he concluded that the attunement process itself occurs largely out of awareness.

Stern also experimented with perturbing attunements, and showed that infants were indeed aware of attunements and affected by their perturbations. After viewing the videotape together, Stern and the mother "tailor-made" a perturbation, based on observation of a specific attunement to a frequent infant behavior. The mother agreed to play with the infant again, to pretend that she perceived the infant as, for example, less excited than he really appeared to be, and to slightly misattune accordingly. During the perturbation misattunements, the infant completely stopped playing and looked over to the mother. By contrast, in the first interaction, during ongoing natural attunements, infants simply continued to play without missing a beat.

In discussing the possible functions of attunements Stern differentiates between communication and communion. Examples of the functions of communication include: to imitate, to tune the baby up or down, to restructure the interaction, to reinforce, or to teach. Communing is something very different: to participate, *to share without altering,* to maintain the thread of feeling-connectedness. Affect attunement is a form of communing.

To demonstrate the potential power of attunements, Stern described two mother–daughter pairs playing in the same free-play set-up. Molly's mother tended to match when Molly was on the way up the crescendo of exuberance. Annie's mother tended to match when the bubble had just burst. Stern described the two styles as attuning to enthusiasm vs. "exthusiasm." Each style, when exaggerated, can introduce a selective bias, placing the opposite pole outside the "shareable universe."

It is important to note that Stern does not consider affect attunement equivalent to empathy, although both concepts share the phenomenon of emotional resonance. Whereas attunement occurs largely automatically and out of awareness, empathy requires the mediation of cognitive processes (see Basch 1977). "Attunement is a distinct form of affective transaction in its own right" (Stern 1985, p. 145) and need not proceed toward empathic knowledge.

Unlike imitation, attunement shifts the focus to the quality of feeling that is "behind" the behavior. It treats the feeling quality as the referent, and the overt behavior as one of several possible expressions of the referent. "Attunement takes the experience of emotional resonance and recasts that experience into another form of expression," by way of nonverbal metaphor and analogy (Stern 1985, p. 161). For example, the same level of exuberance might be expressed as a facial expression, a vocalization, or a gesture. All three overt behaviors would refer to the same inner state. Stern considers how perceptual qualities, such as forcefulness, crescendo-decrescendo, rhythm, or activation could be translated into feeling states. He uses Suzanne Langer's (1967) argument that the organization of the perceptual elements in art creates the "illusion" of "forms of feeling," such as vastness or being enclosed, calm or frenzy, advancing or receding. This translation of concrete behavioral dimensions of timing, form, and intensity in the mother–infant interaction into forms of feeling constitutes a significant step in the infant's development of symbolic capacity. Similar to the process when viewing art, we translate the acceleration, speed, and fullness of display of the other's gesture, facial expression, or vocalization into a feeling quality. This is a critical aspect of Stern's theory of intersubjectivity, and it differentiates him sharply from Trevarthen and Meltzoff, who remain at the level of behavioral correspondences. Affect attunement is a critical step on the way to symbolic capacity, organized toward the end of the first year.

Why is intersubjectivity and particularly affect attunement so powerful? Stern suggests that it contributes to attachment and a sense of security, and that it ushers in the capacity for psychic intimacy. The focus shifts from the mutual regulation of behavior to the mutual sharing of experience. Even minor failures in attunement can be experienced as ruptures in a relationship. Each individual learns that some subjective states are shareable, and some are not.

DISCUSSION OF THE THREE THEORISTS OF INFANT INTERSUBJECTIVITY

Meltzoff, Trevarthen, and Stern share a number of central tenets. All three attempt to conceptualize the origins of a theory of mind in infancy. For each, mind begins as a *shared* mind, and the central question is, how could the infant sense the state of the other? All three theories posit that the infant's perception of correspondence is the most central mechanism in the creation of intersubjectivity. The infant's capacity for crossmodal perception is seen as key in detecting correspondences, and in translating from one modality to another. All three conceptualize a highly complex presymbolic representational intelligence, a motivated and intentional (rather than reflexive) infant, capable of distinguishing self vs. environment at a perceptual level. And all three emphasize positive emotion, playfulness, intimacy, and bonding as an essential function of intersubjectivity. Nevertheless, each author has a distinctly different theory of infant intersubjectivity. Two points of difference stand out: the definition of correspondence/matching, and the theory of mind underlying infant intersubjectivity. In addition, the recent discovery of "mirror neurons" may validate key ideas of all three theorists, and may provide a way of further understanding the power of the perception of correspondences.

Definition of Correspondence/Matching

For Meltzoff the definition of correspondence rests on *form*: an imitation model. For Trevarthen, correspondence is defined by behavioral similarities in timing, form, and intensity. Stern uses the same criteria as Trevarthen, timing, form, and intensity, but elaborates these criteria in two important ways: (1) the similarities are crossmodal, rather than within modality, and (2) this crossmodal similarity allows each partner to infer *inner state*, rather than overt behavior.

Whereas Meltzoff uses an experimental paradigm, Trevarthen and Stern study quasi-naturalistic ongoing face-to-face communication. This important difference affects the definition of correspondence. Since Meltzoff studies the behavior of the infant within an experiment, his concept of correspondence is more static, and is by design primarily a one-person view, although he certainly acknowledges the importance of parent–infant imitation games. In contrast, Trevarthen and Stern study face-to-face *two-way communication*. They construe the dyad to be the unit of study, and their concept of matching is more process-oriented, emphasizing shifts over time. Stern and Trevarthen both operate within a mutual regulation model of communication, in which each partner affects the other, in the sense that each partner is predictable from the other, moment-by-moment. Meltzoff does not work within this mutual regulation model.

Theory of Mind

The three theorists hold rather different theories of mind. Meltzoff and Trevarthen describe a capacity for the perception of inter- subjectivity that they consider to be *innate:* a neonatal form of presymbolic representational intelligence. By contrast, Stern ar- gues that "true" intersubjectivity does not begin until the 9–12 month transition to the earliest stage of a symbolic form of intel- ligence. Trevarthen conceptualizes two stages, a neonatal "pri- mary" intersubjectivity, and a "secondary" intersubjectivity at the end of the first year. Thus two very different forms of mind are being considered by these three theorists: presymbolic, and rudimentary symbolic that begins toward the end of the first year.

In Meltzoff's hands, the origin of mind begins at birth with the perception, "you are like me." The key mechanism is the per- ception and production of similarity. The sense of self derives from one's own movements as seen in the actions of the other, and ac- tions of the other experienced proprioceptively as similar to one's own movements. Others have states similar to one's own. Meltzoff's imitation experiments powerfully present a case for the point of view that the infant in the first months of life has a presymbolic *representational* intelligence. This is a fundamental contribution.

Trevarthen and Stern, by contrast, see the origins of mind in the interactive process itself. For Trevarthen, patterns of movement, transferred from subject to subject via form, timing, and intensity, permit the intercoordination of inner psychological states; the key mechanism is the rhythmic coupling of these patterns of movement. From birth, the infant has an inherently emotional and communi- cative brain, a dyadic "conversational" mind.

Stern begins with views of the interactive process rather simi- lar to Trevarthen, but ends up with a very different theory. Because he posits that intersubjectivity begins at the critical shift toward symbolic functioning at the end of the first year, Stern emphasizes that the infant has a theory of *separate* minds. Two separate minds align to a third thing, an inner feeling state. The key mechanism of this alignment is a process of matching in which each partner is "changing with" the other. The crossmodal matching of form, timing, and intensity allows the infant to infer, by metaphor and analogy, forms of feeling "behind" the behavior. The infant detects whether or not the two separate minds are aligned to the same forms of feeling. Thus Stern's theory of intersubjectivity describes the origin of a symbolic mind. Meltzoff's and Trevarthen's theories of (primary) intersubjectivity describe the origins of a presymbolic mind.

The Role of Mirror Neurons in the Perception of Correspondences

The recent discovery of "mirror neurons" may increase our understanding of how the correspondences described by Meltzoff, Trevarthen, and Stern work at the neural level. One hot summer day the Italian researcher Rizzolatti, who was studying the premotor cortex in monkeys, took an ice-cream cone. A monkey nearby was watching. As Rizzolatti moved the cone to his mouth and began to lick it, the electrodes implanted in the monkey's premotor cortex became active (see Pally 1999, 2000). After many experiments, Rizzolatti and his colleagues concluded that a class of visual-motor neurons in the premotor cortex, which are active when a monkey performs a goal-directed action himself (such as reaching for an ice-cream cone), are also active when this monkey simply *observes* this same action in someone else (the researcher reaching for an ice-cream cone) (Rizzolatti 1994, Rizzolatti and Arbib 1998, Rizzolatti et al. 1995, Wolf et al. 2001). A number of researchers argue that humans share the mirror neuron system with monkeys in a homologous area, Broca's area, which is responsible for speech production (Fadiga et al. 1995, Grafton et al. 1996, Rizzolatti et al. 1996; see also Wolf et al. 2001). Rizzolatti and Arbib (1998) suggest that mirror neurons provide an "action-recognition" mechanism: the actor's actions are reproduced in the premotor cortex of the observer. Wolf and colleagues (2001) suggest that through mirror neurons, the observer has an enhanced capacity to recognize the intention of the actor. Pally (1999) puts it this way: I understand your intention by understanding what my own intention would be, if I were doing what you are doing.

Mirror neurons can be seen as a "biological correlate" (Wolf et al. 2001) of the correspondences described by Meltzoff, Trevarthen, and Stern. Each of these theorists, in different ways, had the insight that the infant appreciated correspondences between his own action and that of the partner, long before the discovery of mirror neurons. Meltzoff holds that the infant maps the visually perceived behavior of the partner onto his own motor plans, Trevarthen proposes that the cerebral representation of the other is rooted in a motor image, and Stern conceptualizes the infant's capacity to "feel-what-has-been-perceived-in-the-other." The language of Meltzoff and Trevarthen comes very close to that of mirror neurons. The discovery of mirror neurons may corroborate this insight, although the relevant research has not yet been conducted on infants. However, as important as the discovery of mirror neurons is, it does not address, or substitute for, the subtle differences in the ways the three theorists conceptualize how correspondences may work between infants and parents. All three theorists make important contributions to the understanding of how correspondences are played out in behavioral transactions, and how they may be understood by the infant.

3

An Expanded View of Forms of Intersubjectivity in Infancy and Their Application to Psychoanalysis*

BEATRICE BEEBE, JUDITH RUSTIN,

DORIENNE SORTER, STEVEN KNOBLAUCH

In this chapter we consider the relevance of forms of intersubjectivity in infancy to psychoanalysis. Our working assumption is that modes of preverbal communication documented in infant research can, by analogy, describe modes of "nonverbal" and implicit communication in adult treatment (see also Beebe and Lachmann 1998, 2002, Lachmann and Beebe 1996, Lyons-Ruth 1998, 1999, Pally 2000, Schore 1997, Stern et al. 1998). These modes of communication tend to be implicit, operating largely out of awareness (Lyons-Ruth 1998, Pally 1997a,b). Our intention is to explicate as well as to critique infant intersubjectivity and its relevance to psychoanalysis. Whereas Meltzoff, Trevarthen, and Stern have used infant research to define correspondence as the core of intersubjectivity in infancy, we build on this work to define a fourth position. Using a more neutral definition of intersubjectivity as

*We acknowledge the contributions of George Downing, Mary Sue Moore, Ken Feiner, Frank Lachmann, Lin Reicher, Doris Silverman, Emlyn Capili, Michael Ritter, Sara Markese, Marina Tasopoulos, and Lauren Cooper.

referring to what is occurring between two minds, rather than a more positive definition implying mutuality, we argue that the full range of patterns of interactive regulation provide the broadest definition of the presymbolic origins of intersubjectivity, with correspondence only one of many critical patterns. In addition we address the place of interactive regulation, problems with the concept of matching, the role of self-regulation, the role of difference, and the "balance model" of self- and interactive regulation. All forms of interactive regulation are relevant to the possibility of perceiving and aligning oneself with the moment-by-moment process of the other. A widened scope of the understanding of intersubjectivity in infancy will set the stage for a more fruitful exchange between infant research and psychoanalysis. Chapter 4 then applies these concepts to an adult treatment case.

First we address those ideas from the three theorists of infant intersubjectivity that have particular relevance for psychoanalysis. We highlight the dialogic origin of mind, the role of correspondences, and the idea that symbolic forms of intersubjectivity are built on presymbolic forms. In the second section, "Matching vs. the full complexity of preverbal communication," we develop our own position, that the reliance on the concept of matching/correspondence in the three theorists of infant intersubjectivity does not encompass the full complexity of the preverbal construction of experience. Additional concepts essential to the potential contribution of infant research to the nonverbal dimension of intersubjectivity in psychoanalysis are briefly reviewed: the place of interactive regulation, problems with the concept of matching, the role of self-regulation, the role of difference, and the "balance model" of self- and interactive regulation.

CONTRIBUTIONS OF MELTZOFF, TREVARTHEN, AND STERN RELEVANT TO PSYCHOANALYSIS

One central arena in which infant research *can* make an important contribution to forms of intersubjectivity in psychoanalysis is the appreciation of correspondences and matching, through the work of Meltzoff, Trevarthen, and Stern. First we address two key ideas important for psychoanalysis that the three infancy theorists share: the dialogic origin of mind and the power of correspondences in preverbal communication. We then pursue specific contributions of each of the theorists.

Shared Contributions of Meltzoff, Trevarthen, and Stern

Dialogic origin of mind. Meltzoff, Trevarthen, and Stern all endorse the position that mind begins as shared mind. The infant has multiple ways of sensing the state and process of the other in the early months of life. The origin of mind is seen as dyadic, dialogic, and (presymbolically) representational. This position has major implications for psychoanalytic theory: the organization of experience begins as dyadic and dialogic. In psychoanalysis the origin of mind has generally been based on reconstruction of what the adult patient might have experienced. The origin of mind has often been conceptualized within a one-person model, as an isolated mind, an autistic mind, or in other metaphors, a reflex arc or a seething cauldron, rather than a dyad in dialogue. Once shared mind is posited as the point of origin, the entire psychoanalytic theory of development shifts. The dyadic, dialogic origin of mind has much in common with Balint's (1992) primary object love, Bowlby's (1969) attachment model, and Sullivan's (1953) view of affect contagion in infancy. It is consistent with the position of relational theorists (Aron 1996, Mitchell 2000) that adult mind is dyadic and interactional, and with Stolorow and Atwood's (1992) "myth of the isolated mind," although the focus of these adult theorists is not on the *origin* of mind. Infant research adds to these psychoanalytic theorists, however, in the description of the early complexity of the dialogic exchange, based on a far more sophisticated infant presymbolic intelligence than was ever imagined.

This position of the dialogic origin of mind is also consistent with two major thinkers of the twentieth century, Mikhail Bakhtin in literature and Charles Taylor in philosophy. Bakhtin (1981) has argued that nonverbal exchanges can be dialogical (see also McCrorie 2000). He distinguished ordinary dialogue from "dialogic relations," which are broader, more diverse, and more complex. Even a monologue, in Bakhtin's view, implies a listener. Charles Taylor (1991) has specifically argued for the dialogic origin of mind:

> The general feature of human life that I want to evoke is its fundamentally dialogical character. We become full human agents . . . through our acquisition of rich human languages of expression . . . I want to take "language" in a broad sense, covering not only the words we speak but also other modes of expression . . . including the languages of art, of gesture. . . . But we are inducted into these . . . through exchanges with others who matter to us. . . . The genesis of the human mind is in this sense not "monological" . . . but "dialogical" . . . the making and sustaining of our identity . . . remains dialogical throughout our lives. [pp. 34–35]

The power of correspondences. All three infancy theorists concur that correspondences, matching, and similarities are an extremely powerful, fundamental aspect of preverbal communication, promoting the possibility of "shared mind." Moreover, Meltzoff and Trevarthen concur that even the newborn is sensitive to corresponding movements and expressions in the human partner through temporal and morphological markers, hence, an intersubjective newborn. The range of meanings given to matching/correspondence by the three theorists speak to the complexity of the concept, and the nuances of nonverbal communication that can be communicated through various forms of matching. This theme of correspondence and matching is not salient in psychoanalysis, which has tended to focus on differentiation, disruption, and conflict. The importance of similarities and correspondences has not received equal play, as a means of sensing and entering the other's process, a way of communicating to the other a feeling of "being with," and a fundamental ingredient of intimacy.

Why is matching so important? The capacity to perceive what is familiar, what repeats, and what is invariant, is a central principle of early cognitive development as well as neural functioning (Bornstein 1985). Based on the capacity to perceive difference as well as similarity, infants select similarities, extract invariances, and use this information to form categories that, when generalized, form the basis of presymbolic representation. The ability to abstract common properties among discriminable entities and generalize on the basis of that abstraction forms the basis of adult forms of representation as well (Bornstein 1985, Stern 1985, Walton and Bower 1993).

The discussions of correspondence and matching by the infant theorists can provide psychoanalysis with detailed ways of conceptualizing how each person senses the state and moment-by-moment process of the other, in the nonverbal and implicit realm. Trevarthen's description of patterns of movement transferred from subject to subject via form, timing, and intensity provides a specificity that is very useful for conceptualizing how one person senses the state of the other. Stern's description of *changing with* the other, through micro-momentary shifts in intensity over time that allow us to feel what has been perceived in the other, further elaborates the process by which each person comes to sense the process of the other. These forms of similarity form the bedrock of experiences of "you are with me; you are on my wavelength."

Of the adult theorists of intersubjectivity described in Chapter 1, Stolorow and colleagues come closest to the use of correspondences in their use of the concept of affect attunement, but this term is used by Stolorow and colleagues in a very general way, to convey optimal empathic responsiveness, without the specificity of Stern's definition of attunement as crossmodal matching of timing, form, and intensity, and the power of Stern's concept of "changing with." Ogden's theory is critically dependent on the analyst's personal reverie as a way of inferring the inner state of the patient. Both Trevarthen's and Stern's descriptions of how this sensing of the other occurs might provide an elaboration of *how* the patient influences Ogden's reverie.

Furthermore, all three infancy theorists point out the special motivational significance of correspondences, organizing dyadic experiences of exuberance, playfulness, and enjoyment. Tronick (1998) suggests that these experiences lead to expanded dyadic states of mind. Still, the idea that correspondence and matching might organize experiences of exuberance, playfulness, and dyadic expansion is not salient in psychoanalysis (as an exception see Winnicott 1965). Stern is the most articulate about the importance of these matching experiences for bonding, attachment, and intimacy. This is a powerful but neglected theme for adult forms of intersubjectivity. All of the infant theorists and none of the adult theorists emphasize the powerful positive emotional experiences made possible by various forms of matching. Experiences of exuberance in the psychoanalytic dyad are an important but neglected source of therapeutic action.

Specific Contributions of Meltzoff

Of the three theorists, Meltzoff is the one whose experiments have documented a rudimentary form of representational intelligence in the early weeks and months of life. In the experiments on infant imitation 42 minutes after birth, Meltzoff holds that the infant is comparing his own action, such as mouth opening, against an internal memory, schema, or representation of the action of mouth opening that he saw the model make. Furthermore, the infant's capacity to use crossmodal correspondences to match the actions of the model provides the infant with a way of apprehending that the partner is similar to the self: in essence, in a presymbolic format, "you are like me." By 6 weeks, the infant can observe the model one day, return 24 hours later, and imitate the action. Meltzoff's work offers a radical change in the way we conceptualize the origin of mind in psychoanalysis. Far earlier than we thought, there is a rudimentary capacity to represent, and to match, the behavior of another person. As noted in Chapter 2, this capacity may be based on "mirror neurons."

Meltzoff's work is potentially relevant to psychoanalysis in a second way. Seeing oneself in the actions of the other, or re-creating the other's actions in the self, can be seen as the reason why mirroring experiences are so powerful. The capacity to detect that "you are like me," or to reproduce the other's behavior, so that "I am like you," is a primal organizing theme of preverbal intersubjectivity. These experiences contribute to feeling "known" or "on the same wavelength" (Beebe and Lachmann 1988). This concept is illustrated through a psychoanalytic case in Chapter 4. Benjamin's (1988, 1992, 1995) theory includes Meltzoff's concept that "you are like me" as an independent agent or subject. She argues that this process ultimately contributes to the formation of identifications.

Finally, Meltzoff's work on the crossmodal perception of correspondence provides one mechanism for the coordination of inner and relational states (Beebe and Lachmann 1998). Through crossmodal matching, the infant translates between environmental information and inner proprioceptive information, from the beginning of life. He can thus bring his internal state and behavior into a correspondence with the behavior of the partner. (Stern's theory of crossmodal matching is similar, but he argues that the relevance of this matching for intersubjectivity begins toward the end of the first year, not at birth.) Ekman, Levenson, and Friesen (1983) have made an argument for adults similar to that of Meltzoff for neonates. Meltzoff argues that this crossmodal matching at birth provides a fundamental relatedness between self and other, between inner state and environment. Although Meltzoff's demonstration is in the modality of facial expression, this principle can be extended to other modalities, such as correspondences of timing (Beebe et al. 1985, 2000, Jaffe et al. 2001). In the psychoanalytic dyad, crossmodal correspondences can allow either patient or analyst to bring internal process (or state) and behavior into a correspondence with the internal process and behavior of the partner. Presumably these correspondences are created largely out of awareness and are subject to the multiple vicissitudes of transferences of both analyst and patient.

Specific Contributions of Trevarthen

Whereas Meltzoff conceptualizes the representational newborn, Trevarthen conceptualizes the dialogic newborn, in a reciprocally communicative dyad. Trevarthen's description of the emotional newborn, participating in protoconversation, takes a step beyond Meltzoff to an inherently dyadic, dialogic mind. Trevarthen extends Meltzoff's imitation argument into a more general statement that human sympathetic consciousness is not an acquired skill but rather an innate ability. This ability allows *both* infants and caretakers to be in immediate sympathetic contact, aware of the other's feelings and purposes without words and language, by matching communicative expressions through time, form, and intensity. This matching regulates both interpersonal contact and inner state. This position is consistent with, but deepens, the contemporary view that adult mind is dyadic and organized in interaction (for example Aron 1996, Mitchell 2000, Stolorow and Atwood 1992). If dialogic communication is *inherent* in the infant's capacity, perhaps it remains a lifelong resource that can be tapped when later aspects of development fail. This position is illustrated by the treatment case described in Chapter 4.

Both Trevarthen (1974, 1977, 1979, 1993a,b, 1998) and Stern (1971, 1977, 1985, 1995) have been influential in formulating a mutual, bidirectional regulation model of communication (see also Beebe et al. 1992, Gianino and Tronick 1988, Jaffe and Feldstein 1970, Sander 1977, 1995, Tronick 1989, 1998). Trevarthen suggests that the capacity for the mutual regulation of joint action is available from birth. Mutual regulation is based on each partner's ability to detect that the partner's behavior is contingent on his own actions, and vice-versa. Positioning mutual regulation as a capacity available from the beginning of life is an essential corollary of Trevarthen's dyadic, dialogic mind at birth. Although mutual regulation is endorsed in varying ways by all adult psychoanalytic theorists described in Chapter 1, as well as by current relational theorists (see especially Aron 1996), the position that mutual (bidirectional) regulation is a central aspect of communication from birth again deepens and extends current psychoanalytic views. Mutual regulation becomes a primary organizing principle of all communication and development.

Although all three infancy theorists would agree that early communicative competence is more fundamental than language, Trevarthen is the most explicit on this point. Following Habermas (1979) and Ryan (1974), Trevarthen (1993a,b, 1998) holds that *linguistic forms of intersubjectivity have their foundation in prelinguistic forms; that intersubjectivity is initially preverbal and dialogic.* Trevarthen's view provides the psychoanalytic dyad with a foundation of communication that initially precedes language, eventually runs parallel to language, and can potentially influence and be influenced by language. The description of the prelinguistic origins of communicative competence is one of the most important contributions of the infant theorists of intersubjectivity. One implication for psychoanalysis is that, when language fails, the psychoanalytic dyad can still have access to prelinguistic and implicit forms of communicative competence and intersubjectivity, as illustrated in Chapter 4. A second implication is that *all linguistic forms of intersubjectivity continue to depend on pre- or nonlinguistic forms.* This second point suggests that all psychoanalytic treatments are dependent on pre- and nonlinguistic forms of communicative competence and intersubjectivity, not just those of the more disturbed patient.

Of the three theorists, Trevarthen is unique in proposing that coupling of rhythms is the key mechanism explaining how the matching of communicative expressions works. He hypothesizes that infant and adult coordination of behaviors depends on a common beat, based on coupled neural oscillators, assisted by mutual imitation and matching. A considerable number of infant as well as adult researchers concur with Trevarthen that rhythmic coordination is a fundamental organizing principle of communication (for example Badalamenti and Langs 1990, Beebe et al. 1985, Capella 1981, 1991, Crown 1991, Jaffe and Feldstein 1970, Jaffe et al. 2001, Warner et al. 1987, Warner 1988). Rhythmic coordination can occur in any modality, such as vocal, facial, gazing patterns, body movement. In mother–infant treatments where the infant does not look, or is limp and shut down, subtle forms of rhythmic coordination with sounds or movements remain a way of reaching the infant (Beebe 2003). A similar concept is illustrated in the adult treatment in Chapter 4.

Striking similarities in the timing and rhythmic coordination of the communicative process across the life-span underscore the importance of Trevarthen's position that rhythmic coupling is a key mechanism for the matching and correspondences of inter-subjectivity in infancy (Beebe et al. 1985). Trevarthen and colleagues (1999) give the example of infant finger movements synchronized with the end of melodic phrases, as if the infant were conducting. Another example comes from the work on vocal rhythms, where mothers and infants regulate the exchange of turns in much the same way as do adults (Beebe et al. 1985, 1988, Jaffe et al. 2001). A "switching pause" is the momentary silence that occurs at the point of the turn exchange, and this pause is matched (correlated) in both adult–adult and infant–adult vocal exchanges. Each person can anticipate how long to wait before taking a turn. Matching the duration of the switching pause is a cornerstone of the structure of adult dialogue and turntaking, allowing a graceful exchange of turns. In adult conversation, if the switching pause is too short, or nonexistent, the person who "cuts in" is experienced as "rude." Individuals who talk on endlessly, without allowing the other a turn, may be experienced as *not recognizing* the partner. The dialogic turn-taking structure of conversation is disturbed in such individuals. Conversely, if the switching pause is too long, the person may be experienced as "out to lunch," not paying attention, "not with me." It is remarkable that 4-month infants with their mothers have this aspect of the regulatory structure of adult dialogue. In this sense, language is built on the scaffolding of earlier coordination of communication rhythms (Beebe et al. 1988).

Badalamenti and Langs (1990) linked different vocal rhythm patterns in adult patient–therapist pairs to depth of narrative imagery, a measure developed by Bucci (1997). Instead of waiting for the switching pause to unfold, therapists tended to interrupt more when patients used less narrative imagery. In contrast, low interruption by the therapist, but not low speech rate, was associated with the highest therapist vocal rhythm influence on the patient's vocal rhythms. High narrative imagery in the patient was associated with less therapist interruption, longer therapist silences (but not lower overall speech rate), and high amounts of "back-channeling" (umm, huh) that kept the ongoing beat of the patient's speech. This research by Badalamenti illustrates how variations in the coordination of vocal rhythms are an important aspect of any treatment (see also Holtz 2001). Knoblauch (1997, 2000) has described the role of rhythm in therapeutic dialogue, illustrating both matching and violations of rhythmic patterns. Beebe (1999) used matching of rhythms of whimper and cry sounds as a way of making contact with a female patient sitting up in analysis who cried most of the time, and who was not able to talk or look. Coupling of rhythms is thus an important organizing principle in psychoanalytic communication.

Specific Contributions of Stern

Unlike Trevarthen, who has formulated all of his work within a theory of infant intersubjectivity, Stern's contributions to psychoanalysis (1985, 1989, 1994, 1995, Stern et al. 1998) are much broader than his theory of intersubjectivity. Perhaps Stern's most fundamental contribution was to bring infant research into a prominent place within psychoanalysis. Nevertheless we limit our discussion to the relevance of Stern's theory of intersubjectivity. We do not address Stern's later work with the Boston Study Group on Change (Stern et al. 1998).

The concept of matching is greatly expanded by Stern. His formulation of matching as "changing with" is fundamentally dyadic and moves the concept into a "process" model. By contrast, Stern (Stern et al. 1985) critiques the model of matching as imitation. Imitation is a more static concept describing a particular moment in time, in which one person matches another, rather than an ongoing two-way communicative *process*. Stern describes "changing with" as "Dynamic micro-momentary shifts in intensity over time that are perceived as patterned changes within ourselves and others" that allow us, rather automatically and without awareness, to "change with" the other, to "feel-what-has-been-perceived-in-the-other" (Stern et al. 1985, p. 263). This is an invaluable concept for the psychoanalyst. It provides a key way of tracking the moment-by-moment dyadic, nonverbal process. The focus on slight *shifts in intensity in both partners* is a fine-grained way of being in the fluctuations of the "moment," where subtle gradient changes within an affect category are more likely than a change of affect category. A further aspect of Stern's description of "changing with" is the notion of "share without altering." This is a powerful concept for psychoanalysis, which we illustrate below with the example of entering the distress state of the other, as well as in the treatment case in Chapter 4.

Stern's emphasis on changing with shifts of intensity or *level of activation* (also key in Trevarthen's theory) has received independent support from the work of Jaffe and colleagues (2001) on the coordination of mother–infant as well as adult (mother–stranger) vocal rhythms. The most pervasive pattern in the data was a correspondence between the two partners of level of activation of vocal rhythms (a correlation of the ratio of sound to silence, within any sound–silence cycle, across the group). By contrast, matching the beat (a correlation of the average duration of the sound–silence cycle) was a rare pattern in the Jaffe and colleagues data. Level of activation is continuously shifting in both partners: as one partner shifts level of intensity up or down, the partner does so as well. The concept of matching level of activation provides psychoanalysis with another subtle means of tracking and reaching the partner.

A second way in which Stern expands the concept of matching is his central criterion for affect attunement that the *inner* state of the partner becomes the referent for the match, rather than the overt behavior itself. Although Trevarthen also argues that matching of patterns of movement permits intercoordination of inner states between partners, in Stern's hands this idea becomes more central and importantly different. Stern argues that the same level of exuberance can be expressed as, for example, a facial expression, a gesture, or a vocalization. Crossmodal matching of behavior, through nonverbal analogy and metaphor, recasts the experience of emotional resonance into a quality of feeling or inner state that Stern terms "forms of feeling." Forms of feeling become the referent for what is matched, ultimately facilitating symbolization. For Stern, affect attunement provides a bridge from the presymbolic to the symbolic mind. Affect attunement is thus very different from the kinds of matching and correspondences discussed by Meltzoff and Trevarthen, and it defines a *critical reorganization of intersubjectivity* toward the end of the first year. This theory makes an important contribution to our understanding of the origins of symbolic forms of representation of feeling.

Stern suggests that experiences that are attuned to define what is shareable, what can be validated; experiences that are not attuned to define what cannot be validated about the self, potential "not-me" experiences. This element of Stern's theory has a strong parallel in Winnicott's (1965) concept of the "not-me" experience. It is also paralleled in Stolorow and Atwood's (1992) concept of "the unvalidated unconscious": affects that were never validated by the caregiver become the source of vague, diffuse, unsettling feelings and sensations that do not become shareable and thus do not become integrated into the self. Stern's concept is important for psychoanalysis because "not-me" experiences can derive from *nonverbal or implicit* forms of failures of validation.

As important as the concept of affect attunement is for psychoanalysis, it is easily misunderstood. It is often used synonymously with empathy, which Stern explicitly rejects, as discussed in Chapter 2. The central criteria of Stern's concept of affect attunement, that it is a crossmodal matching of timing, form, and intensity; a matching of forms of feeling rather than behaviors; and a matching of micromomentary shifts in intensity over time, are lost in most psychoanalytic discussions of affect attunement.

MATCHING VS. THE FULL COMPLEXITY
OF PREVERBAL COMMUNICATION

In addressing the relevance of infant research for theories of
intersubjectivity in adult psychoanalysis, Meltzoff, Trevarthen, and
Stern provide a critical foundation. Apart from Stern's notion of
attunement, it is striking that many of their ideas have not been
used in psychoanalytic discussions of intersubjectivity, as noted
above. However, the reliance on the concept of matching/corre-
spondence in these three infancy theorists does not encompass the
full complexity of the preverbal construction of experience. Nor is
the concept of matching/correspondence sufficiently broad to explicate the relevance of other important infant research findings
for theories of intersubjectivity in psychoanalysis. Correspondences
can be seen as a focal point in a broader field of the complex structure of preverbal relatedness. In this section we build on and expand Meltzoff, Trevarthen, and Stern, developing a fourth position
on the meanings of forms of intersubjectivity in infancy. Although
other dimensions of preverbal interactions could well be addressed,
we draw from research on face-to-face interaction and suggest that
the following issues require clarification and elaboration: problems
with the concept of matching, the role of difference, the place of
interactive regulation, and the role of self-regulation. We close with
the "balance model" of self and interactive regulation, which integrates these issues.

Difficulties with the Concept of Matching

Matching alone does not characterize mother–infant interactions
in the first half year (Cohn and Tronick 1989, Malatesta et al. 1989,
Tronick 1989). Instead, *both* similarities and differences characterize the interaction. By focusing on the perception of correspondence and matching as the key to presymbolic intersubjectivity,
overall the three infant theorists tend to ignore issues of difference,
even though the infant's capacity to perceive differences is equally

developed. For example, DeCasper and Carstens (1980) showed that newborns perceive violations in an expected pattern, and show signs of affective distress following the violation. The one exception to this critique is Stern and colleagues' (1985) demonstration that infants perceive experimental maternal mismatches, and these mismatches disrupt the infant's ongoing play.

In Tronick's (1989) view, the concept of matching has been romanticized. In Tronick and Cohn's (1989) data, mothers and infants match engagement (for example, mutual visual focus on partner's face, mutual positive faces, or mutual focus on an object) only about one third of the time. Malatesta and colleagues (1989) have similar data, showing that mother and infant tend to match facial expression about one third of the time. Instead of matching per se, Tronick and Cohn suggest that we should conceptualize a more flexible interactive process: match, mismatch, rematch. The Tronick and Cohn data show that, in general, given a mismatch (for example, mother with smiling face but infant neutral face), mothers and infants tend to rematch (both partners with positive face) within 2 seconds. Furthermore, a greater likelihood of rematch within 2 seconds is associated with a greater probability of secure attachment at one year (Tronick 1989). The critical issue is "interactive repair," the ability of the dyad to rematch, which has been framed as a disruption and repair process (Beebe and Lachmann 1994). Using this perspective, "rematch" following mismatch may be even more important than matching per se.

The meanings of matching are complex and encompass both "similarity" and "compensatory" forms. The concept of matching is frequently assessed through correlational techniques, where the sign can be positive or negative. For example, in the data on mother–infant vocal rhythm matching (Beebe and Lachmann 1988, Beebe et al. 1997, Jaffe et al. 2001), when the sign is positive, as one person increases the duration of a behavior, the partner follows suit: a "similarity" form of matching. As an illustration of a "similarity" form of matching, the switching pause tends to be coordinated with a positive sign so that, at the point of the exchange, both mother and infant wait for a similar duration, thus making the turn exchange more predictable. This finding also characterizes adult conversation (Crown 1991, Jaffe and Feldstein 1970, Feldstein and Welkowitz 1978).

In contrast, when the sign is negative, as one person increases the duration of a behavior, the partner systematically decreases the duration: a "compensatory" form of matching. In the vocal rhythm data of Jaffe and colleagues (2001), vocalizations and pauses tend to be coordinated between partners with a negative sign, which results in a homeostatic "balancing": as one partner's degree of coordination is tighter, the other's is looser, and vice-versa, so that between the two, a more constant activity level is maintained. This mode of coupling constitutes a dyadic regulation of relative tightness of coordination within the turn. Turntaking is facilitated by this mode of rhythmic coupling in the sense that each partner has a model of how to act during his turn: to become more or less coordinated, to move in, or to back off. Here, rather than keeping the behavior similar, as in the switching pause match, the task seems to be keeping a relatively constant dyadic degree of activation across both partners' turns (Beebe and Lachmann 1998, Beebe et al. 1985). The positive and negative signs of the coordination define two modes of rhythmic coupling (Jaffe et al. 2001). The former mode of coupling amplifies dyadic deviations via positive feedback, whereas the latter counteracts deviations, resulting in a more constant dyadic activity level.

Websters (1977) dictionary definition encompasses this double meaning of *matching*: "to join, to fit together," as well as "to provide with a counterpoint or complement." Whereas all three infancy theorists of intersubjectivity use only the "similarity" form of matching, compensatory patterns expand our concepts of matching. The fact that similar patterns of these positive and negative signs of vocal duration coordination can be found in infant–adult as well as adult–adult conversations draws our attention to forms of dialogic timing that are as relevant in adulthood as in infancy. It is clear that similar forms of rhythmic coupling must function in psychoanalysis, but they have yet to be carefully studied (but see Holtz 2001).

Nor do the three infant theorists address the significance of matching positive vs. negative facial-vocal affective states. Field (1995; Field et al. 1990) and Cohn and colleagues (1990) have shown that, in contrast to controls, depressed mothers and their infants tend to match negative, rather than positive, states. Another example of matching negative states is a pattern of "mutually escalating over-arousal" (Beebe 2000). This is a highly disturbing form of interaction in which, as the infant becomes vocally, facially, or bodily distressed, the mother matches the increasing arousal and escalates level of stimulation, as if she may feel increasingly desperate. Each partner then proceeds to match the other's direction of increasing arousal and distress, each topping the other, going up and up and up, until the infant disorganizes, perhaps by vomiting (at four months) or screaming (at 12 months). In one mother–infant pair at four months where this pattern was characteristic of the interaction, and the infant eventually vomited, the 12-month Ainsworth Strange Situation Test classified the infant as disorganized attachment (Beebe 2000).

An interesting analogy to the pattern of mutually escalating overarousal can be found in Shakespeare's *Othello* (Act II, scene iv, lines 89 and following), in which Desdemona and Othello are arguing about Cassio (see McCrorie 2000). Othello suspects Cassio of cuckolding him with Desdemona, while she innocently believes that it is right to advance Cassio's cause in Othello's army. Othello becomes increasingly enraged with Desdemona and she, refusing to answer his pressing questions about a key handkerchief, continues to advance the cause of Cassio. Each continues to escalate until Othello loses all patience and storms off the stage.

By contrast, other forms of matching of negative states provide more successful modes of distress regulation. For example, by matching the infant's cry rhythm (but not the volume), it is possible to create a dyadic synchronization, from which the parent and infant can sometimes both slowly calm down into a slower and slower cry rhythm, facilitating the infant's capacity to re-regulate (see the case of "Elliott" in Beebe and Lachmann 1998, Stern 1985, 1995). Another example can be seen in the mother–infant treatment of Linda and her son Dan (Cohen and Beebe 2003). At 17 months, after positive face-to-face interactions with his mother and then his father, Dan played with a stranger (Beebe). Following several minutes of positive play with the stranger, Dan suddenly became completely still, collapsing tonus with his head down. The stranger became similarly still, and waited. After half a minute, Dan looked up from under his brows, with his head still partially down. The stranger very softly said, "Hello, it's okay." Dan then looked down again, and became motionless. Dan and the stranger cycled through this pattern many times over, for about 2½ minutes. Then, as suddenly as it came, it went, and Dan emerged looking, partially smiling, and gradually resumed play with the stranger. This interaction is an example of distress regulation by "matching" or "entering" a dampened state without trying to shift it. Beebe (1999) described a similar form of matching dampened distress states in the psychoanalytic treatment of Paulina, who did not look or talk, and spent most of the time sobbing. Knoblauch (1997, 2000, 2001) has also discussed certain forms of "matching" as distress regulation. Various forms of distress matching are illustrated in the treatment case in Chapter 4.

Is matching of "negative" states the kind of matching that Trevarthen and Stern had in mind? We argue that it is certainly one way of sensing the state of the other, and thus highly relevant to a theory of intersubjectivity in infancy. Does it make a difference to the meaning of "matching" whether the state of the infant is exuberance, interest, distress, avoidance, or deadness? We will return to this important question shortly.

The Role of Difference

Of the three infant theorists, Stern is the only one who discusses differences in any detail. His theory of affect attunement rests on the assumption that the infant indeed perceives a lack of matching on the part of the caretaker, constituting a failure of attunement. Systematic nonattunement in a particular arena of functioning would lead to the infant's experience that this arena is not "share-able," thus potentially eventually "not-me." Stern implies that fail-ures of matching, that is, certain forms of difference, lead to failures of attunement, or failures of intersubjectivity.

The *American College Dictionary* (1962, p. 1205) defines "sub-jective" as "existing in the mind, belonging to the thinking sub-ject, rather than belonging to the object of thought." The definition of "inter" is "between, together, mutuality, reciprocity." One read-ing is that "intersubjectivity" refers to what is going on between two minds. This is a more general and more neutral definition. A second reading suggests that intersubjectivity has to do with mu-tuality between two minds. This reading contains a bias toward the positive—mutuality or reciprocity. There is a tension between these two readings in both the infancy and the adult theorists.

We prefer the first, more neutral reading. Intersubjectivity, defined as "what is between two minds," encompasses the full com-plexity of how two minds interrelate, align, fail to align, or disrupt and repair alignment. We argue that differences are an intrinsic aspect of the structure of intersubjectivity in infancy (see Slavin and Kriegman 1992, for adults). Even if the "positive" meanings of intersubjectivity are emphasized, such as shared mind, or mu-tual recognition, *it is the process of moving back and forth between similarity and difference that constructs and fine-tunes the alignment* (see Knoblauch 2000). We endorse Tronick's (1989) view that in-teractive repair is more ubiquitous and organizing in development than matching per se.

Many examples of difference or disjunction could be offered, such as the pattern of "chase and dodge," described by Beebe and Stern (1977). This is a complex, reciprocally regulated pattern, in which the mother's movements of head and upper body toward the infant predicted the infant's movements of head and gaze away; reciprocally, the infant's movements away from the mother pre-dicted the mother's movements further toward the infant. This pattern disturbed the infant's use of looking away as a form of self-regulation to reduce arousal (Field 1981), since the mother esca-lated activity just as the infant was re-regulating down. The chase and dodge pattern is a familiar one with premature infants and some infants whose mothers are depressed (Field 1981, 1995), in dyads where the infant is later classified as insecure (Langhorst and Fogel 1982), and in mother–infant pairs who present for treatment (Beebe 2000, 2003). Using the definition of intersubjectivity that emphasizes (positive) mutuality between two minds, the chase and dodge interaction might be considered a failure of intersubjectivity. But using the more neutral definition of intersubjectivity as refering to what is between two minds, we can consider the chase and dodge interaction to be one form of intersubjectivity, albeit disjunctive, that this particular mother–infant pair has constructed.

Maternal disturbances of infant self-regulation can be found in other interactions in addition to "chase and dodge." "Oral teasing" is a pattern in which the mother repeatedly moves her finger in and out of the infant's mouth: the mother pulls the finger out and the infant pulls it back (Beebe 2000). The infant learns to depend on the mother's finger rather than other forms of regulation over which he would have more control, such as putting his own finger in his mouth, or various forms of self-touch. As the mother pulls her finger out, the infant fusses loudly; as she puts it back in, the infant quiets. Another example of disturbance of infant self-regulation can be found in interactions where the mother pulls the infant's hand away just as the infant has begun to self-soothe by fingering a piece of clothing or the strap of the seat (Beebe 2003). Maternal disturbance of infant self-regulation is an important form of difference, disjunction, or conflict. The two partners have different agendas at such a moment (Slavin and Kriegman 1992). The infant's agenda is one of regulating arousal down to a more comfortable range, whereas the mother's agenda may be an attempt to re-engage the infant or an attempt to soothe in a way that unwittingly disturbs the infant's own autonomy.

Perhaps the most extreme form of difference/disjunction at 4 months can be found in mother–infant interactions where the infant is subsequently classified as disorganized attachment in the Ainsworth Strange Situation test at 12 months. In the 4-month face-to-face interaction, the infant often shows extreme forms of distress and attempts to self-regulate, and the mother acts as if the infant is "fine," almost as if she is with a different infant than the one in front of her. The infant has prolonged periods of vocal distress, frequent and prolonged periods of gaze aversion, moments of full head orientation away to 90 degree aversion, accompanied by arching the body away, and moments of loss of tonus, going limp and utterly still. The mothers often smile as the infant is distressed (an example of Lyons-Ruth's [1996] "interactive error"), keep up a rapid pace of vocal, facial, and touch stimulation with little pausing, frequently stimulate while the infant is oriented away and not available for engagement, and often escalate negative facial and vocal expressions of the infant. This picture of the disorganized infants is based on the Jaffe and colleagues (2001) data set, and the description of disorganized infants from the Lyons-Ruth (personal communication, August 18, 1999) data set is remarkably similar. In these disjunctive interactions, the mother essentially denies the infant's distress, and there is a failure of "mentalizing" (Fonagy 1994, 1995): she does not wonder what is wrong, nor does she make attempts to repair. Perhaps this distress is something she cannot bear, because of her own unresolved traumatic past (Main and Hesse 1992, M. S. Moore, personal communication, July, 1999). The infant's extreme forms of self-regulation, finally going limp and utterly still, seem to be a form of "playing dead," or "playing possum," described by Beebe and Stern (1977) and Papousek and Papousek (1977, 1987), as if going dead might make this stimulation stop.

SIMILARITIES AND DIFFERENCES HAVE DIFFERENT MEANINGS IN DIFFERENT INFANT AFFECTIVE CONTEXTS

Infants have a wide affective-engagement range. Using the dimensions of infant orientation to partner, gaze at partner, facial expression, vocal distress, bodily tonus, and physiological arousal, the following range can be roughly schematized (see Figure 3–1):

exuberant face and vocalization, positive face and vocalization, interest face and vocalization, neutral face, negative face (frown, grimace) and vocalization (fuss, cry), loss of tonus (head hangs limp), bodily agitation (feet rapidly moving, head and body arching away), physiological disorganization (vomit). Given these different infant affective contexts, similarities and differences have different meanings, illustrated in Figure 3–1.

Matching interactions in the range from exuberance to neutral seem to be the subject of the three infancy theorists of intersubjectivity. Matching in this range might generate experiences of intimacy, expansiveness, and "shared mind." Matching interactions in the range of negative face or vocalization might characterize optimal forms of distress regulation, where the caregiver temporarily

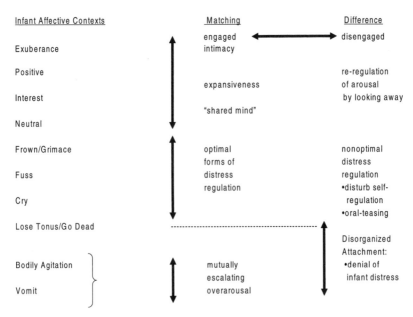

FIGURE 3–1. Similarities and Differences Have Different Meanings in Different Infant Affective Contexts.

Reprinted with permission from Beebe, B., Rustin, J., Sorter, D., and Knoblauch, S. (2003). An expanded view of intersubjectivity in infancy and its application to psychoanalysis. *Psychoanalytic Dialogues* 13(6):805–841.

"joins" the infant's distress, but stays under the infant's level of activation and arousal. Matching infant loss of tonus is rare. It occurred once in the "chase and dodge" interaction, where the mother hung her head, limp, for several seconds, while the infant was engaged in this behavior as well. This form of joining may signal maternal feelings of defeat or despair. Matching of agitation in the form of mutually escalating overarousal would be considered a disruption of the ongoing exchange.

Difference interactions in the range from exuberance to neutral can be considered "usual" disengagements within the ongoing flow of engagement and disengagement, and match, disruption, and repair. These are moments in all interactions, well-described by Tronick (1989), Field (1981), as well as the early work of Stern (1971, 1977, Beebe and Stern 1977) that was not specifically concerned with intersubjectivity. Difference interactions in the infant range of negative face and vocalization, loss of tonus, agitation, and physiological distress, can also be considered "usual," since there are other ways of consoling an infant than matching these distress behaviors (the most obvious of which is physical holding). However, difference in the form of a different agenda from the infant, such as disturbing infant self-regulation attempts, or oral teasing at distressed moments, can be considered forms of disjunction or conflict. When the infant loses tonus and "goes dead," one facilitative form of regulation might be a partial match of the infant by joining the dampened state and waiting, as described above in the case of Dan and Linda (Cohen and Beebe 2003). This response facilitated Dan's return to the engagement. But a full match by losing tonus in a limp head-hang would not seem an optimal form of response for the adult partner, possibly indicating defeat or despair. Finally, the interactions of infants later classified as disorganized attachment described above illustrate difference in the form of severe disjunction, such as maternal teasing, ignoring, laughing, or intrusive response to infant facial and vocal distress, arching away, or losing tonus and playing dead.

The preceding description of variations in the meaning of both matching and difference is an attempt to illustrate the complexity of these early interactions. "Matching" or "correspondence" can be both optimal and nonoptimal for the ongoing exchange. Similarly there are more "usual" as well as "disjunctive" forms of difference, both of which must be included in a theory of the origins of infant intersubjectivity. Particularly the more usual forms of difference (such as infant looking away, re-regulating arousal to a lower range, while partner pauses) are part and parcel of the ongoing regulation of the moment-by-moment exchange.

The Place of Interactive Regulation

If behavioral similarities are the core of intersubjectivity, as the three infancy theorists propose, how do they work? Crossmodal matching is one mechanism common to all three; rhythmic coupling is a further mechanism proposed by Trevarthen. What is implicit, but not developed, is the central mechanism of the mutual regulation model, namely, interpersonal contingencies. All three infancy theorists work with behavioral similarities without attempting to document statistically that each partner is *contingent* on the other, that each "influences" the other moment-by-moment, in the sense that each person's behavioral stream can be predicted from that of the other. Interpersonal contingencies are co-constructed patterns: in most data sets, each person is contingent on the other (for example, Cohn and Tronick 1988, Jaffe et al. 2001). Thus interpersonal contingencies have to do with the *process* of dyadic patterns of relatedness, rather than simply whether the other is similar or different at a particular *moment*.

The infant is a "contingency detector" from birth (DeCasper and Carstens 1980, Papousek and Papousek 1977), detecting predictable consequences of his own actions. For an event to be perceived as contingent by the infant, it must occur rather rapidly, within one to two seconds (Millar and Watson 1979), and it must be predictable, that is, occurring with greater than chance probability, following the infant's behavior. The infant's perception of contingencies, in conjunction with an optimally contingent environment, organizes the infant's expectation that he or she can affect, and be affected by, the partner. This is one crucial origin of the experience of effectance (White 1959) or agency (Rustin 1997, Sander 1977). Contingencies are also associated with affect: confirmation of expected contingent effects leads to positive infant affect; violation of expected contingent effects leads to negative infant affect; and failure to provide contingencies disturbs the capacity to learn (DeCasper and Carstens 1980). Gergeley and Watson (1998) have suggested that the infant's capacity to interpret stimulation as contingent (or not) may well be the most fundamental of the infant's capacities for interpreting sensory information. A similar position is held by Fagen and Rovee-Collier, who have used the infant's capacity to perceive contingencies to document a remarkable array of early abilities to create expectancies of anticipated events, and to remember them across days and weeks (Fagen et al. 1984, Shields and Rovee-Collier 1992).

Murray and Trevarthen (1985) experimentally removed the perception of contingency during mother–infant interaction. First mother and infant interacted normally over closed-circuit TV, in separate rooms. Then each was shown a "replay" of the partner interacting a few minutes earlier. Thus each "looks normal," looking and smiling in the previous ongoing exchange, but then, during the replay, neither partner's behavior was contingent on that of the other. The infant became distressed and avoidant, and the mother became critical and self-focused. The loss of the perception of ongoing contingent responsiveness in the partner disturbs the engagement and generates more extreme forms of self-regulation in both partners.

Matching per se does not imply contingency: matching can be a random event rather than a specific response. For example, each partner might blink at the same time, without being a pattern that is recurrent and predictable. Likewise contingency can occur without matching: my frown can be contingent on your smile. Matching per se does not necessarily indicate a contingent interpersonal influence process through which the behavior of two partners may become similar. Matching does not qualify as an analysis of interactive *process* without explicit documentation of contingencies.

Both Trevarthen and Stern place infant intersubjectivity within a mutual regulation model, but neither empirically consolidates this aspect of their theories. Trevarthen's genius lies in the careful illustration of the single case. However, there are no systematic statistical documentations of interactive contingencies, and he does not address the generalization of the phenomena he describes, so that this aspect of his work remains theoretical rather than solidly empirical. Stern's conceptualization of the interactive process is elegant. But his key matching data illustrating maternal attunement do not address maternal *contingent* responsiveness, and his data do not address the reciprocal process of infant matching mother.

Within the mutual regulation model, each partner experiences both affecting the other and being affected in a predictable process. The content of the influence is not specified. Each could be influencing the other to become systematically similar, matching and being matched. Or each could be influencing the other such that they become systematically dissimilar, which we have described above as "compensatory matching." Either process could be optimal or nonoptimal for the interaction. But both halves of the bi-directional regulation process are essential to consider. Thus we propose that *sensing that one impacts the partner in an ongoing predictable (contingent) way, and that the partner has a reciprocal impact on oneself, are just as important in the origins of intersubjectivity as the perception of correspondence itself.* This concept is dramatically illustrated in the treatment case in Chapter 4 (see also Benjamin 1988).

Differing Uses of the Systems View of Interaction by Meltzoff, Trevarthen, and Stern

Figure 3–2 illustrates the differing uses of the systems view of interaction by Meltzoff, Trevarthen, and Stern. For Meltzoff, the line representing the experimenter's (E) impact on the infant is darkened. The reciprocal route of the infant's impact on the experimenter is

MELTZOFF—birth

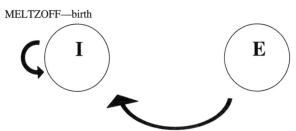

Infant makes crossmodal match (imitation) of experimenter's (E) expression, utilizing proprioceptive feedback from facial movement to match the form of the model's expression. Other is experienced "like me." Meltzoff does not address the impact of the infant on the experimenter.

TREVARTHEN—birth

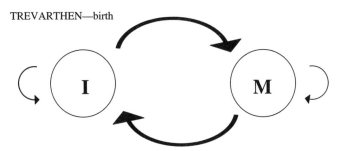

Mutual matching of movement patterns, via time, form, intensity, and coupled rhythms permits intercoordination of inner states. The self-regulation process is not elaborated.

STERN—9–12 months

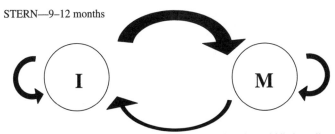

Intersubjectivity is a mutual regulation process, "changing with" the split-second shifts of the partner. Affect attunement = mother's crossmodal matching of timing, form, and intensity of behaviors. Inner states are matched and regulated. Mother's role more elaborated than infant's.

FIGURE 3–2. Systems Model of Interaction: Comparison of Meltzoff, Trevarthen, and Stern.

Reprinted with permission from Beebe, B., Rustin, J., Sorter, D., and Knoblauch, S. (2003). An expanded view of intersubjectivity in infancy and its application to psychoanalysis. *Psychoanalytic Dialogues* 13(6):805–841.

not explored in Meltzoff's work. The line representing the infant's self-regulation is also darkened, representing the infant's own effort to match, with successive approximations, using proprioceptive feedback. The advantage of Meltzoff's approach is that it isolates a particular mechanism, facial imitation. The disadvantage is that intersubjectivity is an inherently dyadic and communicative phenomenon, so that his experimental approach cannot capture the whole process. Meltzoff makes a profound contribution, but his work needs to be integrated with approaches that address the ongoing regulation of the communicative process itself. *Meltzoff's approach privileges the infant's mind, at the moment of matching the other.*

Trevarthen endorses a bidirectional model of interactive regulation in his "psychology of mutually sensitive minds," in which the infant is aware of contingent effects, and the brain is specialized for the mutual regulation of joint actions. For Trevarthen, the lines representing both the infant's impact on the mother, and the mother's impact on the infant, are equally darkened in Figure 3–2. The routes representing mother and infant self-regulation are present, but not darkened. Inner states are coordinated through the interactive process, but this aspect of Trevarthen's theory is not as well-developed as interactive regulation. *Trevarthen privileges the moment of immediate sympathetic contact between two minds.*

Stern began his career with a study of the interactive process between a mother and her two twins (Stern 1971), an elegant statistical analysis of split-second bidirectional contingencies of head orientation and gaze changes. Consistent with this work, Stern conceptualizes intersubjectivity as a mutual regulation process, with each partner changing with the shifts of the partner. But curiously, his core concept of intersubjectivity, affect attunement, is illustrated with data documenting the mother's matching of the infant, but not the infant's matching of the mother. The infant's primary role seems to be a perception of whether or not the parent attunes. Thus for Stern, the lines representing both the infant's impact on the mother, and the mother's impact on the infant, are darkened in Figure 3–2, but unequally, emphasizing the mother's attunement to the infant. The routes representing both mother and infant self-regulation are darkened, consistent with Stern's emphasis that the matching process of intersubjectivity regulates the *inner state* of each partner. But Stern seems to lose the interactive dance in his descriptions of affect attunement. *Stern privileges the moment in which the parent attunes to the infant.*

The Role of Self-Regulation

Overall the three infancy theorists omit self-regulation as a critical aspect of intersubjectivity. Of the three, Stern conceptualizes self-regulation somewhat. But inner states of activation and arousal are simultaneously regulated within the organism, as well as through interaction with the partner. A theory of interaction must address how each person is affected by his own behavior, as well as by that of the partner (Beebe and Lachmann 1998, 2002, Beebe et al. 1992, Sander 1977, Thomas and Martin 1976, Tronick 1989). Furthermore, the nature of the self- and interactive regulation continuously affect each other (Gianino and Tronick 1988). Thus a theory of intersubjectivity in infancy must include issues of self-regulation as a central feature.

Infant research on face-to-face interaction addresses self-regulation patterns in the context of the interaction with the partner. The core question of the three theorists, that is, how infants could sense the state of the partner, will of necessity be affected by how infants sense and regulate their own states, as well as how they perceive and align with the state of the partner. Other research designs, such as that of Sander (1977, 1995) on the regulation of the 24-hour cycle, or that of Demos (1989; Demos and Kaplan 1986) filming the infant while alone, can address another aspect of self-regulation, having to do with "alone states." This aspect of self-regulation can be related to the capacity to be alone (Winnicott 1965), the private self, moments of absorption in the environment, or Winnicott's (1965) incommunicado self. Alone states are not part of the research design of the study of face-to-face interactions.

The study of self-regulation within the face-to-face exchange is still sparse (Beebe and Jaffe 1999). Tronick (1989; Gianino and Tronick 1988) has shown that infants of depressed mothers are preoccupied with self-regulation (oral and tactile self-touch) at the expense of interactive engagement, in the face-to-face exchange. Recent work by Koulomzin (Koulomzin et al. 2002, Beebe and Lachmann 1998) documented difficulties in self-regulation in 4-month infants who were classified as avoidant attachment at 1 year. In contrast with those who would be classified as secure, avoidant infants at 4 months looked less at mother. Only with a self-touch form of self-comfort could these infants sustain vis-a-vis orientation and looking at mother comparable to the secure. Thus issues of self-regulation affect the nature of the interactive regulation, and vice-versa.

The issue of self-regulation is particularly critical during infant distress. A continuation of matching infant escalating arousal can lead to mutually escalating overarousal, as described above. Instead, caregiver responses that assist infant self-regulation, facilitating infant down-regulation of arousal, are more optimal.

Self-regulation is also organized at the physiological level. It is essential to understand how inner and interactive experiences are linked at a physiological level, which none of the three theorists addresses (Beebe and Lachmann 1998). For example, examining the lateralization of the brain for positive and negative emotion using EEG, Davidson and Fox (1982) have shown that, even *in the absence of a matching behavior*, the mere perception of emotion in the face of the partner creates a resonant emotional state in the infant. This kind of research calls into question the exclusive reliance of all three theorists on behavioral correspondences in understanding how the infant could sense or align with the state of the partner.

A vignette from a videotaped psychoanalytic session in which the female patient sat up can illustrate the relevance of self-regulation for psychoanalysis. This description primarily addresses the nonverbal and implicit modes of the interaction. The patient was increasingly distressed, gesturing rapidly with her hands, torso leaning forward tautly, face screwed into a pre-cry, speaking tensely. The analyst was silently listening, his face very attentive. As the patient's agitation began, the analyst slightly shifted the orientation of his chair toward the patient. Both maintained continuous eye-contact. As the agitation mounted, the analyst's foot made intermittent brief rapid jiggles, matching the rhythm of the patient's body. He then moved slightly forward in his chair. At this point the heads of both analyst and patient went up in synchronous movement. At each escalation of the patient's agitation, the analyst participated, crossing and uncrossing his legs, and nodding his head up and down in rhythm with the patient's movements, each time saying "yes," softly. Gradually the patient began to calm down; the analyst's head movements became slower. There were several long moments of silence. Then slowly they began to speak to each other.

In this vignette, the analyst participated in the sequence of escalating agitation and calming down. Although the patient's sequence can be conceptualized primarily in terms of self-regulation, presumably the analyst's movements also influenced her management of the arousal. The analyst did not match the patient's level of arousal. Instead, at critical shifts in the patient's arousal (increasing and decreasing), the analyst "marked" the shifts with ones of his own. The analyst's own self-regulatory movements revealed his inner state as a response to the patient. His efforts to regulate his inner state showed the patient that he was *with* her: these efforts are simultaneously self-regulatory and communicative to the patient, presumably out of awareness of both.

THE BALANCE MODEL OF SELF- AND INTERACTIVE REGULATION: THE OPTIMAL RANGE

The concept of match or correspondence addresses *a particular moment in time.* In contrast, the mathematics used to assess interactive contingencies deals with the interpersonal *process of predictability over time.* The terms *tracking and being tracked* (Beebe and

Lachmann 1998, Beebe and McCrorie 2003), *coordinating, or looser and tighter coupling* (Jaffe et al. 2001) may better capture the process quality of these exchanges. Tracking, coordination, and coupling are synonymous with "contingency" or "influence."

The meaning of *degree* of coordination remains controversial. The adult empirical literature has debated the varying positions that high coordination is optimal (Chapple 1970), high coordination indexes distress (Gottman 1979), and midrange coordination is optimal (Warner et al. 1987). This debate has not been widely aired in the infant literature (see as an exception Cohn and Elmore 1988, Dunham and Dunham 1990, Jaffe et al. 2001). *This issue has not been addressed at all in theories of intersubjectivity, infant or adult.*

Jaffe and colleagues (2001) documented a continuum of *degrees* of interactive coordination of vocal rhythms between mothers and infants, and strangers and infants, at 4 months, which predicted infant attachment outcomes at 1 year. This continuum ranged from high coordination, or tight coupling (vigilant), to low coordination, or loose coupling (inhibited). *Midrange* interactive coordination predicted secure infant attachment, whereas scores outside the midrange predicted insecure. Thus *degrees* of interpersonal contingencies are essential to consider within the broader concept of mutual regulation. A number of other infant studies have also documented that midrange degrees of interpersonal contingency in the middle of the first year predict secure attachment outcomes at one year (Isabella and Belsky 1991, Lewis and Feiring 1989, Leyendecker et al. 1997, Malatesta et al. 1989). Thus the entire consideration of matching and correspondence needs to be refined by a consideration of *degrees of interpersonal contingency in the process of becoming more (or less) similar over time. The concept of degrees of coordination refines the mutual regulation model.*

Elaborating on the theory of interaction of Sander (1977, 1995) and Tronick (1989; Gianino and Tronick 1988), and building on the Jaffe and colleagues (2001) finding that midrange coordination predicted secure attachment, Beebe and Jaffe (1999) and Beebe and McCrorie (2003) have conceptualized a "balance model of self- and interactive regulation." This midrange balance model can be integrated into both Trevarthen's and Stern's views of the origins of intersubjectivity. The "balance model" builds on the Jaffe and colleagues (2001) findings of interactive regulation and adds self-regulation, hypothesizing a midrange optimum in both, illustrated in Figure 3–3. The balance model posits that in the midrange, interactive coupling is present but not obligatory, and self-regulation is preserved but not excessive (Beebe and Jaffe 1999). Optimal social communication and development is hypothesized to occur with flexibility to move between self- and interactive regulation, presumably facilitating disruption and repair processes, and yielding relatively optimal levels of infant attention, affect, and arousal. For each partner, operating outside the midrange may index an attempt to cope with a disturbance in the interaction. An excessive monitoring of the partner, at the expense of self-regulation, defines one pole of imbalance, "interactive vigilance"; preoccupation with self-regulation, at the expense of interactive sensitivity, defines the other pole of imbalance: "withdrawal" or "inhibition"

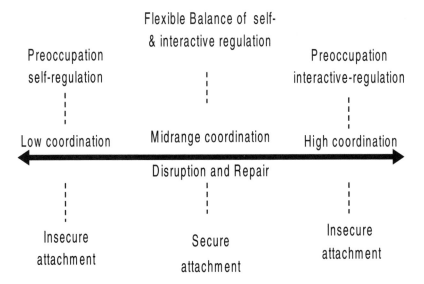

FIGURE 3–3. The Midrange Model of Self- and Interactive Regulation.

Reprinted with permission from Beebe, B., and Lachmann, F. (2002). *Infant Research and Adult Treatment: Co-constructing Interactions.* Hillsdale, NJ: Analytic Press. p. 105.

(Beebe and Jaffe 1999). Tronick (1989) documented that various failures in interactive regulation in depressed mothers and their infants, without repair, were followed by infants' preoccupation with self-regulation of distress states on their own. Applied to the concept of intersubjectivity, the balance model adds self-regulation, expands the issues of similarity (or difference) into a broader realm of degrees of contingency, and posits optimal and less optimal integrations of self- and interactive regulation. Chapter 4 illustrates the use of the balance model in an adult treatment.

In summary, building on Meltzoff, Trevarthen, and Stern, we have articulated a fourth position, suggesting that matching positive and negative states, difference states, modes of disruption and repair, distress regulation, and in fact *all patterns* of self- and interactive regulation, including vigilant, midrange, and inhibited contingencies, as well as the loss of the dialogue in states of loss of tonus or "deadness," are relevant to early presymbolic forms of intersubjectivity. All forms of interactive regulation are relevant to the possibility of perceiving and aligning oneself with the moment-by-moment process of the other. These forms of intersubjectivity documented in infant research are profoundly relevant to psychoanalytic forms of intersubjectivity, as we illustrate in Chapter 4.

4

Faces-in-Relation: Forms of Intersubjectivity in an Adult Treatment of Early Trauma*

Beatrice Beebe

Although the co-construction of the intersubjective field is currently of great interest to psychoanalysis, detailed clinical material illustrating the nonverbal and implicit dimension of this process remains rare. As Lyons-Ruth (1999) notes, much remains to be learned about how implicit modes of intimate relating are transformed, and about the analyst's specific, collaborative participation in this process as a "new kind of relational partner" (p. 612). This paper details aspects of verbal as well as nonverbal, implicit process in the ten-year treatment of Dolores, and particularly my collaborative participation.

*The contributions of Steven Knoblauch, Judith Rustin, and Dorienne Sorter, and particularly their help in analyzing the nonverbal communication of the videotapes, are acknowledged, as well as the contributions of George Downing, Michael Eigen, Adrienne Harris, Alexandra Harrison, Michael Heller, Ted Jacobs, Barbara Kane, Jennifer and Peter Kaufmann, Frank Lachmann, Regina Pally, Lin Reicher, Estelle Shane, Doris Silverman, Suzi Tortora, Sara Markese, Marina Tasopoulos, Lauren Cooper, and Jessica Sarnicola, and Hwee Sze Lim.

Dolores suffered early maternal loss and trauma. Many aspects of her traumatic experiences were communicated to me in non-verbal and implicit modes. She was preoccupied with faces, and she clung to the memory of her first mother's lost face as a beacon of her identity. I concentrate on two themes of the 10-year treatment conducted on a 3-times-per-week basis, sitting up: (1) the integration of the "faces" of Dolores herself, her multiple early attachment figures, and my own, particularly as we struggled to regain "face-to-face" relating in the process of developing a deep mutual attachment; and (2) traumatic loss and mourning. Many other important aspects of the treatment will not be addressed. Although Dolores wanted to be able to find her own face in mine, she could not look at me, she shut her own face down, and she was often silent or dissociated. My response to Dolores was shaped both by my background as a psychoanalyst and as an infant researcher, particularly my own work on facial mirroring and vocal rhythm coordination in the mother–infant face-to-face exchange. In this way, we were matched: we both had a preoccupation with facial dialogue. Dolores reminds us how powerfully, and how early, we are affected by the "face dialogue."

THE FACE IN PSYCHOANALYSIS

Facial communication operates at the nonsymbolic, implicit/procedural level, largely out of awareness. Research using brain imaging suggests that faces enjoy a special status in the brain, because neural activity in the temporal lobes (fusiform gyrus) surges twice as much when adults watch faces vs. other objects (Bower 2001).

The role of the face in psychoanalysis is directly linked to seeing and being seen. Unless the treatment is organized in a sitting position, the face obviously plays a far diminished role, but it is still important in the interchanges around greeting and separation. Seeing and being seen carry many connotations, from Freud's (1913) view that the therapist's being seen dilutes the transference, to Sartre's view that seeing and being seen can objectify the self and other (see Eigen 1993), to the view that being seen and re-sponded to by the other is constitutive of the self (Bion 1977, Kohut 1977, Winnicott 1965).

Winnicott has been very influential in his understanding of mother–infant communication and its analogies in adult treat-ment. One of his most famous descriptions is of facial communi-cation. Winnicott (1974) asks what the infant sees, when he sees his mother's face; and Winnicott's answer is that the infant sees himself. Here we are alerted to the tremendous power of the mother's facial response, and its role in shaping the sense of self. However, this famous concept emphasizes the mother's impact on the infant, matching or reflecting back the infant's affective state, omitting Winnicott's equal appreciation for the role of the infant. The infant's facial-visual responsivity has a reciprocal power in affecting the mother's feeling of being recognized and loved by her baby (see Tronick 1989).

Eigen (1993) notes, "The centrality of the human face as sym-bolic of personality permeates the fabric of human experience" (p. 49). He suggests that the human face is the most prominent "organizing principle in the field of meaning" (p. 56). He argues that psychoanalysis must concern itself with the face, particularly in the early disorders of the self, because of the central importance of the face of the other in the formation of self-feeling (see also Kohut 1977, Weil 1958, Winnicott 1965, 1974). These patients are often unable to create an enduring image of the therapist's face, which is a critical aspect of the treatment. Eigen argues that the therapist's facial behavior plays an essential role in evoking and broadening the patient's capacity to experience. He describes the work of Levinas (1974) who argues that the birth of the human personality is associated with a positive experience of the face.

A substantial body of experimental adult literature demon-strates that facial action is simultaneously communicative and self-regulatory, modulating physiological arousal and subjective experience. Tomkins (1962, 1963) considered the face central, ex-pressing emotion both to others and to the self, via feedback from the tongue and facial muscles, the sound of one's own voice, and changes in blood-flow and temperature of the face. Changes in facial action are associated with subjective changes, either intensifying or inhibiting the experience of the emotion (Tomkins 1962). Facial action can influence subjective experience of emotion without awareness (Adelmann and Zajonc 1989, Ekman et al. 1980, 1983, Izard 1979, Levenson et al. 1990).

Because a particular facial expression is associated with a particular pattern of physiological arousal (Ekman et al. 1983), matching the expression of the partner produces a similar physiological state in the onlooker. Thus matching of expressions is an important way in which the emotional state of the individual can be transmitted to the partner (Adelmann and Zajonc 1989, Izard 1971, Laird 1984, Winton 1986). Other research shows that even without matching of facial expression, *the mere perception of emotion in the partner creates a resonant emotional state in the perceiver*, for infants as well as adults (Davidson and Fox 1982). Both positive and negative emotional "matching" reactions can be evoked out of awareness, so that important aspects of face-to-face communication occur on a nonconscious level (Dimberg et al. 2000). The Heller and Haynal (1997) study described in Chapter 1, the doctor's face as a mirror of his patient's suicidal projects, dramatically illustrates this nonconscious facial communication.

INTRODUCTION TO DOLORES

Dolores was a brilliant and accomplished professional woman, and capable at times of highly articulate self-reflection. She was very gifted at language. She was preoccupied with very early, nonverbal experiences, but nevertheless she possessed a remarkable ability to put her experiences into words. Her descriptions were often poetic. She was very interested in mothers and infants, and she read widely. Because of her own remarkable abilities and resources, aided by three previous treatments, Dolores was able to maintain a high level of professional functioning while simultaneously participating in an intense, difficult, and at times terrifying and destabilizing treatment with me. Aspects of the treatment described are disquieting.

Despite Dolores's language gifts, because of her long periods of profound dissociation, and because of her very early maternal loss, much of the early progress of the treatment occurred through the "action-dialogue" of our nonverbal communication. I used all modalities to try to reach her: the rhythm and intonation of our voices, our breathing rhythms, our head and bodily orientation, as well as my steady gaze, the dampening of my bodily activity, and my facial response. Although I was aware of some of my non-verbal behavior, most of it was out of my awareness. Only after reviewing in detail the videotaped interactions presented below, in preparation for writing this chapter, did I become aware of much of my nonverbal behavior with Dolores.

Derived from my research background with videotape micro-analysis of mother–infant interactions, I made an unusual inter-vention in the second year of treatment, taking a series of videotapes of Dolores and me together, and of my face only while interacting with her. I was familiar with using videotape viewing to facilitate understanding of nonverbal communication patterns in treatments of mother–infant pairs (Beebe 2003, 2005, Cohen and Beebe 2003, Downing 2001). I became interested in videotaping as a possible aid to reaching Dolores because, despite her gifts, in very central ways she was deeply shut down and difficult to engage. The paper describes some of these videotaped interactions, and the impact of the videotaping on the treatment. Through the analyses of the videotapes I came to understand a great deal more about the non-verbal and implicit aspects of my own collaborative participation. The paper attempts to find a language to describe our experiences together struggling with the sequelae of Dolores's early trauma, staying as close as possible to the actual words and actions of the two partners. Although most of this 10-year treatment was con-ducted as an ordinary psychoanalytic exchange, sitting up, in this paper I focus on the unusual videotaping rather than the back-ground of usual therapeutic exchange.

The chapter is organized with two intersecting goals. The first is a description of clinical material from various points across the 10-year treatment, selected particularly as it is relevant to Dolores's concerns about the face, and her traumatic loss and mourning. Some of the material is based on notes taken during sessions, and some from videotapes taken of my face only, as I was interacting with Dolores. The videotaped sessions occur 1½ years into the treatment. Whereas the material taken from notes describes the verbal interaction, the material taken from videotapes depicts the nonverbal and implicit process as well.

The second goal of the chapter is an ongoing commentary on this clinical material to illustrate the concepts from Chapter 3. Through this clinical material we revisit the central concepts of Meltzoff, Trevarthen, and Stern: the dialogic origin of mind, the role of correspondences, and the idea that symbolic forms of intersubjectivity are built on presymbolic forms. In addition we revisit from Chapter 3 various concepts offered to broaden a definition of the presymbolic origins of intersubjectivity: interactive regulation, the role of self regulation, the role of difference, distress regulation, and the "balance model" of self- and interactive regulation.

Dolores is a 40-year-old biology professor, very attractive, and sociable with students. An early marriage ended unhappily. Since then she has had some long friendships with men, including a long relationship with a boyfriend that did not work out, but she never remarried. Despite a few close and devoted friends, overall she is isolated and spends a great deal of time alone. Her primary mode of adaptation is to withdraw. Although she has been successful in her teaching career, she has difficulty thinking and writing alone. This is her fourth attempt at treatment. Dolores and I have been working together for 10 years in a 3 times per week, sitting-up, psychoanalytically oriented psychotherapy.

For the first year of the treatment, Dolores and I lived in the same city. However, when she obtained a teaching job three hours away in a neighboring state, where there were no adequate mental health facilities, Dolores and I decided to continue the treatment. Every other week she came into the city for two double-sessions in person, on two adjacent days; otherwise the treatment took place on the telephone.

For the first two years of her life Dolores had a foster mother with whom she had a close and affectionate relationship. Then her biological mother reclaimed her, and she never saw the "good" foster mother again. During the period with her biological mother, approximately ages 2 to 4, Dolores was emotionally, physically, and sexually abused. When she was 4 years old she became mute, which precipitated a year-long hospitalization. A photograph taken at this time shows a swollen, bruised face with a sullen stare. After a year in the hospital Dolores was adopted by a loving family. She thus had multiple abrupt, total changes of her attachment systems, including the early disruption of the bond to the original biological mother.

Dolores was preoccupied with faces and particularly the face of her first good foster mother. She used the metaphors of the "good face" and the "bad face" for her foster mother and her abusive, biological mother. She longed for an attachment to me, and yet she could not look at me, and often could not talk. Her facial and bodily expressiveness was inhibited, shut-down. For the first portion of every session she wore her sunglasses. She took them off only after considerable prodding. She appeared shy, hesitant, wary, low-key. At times she was severely dissociated. The treatment was a struggle to regain face-to-face relating and to create a secure attachment. Now, a decade later, she does look at me with a reasonably normal gaze pattern, most of the time. The attachment is progressively more secure, but much remains to be done.

At the beginning of the treatment Dolores and I sat face-to-face at the usual psychotherapy distance. The following process is based on notes taken during the first 6 sessions at the very beginning of the treatment. She glanced intermittently during these sessions but made no sustained eye-contact. Dolores had discussed some good memories of the good foster mother.

THE "GOOD FACE" OF THE FIRST MOTHER:
A FRAGMENT FROM THE FIRST SESSION

> Dolores: [speaking slowly, in a childlike voice] I do have the
> good face. It made me survive. I know that face, looking
> at me. I make that face happy, I know how her face goes.
> When I get so isolated, I'm missing someone I can give
> this to.
> BB: Yes.

Her comment that she can make the face happy, and when she
is isolated she is missing someone she can give this to, illustrates the
bidirectional model of influence that is so central in infant research
on face-to-face interaction. She describes the experience of the child
who makes the mother's face come alive. This is the other side of the
usual description of the mother echoing the child's own facial affect.
It is interesting that she speaks of "the" face, not "her" face.

> Dolores: The good face doesn't want my badness though, and
> then—I'm all alone. Then I can't find the good face any
> more. I know it's there, but I can't find it, I just can't find
> the good feelings in me. . . .

Here she illustrates the dyadic organization of experience: her
own good feelings are organized in relation to the good face. If her
relationship with the good face is disrupted in her own mind, then
her own goodness is lost.

> Dolores: I remember a time playing with my [adoptive]
> mother. I looked at her face, but I remembered *another*
> face. I remembered it so vividly that I felt I actually saw
> it. When I saw this face, I felt *alive* and good. I *was* good.
> I felt it in my molecules, the face, and how it tells me I
> am. I know from the face what I can be, and what it wants
> from me: when to be happy, and when to be scared; when

I'm good, and when I'm not. I know everything about me from the face. It tells me what's next. I know when it will love me, and when it won't. . . .

Her description captures the concept of "expectancies" in infant research: the idea that the infant comes to expect the moment-by-moment sequence of how the faces go, and what will be next. Here, however, she frames the description more in terms of the impact of the adult's face on the child's face. Her description also evokes the visual cliff experiment (Klinnert et al. 1983) in which a toddler is placed on a glass table, next to mother. Under the glass table, there is a "visual cliff." At the far side of the table are some very interesting toys. As the child begins to cross the table toward the toys, eventually he or she notices that it seems as if there is a cliff. The child looks back to mother. When the mother is instructed to show a smile face, the child proceeds without hesitation to the toys at the far end. When the mother is instructed to show a fear face, the child does not cross the "cliff." The child thus knows what to feel and what to do, whether to be scared and not cross, or to be unafraid and cross, from the face of the mother.

Her use of the word "molecules" links the words to the visceral, bodily level of experience, reminiscent of Loewald's (1980) concept of "linking" of words to preverbal experience (see Mitchell 2000). Bucci (1997) also emphasizes the link between visceral, bodily experience and emotion in language, through her concept of depth of referential imagery. Dolores's own capacity to make these links was a rich resource in the treatment.

> Dolores: I don't want to be so angry at the good face; I want her to help me.
>
> BB: You're angry at the good mother because she left you, and you're worried about being angry?
>
> Dolores: Yes. But I'm so ashamed of what happened, I don't want the good face to know about it. The good face didn't come back to get me, because she knew I was bad.

Her fear of shame, and of exposure of her "badness," may have contributed to her fear of looking, of being seen as well as seeing. Perhaps the good mother would see something bad in her face.

> BB: I can understand how you came to think this way, even though somewhere you know that no baby is bad. That is a 2-year old's theory. I think you are telling me that it is so important for you to remember the love that was there for you from the good mother, even though you were later abused.

Here I affirmed her love of the foster mother. I sensed the pivotal importance of this love. I also learned here how her shame over whatever happened in this period, and her anguish over being left, disturbed her contact with her memory of her good foster mother. Much later we delved into the storm of her rage at the foster mother for letting her go. Eventually I learned that the biological, abusive mother had told her that the foster mother had left her because she was a bad little girl; that the foster mother had found another, good little girl to take her place; and that is why the foster mother never came back.

> Dolores: Can you help me let the good face know what happened, and see if she still thinks I'm good?
> BB: Maybe you and I together can let the good face know what happened. You so long to feel the good mother's face. Without her, it seems so hard to feel that you are good yourself.
> Dolores: Maybe if you know that babies aren't bad, maybe you and I could say, that there still could be a good face of the mother and a good face of the baby? I don't want to leave the session. I need you to hold the two faces together.
> BB: You are struggling to hold together the face of the good mother, and the face of the good baby, even though you were abused.

Dolores: If the good mother knew the bad things, the baby
          would still be good?
BB: Yes.

I respond strongly that the child is good, setting the frame of
the therapy. In asking if I can help her let the good face know what
happened, she goes right to what she needs. In this segment I join
her capacity to be in the Winnicottian transitional play-space:
"Maybe you and I together can let the good face know what happened." Together we created a capacity for play, improvisation, and
at times, humor. Her capacity to be in this play-space, and to directly invite me in, was another rich resource of the treatment.

Her urgent request that the two faces be held together, that
she can't proceed with her development without being able to hold
the two faces together, her own and that of the good mother, can
be related to the "dialogic origin of mind" proposed by the three
infant theorists. She needs to be able to hold onto that early "face
dialogue." As Meltzoff, Trevarthen, and Stern have so eloquently
argued, there is a rich face (as well as vocal and touch) dialogue
prior to language, nuanced and complex, as Dolores was well aware.
My own background in research on face-to-face interaction led me
to think of the face dialogue (as well as gaze, orientation, voice) as
a complex arena for expressing and responding to emotions (rather
than a mimicking or manipulation of faces). This fragment illustrates
one of the major themes of the treatment, how Dolores engaged me
to help her in her quest to integrate her different mothering experiences, with such radically different sets of expectancies.

NOT BEING FOUND BY THE ADOPTIVE MOTHER'S FACE: FRAGMENT FROM THE FIRST WEEKS OF TREATMENT

Dolores: I searched my [adoptive] mother's face, and there
          was no rest for me there, where faces meet and match.
          This is what I lost, though I know I *did* once have it. Help
          me wake up. I do not want to go dead. [pause] I know I

did not look right to my [adoptive] mother. I didn't know why, I knew my face wasn't right. I couldn't look at her, and find me. [pause] I had it once, though not for long, I know I did. And that is what is here with you.

BB: That is what you came looking for?

Dolores: You can help me find it. I have a resting place here, a coming alive, feeling recognized, someone who doesn't turn away. I won't live if I don't get it. [pause] My [adoptive] mother needed to stop me. She never found herself in me, so I never found myself in her. I shut down. Though once I had it, I know I did.

Dolores describes the terrible impact of a disruption in the mutual facial mirroring process between her and her adoptive mother, and the disaster of not being "found" (Winnicott 1965, 1974). I admired her striving to hold onto "the good face," and to her aliveness. When she described the powerful impact of feeling me respond to her, it drew me closer. I was very affected by her invitation, but I also heard the panic: she won't live if she doesn't get it. This made me feel worried as well.

"Where the faces meet and match" is reminiscent of the description of matching found in the three infant theorists of intersubjectivity. This "meeting and matching" seems to be the essence of a certain kind of aliveness for her, and without it she will "go dead." A central dilemma is that she urgently wants this meeting and aliveness, and yet she cannot do it. "Going dead" is reminiscent of the infants who are later classified as disorganized attachment at 12 months (Jaffe et al. 2001, Lyons-Ruth, personal communication, August 18, 1999). At 4 months these infants lose postural tonus and go limp, "playing possum" (see Papousek and Papousek 1977) or "inhibiting responsivity" (see Beebe and Stern 1977), presumably in a move of conservation-withdrawal (Perry 1996). Eventually a feeling of inner deadness became one of the most pressing issues of Dolores's treatment, reminiscent of deadness as a core clinical concern in Ogden's theory of intersubjectivity.

Dolores seems to "recognize" in me someone who "recognizes" her. This bedrock of the treatment was established almost immediately. Her determination to regain the feeling of being alive, to find the place where "faces meet and match," to find herself in the face of the other, continued to be a source of hope in the treatment, a counterpoint to her deadness.

"I DON'T HAVE A FACE OF MY OWN": FRAGMENT FROM THE FIRST WEEKS OF TREATMENT

> Dolores: You know, there is a lot of confusion about my face. When I'm more stressed bad things happen. Sometimes I feel very young. I have the sensation then of a thin piece of skin over my eyes, and the sensation of my face turning to stone.
>
> BB: It seems you feel your face stopped moving and your eyes stopped seeing, in reaction to not having your good mother's face to respond to you. You must have been so terribly depressed with the abusive mother.

I am tender, warm, worried. Here she returns to a visceral experience of deadness, the face turning to stone. Her face went dead after she lost the good foster mother, and she sadly did not regain the aliveness of her face with her adopted mother. The face going dead seems to be a metaphor for the self going dead, after losing the good foster mother. Her state at that time, without an attachment partner, without a face-dialogue, and prior to a strong, symbolic, evocative capacity, constituted the loss of any possibility of intersubjectivity, however defined.

> Dolores: (continues): I feel alienated from my face. My face doesn't *feel* like *me*. *I don't have a face of my own.* I look at *other* people's faces to see what *my* face looks like. My adoptive mother looked at me like a stranger. I didn't feel my face looked right. I couldn't look at her and find me.

BB: It seems that your adoptive mother wasn't able to be *responsive* enough to your face, both of you couldn't really respond to the other, and then you developed the idea that there was something *wrong* with your face.

Dolores: Maybe *you* could understand [pause] that I might not *have* a face. Maybe something *is* wrong with my face. Maybe I *do* have a bad face. I need to see your face, to feel that I am looking at the good face, and to feel good myself.

Dolores has two traumatic ideas here; that she has a bad face, or worse, that she might not have a face at all, and that her face turns to stone: her face is dead. These experiences of her face are presumably coordinated with an unresponsive or an abusive partner. She again states one of the core issues of the treatment, that she needs my face to regain her own inner aliveness and goodness. Yet, she cannot look at me.

BB: A child gets her own face from the face of the mother, and the mother gets her feeling of being a mother from the face of her child. You feel that you had it, and then you lost it. Then evidently all you had was the bad face. That made you feel like your own face is bad. Now you want to see my face, to reflect back to you your own good face. But it's very hard for you to look.

Dolores: I understand. I have to find you, to find your face, to find my own face. I don't like feeling like I don't have a face. You recognize me. Maybe you could understand that I might not have a face.

It is remarkable that Dolores knows that she must find my face to find her own. In some very palpable sense, it is true that Dolores does not have a "face," or facial-visual responsiveness, that she can use in co-creating our engagement. She essentially defines for us one of the most central goals of the treatment. Her ability to reflect on the process in this way was another essential resource. My comments emphasize that Dolores's experience of her face was developed in relation to a lack of appropriate responsivity in both the abusive, biological mother and the later adoptive mother. I was very touched by Dolores. I responded to her longing for engagement with me.

I was moved by the horror of her early childhood. My experience of her terror was perhaps most palpable when I would approach her warmly in the waiting room to greet her. She would back away from me, with the look of a frightened animal. I learned to approach her very slowly, and to keep my distance at first. In the Ainsworth separation–reunion test of attachment at 1 year, backing away from the mother upon the reunion is a behavior characteristic of infants classified as disorganized (Main and Hesse 1992).

MY DIFFICULTY REACHING DOLORES

Following a half dozen initial sessions in which she told me her story in a halting manner, filled with intense emotion, and quite coherent, Dolores began to sit with her body oriented away from me, without looking, barely talking. She seemed out of contact, dissociated. At this early point in the treatment I tried many different strategies of making contact with her. I began to notice that at various points, without looking, she oriented toward and away from me. I suggested that, instead of trying to talk, perhaps we could begin by trying together to become aware of when she was able to move her body to be oriented to me, and when she oriented away. Over the course of the ensuing months Dolores began to elaborate on the metaphor, saying "I'm in your orient," or "I'm falling out of your orient." Dolores's ability to respond in this rather poetic way was very touching, and it helped us work on maintaining a sense of a bond. But it continued to be difficult to make contact with her with a more usual verbal narrative, and she continued to be dissociated for long periods without speaking. Eventually I experimented with moving my chair into a more "biological" face-to-face distance, the two chairs at right angles, with a small table in between. This distance is approximately that of usual adult face-to-face interaction distance, closer than usual face-to-face psychotherapy, but not as close as that between mother and infant. This arrangement somewhat facilitated making contact with Dolores: she seemed more aware of my presence, and the long dissociated periods became less frequent and prolonged. We have maintained this arrangement.

How was I affected by the fact that I could not "get" Dolores's gaze or face? I experienced her muted face and voice as fear, rather than as withholding. I felt patient, very similar to interacting with the infants of my research. I tried to have no agenda but to stay with her, to try to sense what she felt, and follow what she said. Dolores frequently told me how important I was to her. I am certain that if she had not been as forthcoming in this regard, I would have had a much more difficult time, and the treatment would have taken a very different course. Her own generous and loving approach to me was a critical catalyst in the treatment.

Because after the first year of treatment Dolores's teaching position required that she live at a considerable distance from my office, much of treatment was conducted on the telephone. The sessions in person every other week were usually long double sessions. Whereas we were usually successful in generating a genuine engagement for some period in the sessions conducted in person, over the telephone the sessions were very difficult. Dolores was often completely quiet for long periods. And she was in agony over the long periods without seeing me in person. She explained that she could not remember me in between sessions. She had tried and tried to remember the good foster mother. Every day she had thought that today, maybe she will come back. And day after day after day, the mother did not come back. Until eventually, one day, Dolores described that her "mind snapped: it was a physical feeling of breaking." After that, something changed, something was broken.

INTRODUCTION OF VIDEOTAPING

About a year and a half into the treatment, when Dolores was having a great deal of trouble adjusting to seeing me less in person, she brought up the idea of videotaping some sessions. She knew that my research involved videotaping mothers and infants. We discussed it, and we were both interested in the idea. Because Dolores could not look at me, I thought that the videotape might help her sense more of my feeling for her. I believed that her ability to engage with my face would be essential in reclaiming her relatedness and aliveness. Some of the footage was of Dolores and me together, but some of it was of my face only, as I interacted with her.

I will describe several brief sections of videotape from this period 1½ years into the treatment. At this point, Dolores barely looked at me, with the exception of a rare fleeting glance. However, out of her peripheral vision she could certainly detect my body movement and facial changes, although not the exact facial expression. Obviously she could monitor my vocal rhythms, contours, and cadences. I selected sections that I have permission to show to professional audiences, where only my face is visible. My face reflects what I see in her, what I see her feel, as well as my own response. Her face is omitted according to her wishes. In this portion of the videotape her speech was nearly inaudible, requiring close attention to understand it. Her voice was muffled and childlike.

The following sections are based on close videotape analysis. In my descriptions I distinguish vocal rhythm (see Jaffe et al. 2001), vocal contour (Fernald 1987), and pitch. I also comment on my degree of bodily activation, self-comforting self-touch, hand gestures and face (see Beebe 2003, 2005). Often Dolores's words are barely audible from the videotape, but the rhythm of her words is usually detectable. I generally repeat what I hear her say, because I am straining to understand her words. Although I may have been aware of some of my nonverbal behavior, most of it was out of awareness. For example, I know that I was being "quiet" with my body in the first section below, but only after I examined the tape did I realize how completely quiet I had become, to adjust to her level of fearfulness. I am aware that I also slow down and reduce my level of activity when I interact with infants. But for Dolores I did this in an even more dramatic fashion.

MOMENTS IN WHICH DOLORES AND I REACH
EACH OTHER: VIDEOTAPE ILLUSTRATION 1,
1½ YEARS INTO THE TREATMENT (2 MINUTES)

As this moment opens, my face is in side-view. My body is completely still. I am careful not to make sudden movements. In contrast to my more usual high-energy style, I have lowered my arousal to the very bottom of my range. I am leaning forward, with an intent, direct, sustained focus. I am paying very focused, tender attention to Dolores, listening to every word, and clearly working hard to understand what she says. It is as if nothing else in the world exists for me except for her. Dolores does not look at me.

> Dolores: In the, in the [pause] good way [pause] that [pause]
> that I [pause] that I feel [pause] complicated about—

Dolores' speech is hesitant, dampened, stop-start, stuttering, fragmented, with a staccato rhythm. She seems to be in considerable distress, and struggling to express a complicated feeling.

> BB: In that good way? In the good way that you feel compli-
> cated about?

My tone is very soft. I repeat her phrase, but bring it into a more flowing and coherent rhythm. I don't hesitate. The contour rises by the end of the sentence, with a feeling of "questioning" and "opening." The rising intonation at the end is slightly enlivening. It is as if I am sensing her longing to connect to me, despite her terror, and I am elongating the moment, as if to say, "Stay here in this moment with me." As I work hard to understand her words, my rhythm and tone render her fragmented communication more coherent, as I convey "I am getting it." As I say, "In that good way," my chin is tilted upward, and my left hand holds my chin. But as I continue with, "In the good way that you feel complicated about," my hand moves upward, and I hold the side of my face and forehead. My own self-soothing acknowledges her level of distress. This interaction illustrates not a "matching" but a "difference" response. My rhythm is clearly different from hers, but it facilitates the relatedness. I provide more opening, enlivening, and coherence that she then partially joins, when she reaches "good but sad," below. This interaction illustrates one form of distress regulation: I enter the rhythm and cadence of her distress, but I also slightly transform the expression of it.

>   Dolores: Uh-huh.
>   BB: The good way of being connected to me that's so complicated?

Here I repeat her phrase but elaborate it, adding the phrase "of being connected to me," a symbolic elaboration. My rhythm is flowing. I emphasize her longing to connect.

>   Dolores: [long pause] Good but sad.

"Good but sad" is an important integration that Dolores achieves here. Her rhythm here is flowing, more organized. Perhaps my increased coherence through the rhythm of my speech, and my symbolic elaboration, enabled her to describe this poignant dilemma.

>   BB: You feel good but *sad*? [pause] Good but *sad*? [long pause]

Here I match the rhythm of her phase, but again slightly elaborate on it as well. I use a rising intonation and elongate the word "sad," with a question intonation, conveying an opening quality. By repeating her phrase twice I tarry in the feeling of it, giving us both a moment to absorb it. My intent face conveys the intensity of my listening. Dolores's ability to endorse both the positive and the negative feelings is extremely important, and my repetition underscores it. This interaction again illustrates a form of distress regulation, in which the matching aspect of my response constitutes entering her distress, but my elaboration on her rhythm is a form of slightly re-organizing it.

> BB: Is the complicated part about having to leave? [pause] Are you thinking about that right now? And whether you'll turn to concrete?

I connect her feeling to the imminent end of the session. "Turning to concrete" is a phrase she had used earlier in the session to describe her feeling about leaving. With each sentence, I slightly change the pattern of the way my hand is self-soothing my face, registering my own efforts to regulate my intense feelings with Dolores. Dolores's feet are visible in the videotape at this moment, and her toes wiggle, then rub up against each other, self-soothing.

> Dolores: [inaudible]
> BB: [repeating what I think I hear] "But you're planting a flower before you leave?"

My chin moves upward, in a greater focus of attention, and my body is completely still. This may convey to Dolores how intent I am on what she is saying and feeling.

> Dolores: [inaudible]
> BB: You're planting a flower that you're coming back?
> Dolores: [inaudible]
> BB: Before you turn to concrete?

My eyebrows go up in a concerned expression. The more hope she has, the more she dreads that she may lose me. Leaving is excruciating. On the other hand, in this vignette she integrates the opposites of her experience: good but sad, alive flower and inanimate concrete.

The next time that Dolores came to a session in person, together we watched this videotape that we had made. She watched the video without taking her eyes off it. She was riveted, and tearful. This was the first prolonged period that she had been able to see my face, and she was so moved to see me. We talked about how she still could not look at me while we actually interacted, but how important it was to her to be able to see me on the video.

REACHING EACH OTHER WITH AN EXPANDED RANGE: VIDEOTAPE ILLUSTRATION 2, 3 MONTHS LATER (1 MINUTE)

In this session my body moves around slightly, with greater range, suggesting that I sense at this moment that Dolores is not as vulnerable as she was in the earlier session, in which my body (although not my hands) stayed completely still. My body uses the three dimensions of space, shaping the space in a more open, embracing way than in the previous vignette. My chest has a concave shape, similar to that of a mother snuggling her baby into her chest. My gestures have a soft, circular, undulating quality. My head tilts and bobs at times, and overall the movements of my body are more playful.

> BB: You told me something important that will help us, with why it's so hard. [pause] You told me that if you look at me [my head tilts, I lean forward, and I gesture with my right hand], maybe I'll become the mother you'll never see again. [pause] If you let yourself *have* my face, it will be like the mother whose face you *lost*. That if you *look* at me, you'll never *see* me again. [pause] So no wonder you wouldn't want to look at me [my eyebrows go up]. [long pause]
>
> Dolores: unh.
>
> BB: If you don't look at me, it won't happen. That's your idea, right? [long pause]
>
> BB: [slight smile, with soft sadness: I see something on her face] You're worried about leaving aren't you? [long pause]

> Dolores: If I don't look at you, it won't happen. [for a split-second Dolores glances at my face]
> BB: [big, soft smile]
> [a few minutes later in the same session]
> BB: [picking up on something she has just said] [smiling] If you look at the *videotape* it will put my face in front of your eyes, but not through *your* looking.

I am referring here to the fact that the first time she really looked at my face for more than a split-second occurred when we both watched the first video of a session together, a few months earlier. She had been very moved to see my face, and tearful. She could tolerate seeing me in the videotape better than in vivo. My tone is playful, with rising contours. I am gently teasing her about not looking at me, and we are sharing some humor. Earlier in the exchange, my head tilt, leaning forward, with a hand gesture, served to emphasize my verbal communication. Head tilting or slight shifts of head orientation, as well as orientational changes and hand gestures, are important markers of the exchange, accentuating the moment.

> Dolores: [inaudible]
> BB: [repeating what I think I have heard her say] My face jumped into your eyes, for one little second? [pause] Really? [pause] Well, *that's* good.

My eyebrows go up, I have a big smile, and the phrase "Well, that's good" has a "sinusoidal" contour, known in infant research as a "greeting" contour. I am greeting her playful effort at engagement.

> [Big shift: I see something on her face]
> BB: You feel sad.
> Dolores: [inaudible]
> BB: [repeating what I think I have heard her say] Leaving is the *worst* thing that could happen?

Her positive feelings rapidly move to sadness. I match the rhythm of her words, including her emphasis on "worst." I add a slight questioning intonation at the end. My body becomes very quiet. I briefly close my eyes, and I let out a soft sigh. This interaction illustrates a form of distress regulation that is very close to an exact matching. I elaborate in two subtle ways: the questioning intonation, which leaves open the possibility of other feelings, and the sigh, which elaborates on the sense of loss.

Dolores: [inaudible]
BB: All the wrong faces will come back?

I repeat her sentence, but add a question intonation at the end. Again, this slight elaboration of the question intonation holds open the possibility that this might or might not happen.

Dolores: Unh.
BB: And will you get rid of *my* face?

I want to help her to connect to my face in every possible way. I imply that she is active in keeping or losing my face. This is where I hope the treatment is going (see Loewald 1980, Kohut 1977), although at this point she seems to have very little ability to hold onto the image of my face. [long pause]

Dolores: [inaudible]
BB: You won't be able to take the subway to come see me.

Here I exactly match the rhythm and contour of her statement. There is no question that she will not be able to take the subway to see me during the next period when the sessions will be held on the telephone. My face has a "woe-face" expression, giving a palpable form to the feeling in her words.

Dolores: [inaudible]
BB: Or call up down the street.

Dolores is referring to the fact that the next period of sessions will be on the telephone, and she lives so far outside the city that she will not just be able to take a subway to see me, as she could if she lived in the city. On this particular day she had called me from her cell phone down the street as she was coming to the session.

I nod my head. My face is quiet. But my head and my words exactly match the rhythm and contour of her statement without changing anything. Exact matches can constitute a very particular form of empathy; here I have no agenda but to stay exactly in her feeling. I am accepting her very coherent statement of loss, exactly how she expresses it. This interaction also illustrates a form of distress regulation that I term, "joining the dampened state" (see Beebe 2000, 2003, Cohen and Beebe 2003). The crossmodal matching of my head and her words illustrates Stern's concept of affect attunement.

Dolores: [says something inaudible; I don't repeat it.]
BB: [gentle laugh; body moves]

In this fragment of the session Dolores is experimenting (ever so slightly) with looking at me. After I elaborate on her own interpretation of why she does not look at me (that I might become the mother she will never see again), she glances at my face. Then I gently tease her about looking at me, and she glances at me again. My expanded nonverbal range, with more bodily movement, laughing, without marked self-comforting self-touch, parallels Dolores's own increased engagement and verbal participation. It contrasts with the session 3 months earlier in which my own nonverbal range was more constricted, presumably in an effort not to over-arouse or frighten her, and in an effort to stay closer to her own range of activation. Immediately following the increased engagement and aliveness of the first portion of this vignette, Dolores goes into the sadness of the imminent end of the session, poignantly expressing her feelings. But by the end of the vignette, Dolores again introduces some gentle humor, and I softly laugh. In this approximately 1-minute vignette, Dolores integrates experimentation with looking, sadness about loss, and humor, showing an expanding range.

THE STRUGGLE TO DISCUSS DOLORES'S EARLY
HISTORY: SECOND HALF OF SECOND YEAR

These videotapes document aspects of our slow, careful work of bonding. They show how we both contributed to the possibility that Dolores might feel less distressed, more engaged, and at times comforted. A period then followed in the second half of the second year in which Dolores made a concerted effort to tell me some more about her early history. It was extremely difficult for Dolores to tell me anything concrete. We might spend an entire session struggling to make it possible for Dolores to communicate one piece of information.

During this period, at the point at which she might begin to discuss any of the details, she would become agitated, her body would tighten, and eventually she would hold her breath, as if in an effort to hold everything in. She would hold her breath for long periods, unable to stop, until she would begin to panic. Eventually I began to try to get her to synchronize with my breathing. I made soft, rhythmic sounds as I breathed in and out. Dolores called it the "breathing song." Together we began to be able to anticipate when an episode of breath-holding was about to begin, and to do the breathing song together before she became extremely agitated. Over the course of the next couple of years the breathing symptom gradually became less frequent.

Another dramatic expression of her difficulty communicating the details of her early history was an abrupt falling into deep sleep after revealing something particularly painful. The sleep would last for the rest of the session, and she could not be wakened. I would sit near her head, and while she was sleeping I would softly tell her what had just happened, and why I thought she had to fall into a deep sleep. Then I would stay next to her while she slept, and every once in a while softly tell her that I was there while she was sleeping. Toward the end of the session she was able to wake up, and to listen while I again told her what I thought had happened. Gradually she would be able to reorganize. I would walk with her around the room until I felt she had regained her full consciousness and could leave. Very often a friend met her at the end of the session.

Going to sleep as a way of escaping these painful memories gradually yielded to a less severe form of retreat, in which Dolores's eyelids would begin to flutter, and she would declare that she was "going behind her eyes." This became a way of communicating to me that she was becoming overwhelmed and needed to retreat. Our validating her need to retreat would very often make it possible to proceed.

During this period she touched the same two scarred areas on her body, over and over, in a quasi-trancelike state, asking me if she were bleeding. From this behavior we were able to understand that she had been beaten. She remembered that she would hide in the closet to escape the abusive (biological) mother. She whispered over and over to me, "Shhh. Don't move. Be quiet. Shhh." Her body was tight with fear.

During the periods in which she was struggling to tell me something about the sexual abuse that occurred during the period with her biological mother, she vomited on her way to the sessions. There was a tightening in her face around her mouth, and she did not want anyone to come near her mouth. These symptoms, together with other memories, associations, and drawings she brought me, were eventually linked to an oral sexual abuse.

During this period of the treatment she reported that she had once gotten on a bus, around the age of 20, and traveled all day and all night, going looking for the first good mother. She had also found a file that belonged to her father, with information about the adoption. In that file she had also found the photograph of the little girl with the bruised, swollen face.

DOLORES'S DISCOVERY OF A MAN IN MY LIFE: TOWARD THE END OF THE SECOND YEAR

Six months later Dolores discovered that I had a man in my life. This reminded her of the last day that she had seen the first good mother, who had left with a man. She developed the idea that "the man" had taken her mother away. She was convinced that "the man" would take me away from her, and that she would lose her "place" with me. Much later in the treatment we discovered that this traumatic theme, that the father figure would take the mother away, was repeated in various ways in all three of her family constellations.

The presence of a man in my own life evoked in Dolores this core traumatic theme that, from then on, became a central aspect of the treatment. Our "honeymoon" was over. She began to struggle with the feeling of being "kicked out," similar to the way she had felt "kicked out" from the first good mother. For the first 6 months after discovering "the man," Dolores barely spoke to me. It was an "ice-rage." The sessions over the telephone were particularly difficult for us. It was quite a loss for me to endure such a profound withdrawal of her love. At first I felt terribly guilty, and it evoked a core traumatic theme in my own early childhood, my own "badness." This reaction of mine sent us into quite a tailspin. My reaction made it extremely difficult for me—and us—to tolerate how enraged she was. Slowly I came to terms with the idea that this theme had to emerge, that it would have happened sooner or later, and that it would be essential to her recovery. I also acknowledged to her that some of our difficulty was coming from something in me, something from my own childhood, that had been re-evoked. This acknowledgment meant a lot to her, and she did not press for details. Slowly she began to talk to me again. Although we have continued to struggle with this theme for the entire treatment, we have increasingly been able to think together about what it means.

DOLORES'S USE OF VIEWING THE VIDEOTAPES TO FOSTER AN INTERNALIZATION PROCESS: MAKING MY FACES ON HER FACE, 2½ YEARS INTO THE TREATMENT

These are notes taken during a session on the telephone. While she was alone, Dolores had been looking at the videotapes taken 1½ years into the treatment, described earlier.

Dolores: I was looking at your face looking at me. I saw the way it's different when I'm with you.

BB: You saw it watching the video?

Dolores: Yes.

BB: What did you see?

Dolores: I saw that you were seeing me. I wasn't seeing you, when I was with you in person, but later, when I was watching the video, and I saw you, I felt much more real.

BB: Wow.

Dolores: Yes. In a way that, when I am with my feelings alone, sometimes I don't. But when I saw my feelings on your face, I felt more, feeling my feelings. I felt kind of familiar. But I don't *feel* them, necessarily, when I'm alone.

BB: That's very interesting. "To feel them" means what, really?

Dolores: When I'm alone with them I feel more confused. When I see them on your face, I can read them better. When I'm having them all by myself, there isn't any sense to them—that's part of what feels so bad, nobody to make any meaning.

BB: Can we make the same meaning when we're talking on the phone, now, without the faces?

Dolores: I need to see, or I need to *feel*. I have the picture of you, looking at me, and I like it; you never take your eyes away from my face. But now, on the phone, your voice floats on the ear, floats away. I want your eyes looking at me.

This session shows how Dolores began to use watching the videotape as an adjunct to the internalization process. Internalization can be reconceptualized as an expectation of an interactive process, in which the inner organization is based on reciprocal coordinations, joint bidirectional interactive patterns, which regulate the exchange (Beebe and Lachmann 1994, Benjamin 1988, Loewald 1980). Watching the videotapes provided a format in which she could actually see and take in more information from my face. This was her idea. From my research on the facial interchange between infants and mothers, I was convinced that she needed to see my feelings for her in my face, as well as hearing my emotions through my voice. The videotape gave us one powerful way to do that. At this point in the treatment she still did not look at me, and we did not yet completely understand the dynamics behind this.

The research of Dimberg and colleagues (2000) can be used to imagine what happened when Dolores watched my face watching her. Out of her own awareness or conscious intention, Dolores's face probably matched my expressions. The work of Ekman and colleagues (Ekman 1983, Ekman et al. 1983, Levenson et al. 1990), showing that particular facial expressions are associated with particular patterns of physiological arousal, suggests that Dolores had visceral as well as facial responses as she watched my face. This research is consistent with Gergeley and Watson's (1998) suggestion that, in the parent–infant face-to-face exchange, one function of facial mirroring is an amplification of the infant's own inner state. Seeing one's own facial expression reproduced or elaborated on the face of the partner may help the infant sense and register his or her own face and associated proprioceptive feedback. Something like this seems to have occurred between Dolores and me. She was learning more about her own feelings by watching me experience her. Her inner registration and identification of her feelings had been difficult for her. When she was able to "see" herself in my face, she was able to sense her own inner state more clearly (G. Downing, personal communication, July 18, 2001). She was also better able to register her own response to me in a verbal mode: she *likes* the feeling of my face watching her so closely. The discovery of "mirror neurons," described in Chapter 2, is also relevant to Dolores's watching the videotapes. Simply by watching my actions, for example a moment of tender response on my face, her own brain was activated in the premotor cortex, as if she were herself performing those actions.

At the end of this section she poignantly reminds us how difficult it is for her on the telephone. She had such difficulty remembering me in between sessions, which was exacerbated by the unfortunate necessity to have so many of the sessions over the telephone.

FURTHER WORK ON INTERNALIZATION: "THOSE GOOD FACE-FEELINGS: THAT IS WHAT I HAVE INSIDE OF ME"

> [Continuing over the telephone one week later]
> Dolores: I'm thinking about how I used the video to remember you. Because I don't look at you when I'm with you. I don't have the memory of my face *interacting* with your face, because I don't *do* that. But when I was *watching* you, on the video while I was alone, I was interacting with your face. When I wanted to have certain feelings, I called up the feeling of your face. *I was making your faces on my face.*

Here her experience is reminiscent of the work of Meltzoff. She is describing a "like me" experience. She can get back to her own experience through my face. First she senses that, as I interact with her, my face is like hers: I feel her and my face reflects what I feel. Then as she matches my face in the video as she watches it, her face is like mine. In this way she has gotten back to her original feeling.

> BB: Like imitating?
> Dolores: Yes but not imitating exactly. More remembering the feeling of your face talking to my face—not the words. I said your 'face-talk' *on my face.* I was getting the feeling for what was happening in the faces, and that's how I remembered certain feelings, certain good feelings—how I remembered feeling comforted—during watching the video, and after—during the good period when I wasn't saying that your face isn't for me, anymore.

Here Dolores is referring to the fact that, after discovering the presence of a man in my life, she felt that her face was no longer for me, and my face was no longer for her: the trauma with the good foster mother. But she continues here to be able to talk about a profound feeling of facial connection between us, nevertheless.

> BB: I'm so sorry that you feel that now. But I still feel that my face *is* for you.
>
> Dolores: You have such good faces. I have those good face-feelings. That is what is *inside me*. I sometimes have bad face-feelings too. Your good faces, the "still-lake-face," the "resting-face"—I like best your "just-watching-all-the-time-face," it makes me safe.
>
> BB: I'm so happy that you can see what my face feels for you. And how did you remember us after you watched the video?
>
> Dolores: I wanted the feeling again. *One strange thing: afterwards I made your face.*
>
> BB: Oh! Which one?
>
> Dolores: A certain face. A picture of my feelings. Deep. Like when you see I'm worried or sad.
>
> BB: Then you made my "worry-sad-face"?
>
> Dolores: Yes. I moved my face. I could just feel you.
>
> BB: You could feel me responding to you?
>
> Dolores: If I don't have a responder, I can't even have that feeling. It's *you*, feeling *me*, and it's *me*, seeing myself on your face. *Then I can feel more real, then I know that it is me.* On the video, when I let myself be with your face, *then I knew that your face was for me*, the second time I watched it. I could see that your face was not bad or scared or mean. The face is the beginning of a person. This face loves me; I'm ok.
>
> BB: I think you felt this once before, with the face of the first good mother, and now you feel it again with me.
>
> Dolores: I guess I took it away from you.
>
> BB: Because you think that my face is not supposed to be for you, anymore, because of "the man"?
>
> Dolores: I don't want there to be three faces. If there are three, only two go together, and my face isn't in it.

BB: You're describing to me a way of using the video to help yourself know that I sense you. But because of this terrible tragedy where you lost your first good mother, and you think a man took her away, your ability to know that my face is for you has been disrupted. This is very difficult and sad for us.

Dolores: All the other times I looked at the video I saw your face, but I didn't let myself *be* with your face, and I didn't let your face *be with me*. This time I did. It caught me by surprise.

BB: You really let yourself have it this time? You need my face to feel my reach for you, and to feel yourself.

Dolores: Otherwise I'm like a blind baby.

She is even more articulate in this session than the last one about how she uses the videotape as an adjunct to an internalization process. Her statement, ". . . those good face-feelings: that is what I have inside of me" is a way of talking about how she can viscerally as well as symbolically sense my appreciation of what she feels. She is active in the process of matching my faces on the video, participating, creating, rehearsing. She also uses her memory of looking at the videotapes to call up certain feelings, and she makes subtle differentiations among my faces. This is a big shift in her own capacity and activity. The discovery of a man in my life threatens to disrupt her emerging but still very fragile internalization of our relationship.

BEING SENSED. ONE YEAR LATER, EARLY IN THE FOURTH YEAR

[Notes taken during a telephone session]

Dolores: When I get so sure inside that I don't have a face, and then I disappear, when I don't have a sensing—I don't know which is first, my face or the other face—then I

don't have my senses, even breathing, because all my
senses are in the face.

BB: In the face of the other person, in relation to your face?

Dolores: Yes—in *your* face. I don't have a face if I'm not sensed.
If I'm not in your senses, then there's no way to be alive.
You don't have any of your own senses or sensings without the other person. Then you can't talk.

BB: Is that maybe why you couldn't talk and went mute?

Dolores: I think so. I did not have any senses. I couldn't sense
anyone else's senses, or anyone sensing me—even the
touching sense—touching is still in the face.

BB: That must have been so terrible.

Dolores: Yes.

BB: And do you feel that way again now?

Dolores: Yes.

In this vignette Dolores tells me how much she needs my sensing her in order to have a sensing experience of herself. This experience of not being sensed by me, and not sensing herself, typically occurred during a telephone session, and almost never face-to-face. She is also very coherent and articulate in this session, particularly in contrast to material from the middle of the second year. Earlier in her life she had had an image of herself as completely alone, a "little creature without a head." My association to this session is that she "took off her head" in response to the traumatic loss of a sensing loving presence when she lost her first good mother. She could not sense herself alone, and she felt she had lost her head.

YOUR FACE IN RESPONSE TO MY FACE: YOU LET ME IMPACT ON YOU. EARLY IN THE FIFTH YEAR

[Notes taken during a session in person]

Dolores: My whole life I have had big feelings about a lost face
I was looking for. It reminds me how I felt after I lost the

relationship with James [the long relationship that did not work out] and I was in unbelievably deep grief and mourning. I don't have the words for it but I know a huge part of the loss had to do with how I had impacted on him, on his face. That was a metaphor, maybe, of a total way of responding. You know, how like a dance makes music visible, a face makes a whole heart visible.

BB: How did you impact on his face?

Dolores: Part of what was so missing was his face—his face-in-response-to-my-face. I learned about myself when I saw my impact on his face. I created something—to see yourself, to see your impact on the other person. I can make that face do a lot of different things. You know, we seek the pleasure and the desire on someone else's face. [long pause] It was not just that I was missing his face, but the conversation, what I could make happen. The loss was, to be able to make a difference. (Dolores cries). When I met you—Sally (Dolores's previous therapist) was quite wonderful, but she kept hiding. She was uneasy about letting me impact on her, except—she would use her own reactions, but only in terms of what I might have evoked in her. The therapist can say, you know, I find myself feeling angry—and can use that to talk about the patient's anger. But do you think a therapist ever says, you know, I found myself feeling loved—

BB: [laughs] I do feel that.

Dolores: That is what is different here. From the very beginning you let me impact on you. That is what I've been missing my whole life.

BB: How did I do it?

Dolores: [Cries] You accepted it, what my feelings were, or what my face was or offered—you met it. You felt impacted or changed by it. Not like Sally. With Sally it was about my unconscious exerting a pressure on her to feel a certain something, and what did that say about me. It wasn't about "me and you," the way it is here.

BB: I did feel so moved by you and by your story. I remember so vividly the first day I met you.

Dolores: You shook my hand in that little waiting room, the first day.

BB: And the next time I saw you I ran into you in the street.

Dolores: You recognized me—

BB: And we were both so surprised and delighted in the moment.

Dolores: Because of the power of our first meeting.

BB: Yes. I know I did let myself be affected by you, by your story. I remember I wrote down some of the things you said about your face, in those first few meetings.

Dolores: Your response to me made me more hopeful. It helped me identify what it was I needed.

BB: I'm so happy you feel this way. (Pause). And will you remember this on Monday?

Dolores: No. I am too upset when I remember it and don't have it. Maybe I remember the loss of it.

BB: Yes. I think so. The loss of our conversation, even temporarily, becomes more salient than what we had. Like the infant research example by Stern of one mother who attunes to enthusiasm, when the little girl is having fun and becoming excited, on the way up the arousal curve; and another mother who attunes to "exthusiasm": when her little girl is on the way down, the blocks fell, don't worry honey we'll build it up again. You code "ex-thusiasm."

Dolores: Therapists are best at entering the patient's distress, not the patient's joy. But the therapist as a person may resist entering the full despair.

BB: And sometimes you feel I have trouble entering the full impact of your despair.

Dolores: Yes.

The remarkable range of Dolores's functioning is again evident here as she describes the lost relationship with James. Her ability to value her impact on James, and on me, helps to repair the profound helplessness of her early years. At the end of the vignette I am again concerned about her difficulty in holding on to these feelings.

TAKING BOTH OF US INTO ACCOUNT. TWO YEARS LATER, SEVENTH YEAR

[Notes after a session in person]

We uncovered her feeling that her face does not have enough to give me. It was at a moment of her deep despair, when I had been feeling that I did not have enough to give her. Her association was that she must have felt that was the reason why the first good mother left her, that her own face did not have enough to give, and that perhaps I experienced with her what she had felt about her first mother. Increasingly now Dolores has a remarkable ability to take both of our experiences into account.

BEGINNING OF THE NINTH YEAR, WATCHING TOGETHER THE VIDEOTAPES WE MADE IN THE SECOND YEAR

This vignette is based on a session in person. Dolores and I are watching the videotape sections from the second year, described above. She has given me permission to show these clips of my face to a professional audience, and she wants to review them. The following exchange is based on notes taking during the session. We are looking at the section where I am saying, "Good but *sad*? Good but *sad*?"

> Dolores: You have an energy here. You have heard something. It marks the moment. You have a lot of hope in me. For me it seems like I'm waking up, being discovered. Same as now. You bring me alive. I was feeling that leaving would turn me to concrete, like going into a coma. You are transforming things—my hope of being found.

[Now we are looking at the section of the video where I am saying, "If you look at me, you feel I'll become the mother you'll never
see again." Dolores says, "If I don't look at you it won't happen."
Then after a long pause she looks at me for a split-second and I
smile.]

Dolores: You are so happy to see me look at you!

[Now we are looking at the video section where we are teasing.]

Dolores: These are the faces that I wait for. They bring me to
life.
BB: These are beautiful things to say to me. [pause] You are
so much more able to look at me now. What do you think
made the difference in shifting it?
Dolores: Your harassment and bullying. [we both laugh] I can
see now that I could come to look at you because you gave
me so much with your face. I couldn't stand, after a while,
not giving you mine. Which I wouldn't know really, if I
weren't looking at this with you now. How could someone being looked at the way you do, not reciprocate?
Because one of the important reasons I feel so dead is in
not being able to give someone my own face.
BB: That is also a beautiful thing to say to me. I think the other
thing that helped us was analyzing the fantasy that if you
looked at me, my face would turn into the monster [one
of her abusers], or I would see you as a monster.
Dolores: I looked at your face. I did not see a monster, so that
could tell me I wasn't a monster either. Your looking at
my faces didn't make you into a monster. You gave me a
good sweet face; it must mean I'm not a monster.

The analysis of Dolores's fantasy that if she looked at me, she
would see the face of a monster, her abuser, or that she herself
would have a monstrous face, went on over the course of at least
half a decade. Only very gradually did this terror decrease until

finally, at this point in the treatment, she seems to feel relatively free of it.

> Dolores: I know the feeling, being on the other side of it. I wonder how *others* perceive it, how close it was to what I felt. What do *others* see about *us*?
>
> BB: I think the audience was very moved by my being willing to show myself to them.
>
> Dolores: But *really* what they were seeing was your willingness to show yourself to *me*. Therapists are not usually willing to show themselves. The face of Jason [one of her former therapists] was like a stone.
>
> BB: I'm grateful that you felt comfortable enough to let me show the videotape.
>
> Dolores: Now that I see it, I feel I'm totally protected.

In this vignette Dolores is able to revisit our early interaction with delight. She takes pleasure in my energy, my happiness when she could look at me even for an instant. She is very clear that my response to her has helped her come alive. She uses this moment to realize that she needed to reciprocate, to give me her own face. This is something so essential that we have been struggling to accomplish. Her capacity for spontaneous delight, for reflection, for humor in teasing me, for appreciation, all indicate a widening emotional range.

DOLORES'S FACE IN THE NINTH AND TENTH YEARS

Dolores's face has undergone quite a transformation. It is soft and hesitant, but her emotions are visible. She is slow to make eye-contact, but can sustain a steady gaze at times. At some point in the session, she can usually open up into a smile. At the beginning of every session in person, there is still a question of how long it will take her to take off her sunglasses. I feel very shut out when she wears them, and it is a sure sign that she is feeling distant when she does not take them off for quite a while. Usually these days she takes them off quickly. But more time will be needed before she will be able to look at me in a more ongoing and sustained way.

MORE WORK ON THE THEME OF BEING KICKED OUT BY "THE MAN"

In the ninth and tenth years we made more progress on the theme of being "kicked out" by the presence of "the man," and her continuing anger at me that somehow, whatever I do, it is not right, or not enough, or not what she needs. This anger was usually very palpable on the telephone, hanging heavy in the long silences between us. We were able to agree that her silences on the telephone are her way of pouting and protesting, without putting into words how neglected she feels. She was able to comment that she knew her feelings did not really quite make sense, even though she still felt them as strongly as ever: she is "squeezed in, stuck on, a 'post-it.'" Eventually she was able to tell me, "If I don't hold myself back, angry and stony, I'll just be begging you not to leave, not to end the session. I'm always on the verge of that. If I don't let myself be with you, I won't be in a state of panic when the session ends. I feel powerless: it doesn't matter what I feel or want, I'm not going to get what I need, because of the man. Which I know isn't really true."

In addition, Dolores was now developing a new, tentative relationship with a boyfriend. Although the increased security in our relationship together had made this new boyfriend possible, she felt that something more needed to shift between us if this new relationship was to be possible. Thus the new boyfriend added a new urgency to our need to solve this problem.

In an important series of sessions, she commented that she is always in "waiting mode," waiting for the time that she will really have me, but she never does. She feels not alive, spending her life waiting. In a very familiar vein, I commented on how painful it was to be waiting for the mother who never came. But then I suggested that perhaps she had a fantasy that someday she would really "have" me—maybe like a mother or a "primary partner"—so she doesn't have to be alive now, or really use what we do have now. Instead, she stays half-dead, waiting, until she gets her mother back. Dolores could not in this session focus on or hold on to this idea. In the next session [in person], however, Dolores was more forthcoming:

> Dolores: In between our sessions, the waiting is interminable. I'm protesting the waiting. Even though I know that it's not really *you* who made me wait. This is what I feel when we talk on the phone, angry, you've made me wait, the way I had to wait for my mother, and she never came.
>
> BB: [I referred back to the previous session's idea that she has a fantasy that she will eventually "get" me, so she doesn't have to use me now.]
>
> Dolores: What I have with you is not sufficient, so I'm not going to settle for it. I'm not going to let it count as the real thing.
>
> BB: The "real thing"?
>
> Dolores: Something that can never be. Something that I never had, a better past, a real mother. If I make it ok, what I have with you—though it is wonderful—then I would have to accept what has already happened, and what will never happen.
>
> BB: You seem to have the idea that the loss is not irrevocable, you could get her back, you could get me back, it could be "just you and me" the way it was originally just you and your first mother.
>
> Dolores: Probably. I know I can't go back to being a *baby*. "The man" has something I want; he has the advantage; I'm diminished.
>
> BB: You are having difficulty mourning for the terrible, irrevocable loss. You are holding out for something else, something better, getting your mother back, getting us as a primary mother–child unit, that I could somehow

be the real mother. And you had these difficulties before "the man" entered the picture.

Dolores: I want to go ahead with this new boyfriend—whatever is happening with him is so different—but I have the idea that if I do go forward, I will give up the opportunity to find something that I already lost. A grown-up relationship runs counter to the fantasy of getting my mother back.

BB: To be able to go forward with this new relationship, and to accept that I am your "real" therapist, now, requires facing this mourning.

Dolores: [crying] My only hope was to get her back. I knew it was impossible. I always knew this. But I try anyway. It keeps me from having a life. I can't think about it.

[later in the session]

Dolores: The man—pushes me out—is probably connected to the idea that I can't grieve. If I keep him there, kicking me out from being with you, then I'm holding on to the idea that I *could* have you. It's because of the man that I can't have you, rather than the problem with grieving.

BB: That is such an important realization.

SHARING THIS CHAPTER WITH DOLORES AND THE IMPACT ON THE TREATMENT: TENTH YEAR

In the process of obtaining Dolores's permission for me to write up our treatment, I gave her a draft of this chapter to read. This event became a catalyst for reviewing the treatment together. This vignette occurred over the telephone.

Dolores: In the videotapes you were sitting so quietly, so respectful, so careful. Did you know that you were honoring the potential over-arousal of my longing?

BB: I did feel careful. I felt your fear. I felt your longing, your terror of loss, a huge love, and a huge loss.

Dolores: I was longing for engagement but it was intolerable to get it. I shut down interaction in the arena most important to me.

BB: Yes, you shut down your face, and looking, but you engaged in other ways: you really did talk to me. Even during the periods that you were so dissociated and didn't remember, you were always trying to explain what had happened, and struggling to remember all the traumatic things.

Dolores: I might not have looked at you directly, but I took in enough of your face. I took it in the very first time I met you, the very first minute, in that little waiting room. I *saw* it, and I *had* it. I made it a good face. I had your face instantly. You looked right at me, and I felt totally welcomed. You were totally welcoming me. Any time I did look, your face was always right there, always waiting for me. And your voice always had a face. I got glimpses of your expression, and I got enough to make a strong image of a good face in you.

I believe that, indeed, something very important happened for Dolores as she saw my face for the first time. However, we did continue to struggle in the early years of the treatment: if she looked at me, my face might look like the "monster," or her face might as well. In addition, by avoiding gaze, Dolores was trying to keep out a face that might evoke too much painful longing, or a face that might abandon her. If she looked at me, she might lose me. It took years of testing out to see if my face might be safe to look at.

I FEEL ON MY FACE THE FEELING
ON YOUR FACE: TENTH YEAR

[Notes taken during a telephone session]
Dolores: I was thinking about the "good" between the faces,

and how I hold onto that feeling. When I have to leave you, I feel on my face the feeling on your face, saying "good, but sad."

BB: As you see it on my face, you feel it in yours?

Dolores: Yes. I feel *you* on *my* face. I see your eyebrow furrowed, trying to see something, you're listening to me so intently. And I can *feel* it on my face, in my body-face. I use it on my own face, the good mother face, your face. [pause] When you have the good-face-in-relation-to-the-good-face, you get to be the good face, you get to have the good face.

BB: You remember this, and it became the foundation for your beautiful capacity to love.

DISCUSSION

Dialogic Origin of Mind

One of the central ideas of the infant theorists of intersubjectivity illustrated by this case is the dialogic origin of mind. In early infancy Dolores lost her biological mother. At approximately age 2 years Dolores lost the dialogue—of face, voice, touch, smell, and some words—with her first (foster) mother. This loss was further compounded by the substitution of the abusive mother, and sexually abusive men. The theory of mind based on presymbolic intelligence, briefly described in Chapter 1, posits that the infant codes expectancies of "how interactions go." One aspect of the trauma that Dolores suffered was a profound violation of her expectancies of "how the faces go." She expected a warm and loving face, the face of the first mother that she could make happy—and instead she was "faced" with the angry, hostile mother who told her she was bad, and with sexually abusive men. One reason why she did not look at me was that she anticipated that either she or I would have the "monster face" associated with the abusive men. She essentially learned three different sets of expectancies of interactions, three different sets of implicit relational knowing: one with the good mother, one with the abusive mother and men, and one with her adopted family. We were always working with all three, trying to integrate them, while validating her very different experiences in them.

But eventually her voice and face went mute, at approximately age 4. She described this experience as "going away," "going dead," "defeated," "lost," "in the quiet place." Perhaps Winnicott's (1958) concept of the loss of going-on-being comes close to describing this trauma. This profound disruption in the *dyadic* organization of her experience threatened the dialogic organization of her mind. It resulted in a loss of *all* forms of "intersubjectivity" during this period. This state of mind continued to threaten her as an adult.

The Role of Correspondences and Matching

The central dilemma in the early stages of the treatment was finding a way into Dolores's "closed system," as she later described it. Despite her verbalized longing to "find my face," she was shut down, and inaccessible for long periods. Arranging our chairs at a more "biological" face-to-face distance helped to create more "immediacy" of my presence during periods of her profound dissociation. But a great deal of the work of "finding" Dolores was based on variations in the nonverbal correspondences and matching described by the three infant theorists. These correspondences provided the most basic ways in which I sensed and entered her experience, promoting a feeling of "being with," and "shared mind," as described in Chapters 2 and 3.

The matching concepts of Trevarthen and Stern provided one foundation of the treatment. Trevarthen's concept is that each partner is able to be aware of the other's feelings and purposes without words and language, by matching communicative expressions through time, form, and intensity. Stern's concept of tracking slight shifts in the partner's level of activation of face, voice, or body, and *changing with* the partner, as a way of "feeling into" what the partner feels, adds further specificity to the concept of matching. I felt my way into Dolores's experience through the way her lower lip might tremble, through her rapid foot jiggle when she was anxious, through the muted quality of her face and movements, through her drastically lowered level of bodily activity— the "deadness." I matched her very reduced activity level, her pausing rhythms and long switching pauses, the rhythm and contour of her words. For Trevarthen, rhythm is perhaps the most central mechanism through which immediate sympathetic contact is created in the earliest proto-conversations (see also Jaffe et al. 2001). Since Dolores initially did not make much use of the facial-visual channel of communication, the early phases of the treatment were carried through my rhythms (of voice and body) rather than my face. Matching her rhythms constituted the *process* of how I reached for her, how I tried to sense her state, and how she could come to sense mine. Both Stern and Trevarthen argue that matching of communicative expressions simultaneously regulates both interpersonal contact and inner state. Dolores gradually came to sense a "comforted" inner state as she became more aware of how I matched her. Thus matching of expressions through time, form, and intensity provides a powerful nonverbal mode of therapeutic action.

The video served to heighten Dolores's awareness of my response to her. Perhaps the same results could have been accomplished without the video. But in any case, Dolores felt that the video helped us. I agreed. Like Winnicott's (1971) child in the squiggle game, who becomes aware that another is aware of what the child is aware of within, in watching the video Dolores discovered that I was seeing what she herself "carried" in her face and body, or "sensed" about herself, without being able to describe it verbally. Seeing my face seeing her, and hearing my sounds responding to hers, alerted her to her own inner affective reality. After reading this chapter, she declared, "I recognized myself in your face of recognizing me, for example, when you said, 'good but sad,' and I came to feel myself more, and to feel more alive. I saw myself, and I saw you, recognizing me, and I felt the promise of an 'us' as a new possibility. And I came to feel an inner sense of feeling comforted."

Similar to Meltzoff's description of the infant's face gradually approximating that of the model, by using the proprioceptive feedback from facial muscles, Dolores would find herself "putting on" my facial expressions while watching the video. By "wearing" my face Dolores became more affectively aware of her own inner experience, presumably through the proprioceptive feedback of her face, as described by Meltzoff, as well as the feedback from various physiological arousal systems, as described by Ekman and colleagues (1983). Meltzoff's concept that by imitating, the infant experiences that the other is "like me," is in play here. As she matched my various faces, Dolores experienced that she was "like" me. But since I was trying to sense my way into *her* experience, she found *herself* in my faces. As she watched the video alone, Dolores experimented with letting herself "change with" my face, and thereby to feel what I had perceived in her.

The description of mirror neurons, presented in Chapter 2, may illuminate Dolores's experience watching the films of my face interacting with her, and matching some of my faces. By simply watching my face moving in heightened affective ways, simultaneous activation of mirror neurons in her own brain would provide her with a link between my action and her neuronal "participation" in my action (Pally 2001). But, as Pally (2001) observed, it was not enough for Dolores to simply watch my face in the video; she had to *make the faces herself*. In this way she presumably obtained more overt sensori-motor feedback from her own body. Her own actions of matching seemed to be important in giving her back her feel of herself.

The Role of Difference

As important as these matching interactions were, matching alone did not fully characterize the nature of my interventions. "Matching" is too global a concept. Instead, in most of my responses, both similarities and elaborations, as well as differences, were apparent. For example, I might repeat her phrase that was punctuated with stops and starts, but bring it into a more coherent rhythm. I might add a rising intonation at the end of the sentence, with a feeling of questioning and opening, as if to hold open other options. I might elongate and emphasize a particular word, giving us a longer moment to absorb its impact. If I saw a shift on her face, such as a sudden sadness, or a smile, I tried to put it into words. Usually my face showed the varying emotions that I sensed in her, even though her face usually did not. I might repeat her phrase, but then add a "sinusoidal" greeting contour, heightening positive affect. I might elaborate a moment of humor, with more rising and playful contours than hers, expanding the range of playfulness. At many points I verbally elaborated on what she said, linking it with an earlier comment, or anticipating the ending of the session.

These varieties of matching responses with subtle elaborations and differences were aspects of the regulation of positive states, but they also provided forms of distress regulation, in which I both entered her experience but also slightly added something of my own. They often held open the possibility of just slightly broader ranges of experience, similar to Loewald's (1980) concept that the therapist holds an image of where the patient might be able to go. The moments when I exactly matched without altering were more rare. I consider them to be very particular forms of distress regulation, consistent with Stern's concept of "share without altering," in which I have no agenda but to stay in her feeling, with exactly the range of nuances that she expresses. For example, joining a sad and dampened state without shifting it is a powerful way of sharing and accepting the distress (see also Cohen and Beebe 2003). As Schore (1994) argues, expanding the capacity of the patient as well as the analyst to stay in distress states, and to find more modulated ways of regulating them, is essential to transforming the distress. Cassidy (1994) argues that distress regulation is an essential aspect of the attachment process. On the positive side, Stern and Trevarthen note that expanding the capacity of both partners to join in positive states is essential to creating a secure attachment bond. Schore (1994) argues that expansion of positive states in the dyad will ultimately alter the opiate circuits in the brain associated with positive affect.

The Role of Self-Regulation

Various nonverbal movements of self-regulation provide powerful additional information about the inner experiences of both partners, as well as the state of relatedness. The contribution of my own self-regulation is visible in the videotapes when I might rest my face in my chin, and then slowly move my hand up my face. This movement suggests a self-soothing and holding of distress. Varieties of head tilts function in many ways, including questioning, marking shifts of attention, as well as accenting ongoing verbalizations. Sighing is a release of one's own distress, but it also can communicate an entering of the other's distress. My own self-regulation movements not only highlight the moments in which I am experiencing particular stress, but they also communicate to Dolores my participation in her distress. In one session later on in the treatment when Dolores noticed that I was rubbing my feet together (a self-soothing movement that I recognize from my childhood), she commented that I was doing it while she was refusing an interpretation that I was offering. This moment also illustrated her remarkable ability to hold both of our experiences in mind.

More global forms of Dolores's self-regulation are seen in her drastically lowered level of bodily movement, her childlike barely audible voice, her long periods of silence, her inability to look at me. Ongoing nonverbal signs of Dolores's self-regulation movements are harder to depict because she is rarely in the videotaped segments analyzed. At one moment, however, a rapid foot-jiggle is visible, expressing a moment of tension or anxiety. Another powerful form of self-regulation was wearing her sunglasses in the beginning of every session in person. This presumably provided her with a safer distance: she can see out, but I cannot see in. The light is also dampened, perhaps providing a lowered level of stimulation and some soothing. Whether and when she would take off the sunglasses was a complicated interaction for us. Earlier in the treatment I accepted long periods, perhaps half an hour, with her sunglasses on. But as the treatment progressed, I became more impatient, and gradually more insistent, that she take them off, after 5 or 10 minutes.

The Role of Interactive Regulation

One of the most essential aspects of what was reparative in this treatment was Dolores's sense that she could affect me and that I could affect her. She could sense, and see, and see again in the video, how her agony impacted on me, shifted my face and voice, created tenderness in me, and comforting. She frequently told me how I impacted on her, in both making her feel cherished and making her feel "kicked out," imagining that "the man" was the one that was important to me, and she was not. After reading this paper, she commented on how important it was to her that I had understood "about the profound loss of feeling my impact on the other, of finding my impact on their face."

The basic concept of the mutual regulation model, that each partner affects the other, is broader than the concept of matching. It indicates that each partner senses in herself an ongoing receptivity (or lack of receptivity) to the other, in adjusting, tracking, and being "influenced"; as well as an ongoing impact (or failure of impact) on the other. This is the bedrock of the entire treatment, the foundation of all human communication. Matching is a very specific form of this more general process of bidirectional interactive regulation.

Balance Model

When we began the treatment, Dolores could be characterized as preoccupied with self-regulation, largely sacrificing engagement (see Figure 4–1). She was emotionally withdrawn, rarely looked, with frequent long silences. Essentially she refused a face-to-face exchange. When she did speak it was hesitant, slow, and childlike. Her inner state was one of "icing over" deadness, or terror. However, she did participate in slow dialogic rhythms with me, even though in a halting, fragmented way. And she did at times try very hard to communicate verbally.

For my part, at the beginning of the treatment I could be described as being in a state of "therapeutic hypervigilance": not taking my eyes off her, tracking every shift in her body or voice, straining to catch her words, but drastically lowering my level of activation (in retrospect so as not to frighten her), and when I was not speaking, frequently (out of awareness) keeping my body *perfectly still*. However, this was a very "active stillness" (J. Gerhardt and P. Carnochan, personal communications, November 25, 2001). I did not intrude or "chase." While my body might be still, listening while verbally silent, my face remained open, expressive, and receptive (J. Kaufmann and P. Kaufmann, personal communications, August 12, 2001). I often leaned forward, but remained contained within my own space (S. Tortora, personal communication, June 2, 2002). When I did speak, my vocal rhythms often matched her slow rate, and I participated in very slow turn-taking rhythms, tolerating very long "switching pauses," never hurrying her. My primary mode of interaction was to "go with" the shifts of tone, rhythm, activation, or face that I saw in her, as described by Stern. These adjustments, which I made largely out of awareness, moved me into her range. Much of my nonverbal behavior with her was based on what the infants had taught me. After reading this chapter, Dolores declared, "You insinuated yourself into an interaction with me, into my closed system, where I had shut everything out."

Ten years into the treatment, we have both shifted our positions more toward the "midrange," with a greater balance of self- and interactive regulation (see Figure 4–1). We have regained face-to-face relating, in large part. Dolores is far less preoccupied with drastic forms of self-regulation, and she is much more engaged. She talks more, her voice is more audible, and her vocal rhythms are fluent. She participates in a fair amount of mutual gazing, looking

Initial Years of Treatment

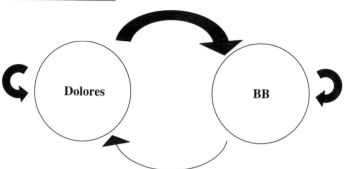

Dolores was preoccupied with self-regulation: withdrawn, muted, gaze-avoidant, regulating terror and deadness. She was intermittently verbally responsive, but childlike. Nonverbally she showed tentative tracking of BB's rhythms.

BB drastically altered her usual range of self-regulation to become slow, soft, with very low activation. BB was verbally and nonverbally a "therapeutic vigilant hypertracker."

9th and 10th Years of Treatment

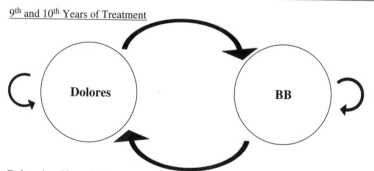

Dolores's self-regulation is less extreme with greater range. She gazes tentatively, is still frightened, but can feel "comforted." She is verbally responsive, reflective, and generative, "thinking together." She is nonverbally responsive.

BB's self-regulation has returned to her usual range, with higher activation, not "careful." BB's tracking of Dolores's verbal and nonverbal behavior is more midrange, no longer hypervigilant.

FIGURE 4–1. Transformation of the Interactive System in the Treatment of Dolores.

Reprinted with permission from Beebe, B. (2004). Faces-in-relation: A case study. *Psychoanalytic Dialogues* 14(1):1–51.

and looking away in a more usual adult pattern. She reports a "comforted" inner state, at least some of the time, particularly when we are physically together, rather than on the telephone. She talks about how hard it was to "relax her grip," to relax "holding onto herself," and that she still has trouble with this. For my part, I'm no longer "hypervigilant" in my attention to her, and I'm no longer dramatically altering my own self-regulation patterns in an attempt to make contact with her. I'm not struggling to dampen down my arousal. My range of body movement is not inhibited, my level of activation of voice and face are more in my usual range, my speech rhythms are not as slow, and I am not as "careful" with her. I can be more relaxed and playful. The narrative is far more coherent. The treatment progresses in a more usual verbal interchange, and the nonverbal communication is generally more in the background. The verbal/nonverbal distinction is not as rigid: verbal and nonverbal create more of a seamless process. A videotape of my face taken 10 years into the treatment shows far more movement in me, particularly head movements. There are no periods where my body is perfectly still. My smiles are softer and have more of a range, my expressions are less "officially nice," and I even allow myself a blank face at one moment. I seem to feel less pressure to be "on," and I am not straining or trying so hard. In this particular videotape Dolores has given me a book, and with her permission I allow myself the pleasure of reading a passage that is particularly meaningful to our relationship. There is "space" for me now, too (M. Heller, personal communication, February 18, 2002). In her outside life, Dolores's relationship with her new boyfriend is progressing. She has become much more involved with professional colleagues as well as friends, so that she is less isolated. But she is still having trouble producing work on her own.

Concrete vs. Constructivist Theory of Mind

At the beginning of the treatment Dolores could be seen as partially stuck in a "concrete" theory of mind (see Chapter 1): it was difficult for her to know that how things appeared to her might not be seen the same way by someone else. She tended to misread her current reality, and conflate it with the experience of the abusive mother, or the loss of the good mother. I addressed her difficulty in comparing old realities with her current life, her difficulty holding together different ideas from different eras of her development. However, increasingly, Dolores did have access to a more constructivist theory of mind, which was a precious resource of the treatment. Increasingly she was aware of how her mental life was both similar to, and different from, that of others. For example she could acknowledge that I might not actually be kicking her out, to go to the man, even though she so strongly felt that I was.

Dolores's tremendous difficulty in mourning the loss of the first good mother derived in part from a concrete theory of mind, in which she believed that she would get the first mother back. This belief became a life-saving fantasy: she felt that it was the only thing she could hold onto to stay alive. Two developments were necessary before we could analyze this fantasy: she had increasing access to her "constructivist" theory of mind, and her relationship with me became sufficiently strong and "real" to her that she could tackle this immense loss (J. Kaufmann and P. Kaufmann, personal communication, August 12, 2001). The analysis of her wish to remain waiting for the first mother to return, and her difficulty in using our relationship to become alive because it was not "the real thing," did not take hold until the 9th and 10th years. It was, however, essential to the treatment. It is here perhaps that the necessity of the explicit, verbal mode of psychoanalytic technique for the treatment is seen most vividly. The nonverbal and implicit relatedness created the foundation of the treatment, but it would not have been sufficient for the treatment to flower (see Bucci 1985).

The Transformation of Implicit Relational Procedures

Dolores can be described as struggling with multiple, inconsistent, and often contradictory implicit relational models, stemming from her three primary caregiving situations, the first good mother, the abusive mother, and the adoptive family (see Lyons-Ruth 1999). Within the model with her first good mother, Dolores had to deal with the radical inconsistency of two realities: she felt this mother really loved her, and this mother "left her for dead." Retaining contradictory, unintegrated images of this first mother was Dolores's way of "using" the image of the good mother who, if Dolores could only wait long enough, would return to reclaim her rightful place as "the real thing." However, this coping strategy had derailed Dolores's development and prevented her mourning. In the course of the treatment she and I together developed a fourth model, in which we struggled to integrate in the same person the good mother and the abandoning mother, and we also developed our own new ways of relating.

The description of this treatment is one response to Lyons-Ruth's (1999) call for greater attention in psychoanalysis to how implicit and nonverbal modes of intimate relating are transformed, and the analyst's specific, collaborative participation in this process as a "new kind of relational partner." She suggests that the creation of new ways of "being with" must be done at the enactive, procedural level as well as the symbolic level. The building blocks for transformations of the system occur in micromoments, small mutually constructed sequences, over an extended period of time. Much of the detailed description of this treatment was an effort to illustrate how these transformations can occur in such micromoments and small mutually constructed sequences. Lyons-Ruth suggests that these transformations of implicit ways of "being with" cannot occur through verbal instruction; instead, they are created through mutually participatory, collaborative "action" dialogues, which are constructed predominantly outside of verbal awareness. Because implicit relational knowing is predominantly outside of awareness, and rarely in focal attention, Lyons-Ruth argues that much of the subtlety and complexity of what the analyst knows is never put into words. It is for this reason that my examination of the videotaped interactions revealed much about my behavior that

I could not have described without them, and why it was difficult to find a language to describe them.

Conclusion

The variety of forms of implicit nonverbal intersubjectivity, including matching, difference, and their subtle intertwinings, patterns of self- and interactive regulation and their balance, and patterns of distress regulation, are many, difficult to catalogue, and probably unique to each psychoanalytic pair. Nevertheless we urgently need to study them. Interactions in the nonverbal and implicit modes are rapid, subtle, co-constructed, and generally out of awareness. And yet they profoundly affect moment-to-moment communication and affective climate, organizing modes of relating, Stern's (1985) "ways of being with." Implicit, procedural, and emotional memories organize transference expectations and provide a degree of continuity and emotional functioning from childhood to adulthood (Bucci 1997, Clyman 1991, Grigsby and Hartlaub 1994, Knoblauch 2000, Lyons-Ruth 1999, Sorter 1994, Stern et al.1998). Critical aspects of therapeutic action occur in this implicit mode that may never be verbalized and yet powerfully organize the analysis. The collaborative participation of the analyst in this process is an essential but little-explored arena. We can teach ourselves to observe these implicit, nonverbal interactions simultaneously in ourselves and in our patients, expanding our own awareness and, where useful, that of the patient.

References, Chapters 1–4

Adelmann, P., and Zajonc, R. (1989). Facial efference and the experience of emotion. *Annual Review of Psychology* 40:249–280.

American College Dictionary. (1962). New York: Random House.

Appelman, E. A. (2000). Attachment experiences transformed into language. *American Journal of Orthopsychiatry* 70(2):192–202.

Aron, L. (1996). *A Meeting of Minds* (2nd ed.). Hillsdale, NJ: Analytic Press.

Atwood, G., and Stolorow, R. (1974). *Faces in a Cloud: Intersubjectivity in Personality Theory*. Northvale, NJ: Jason Aronson.

Bacal, H. (1985). Optimal responsiveness and the therapeutic process. In *Progress in Self Psychology*, Vol. 1, ed. A. Goldberg, pp. 202–227. New York: Guilford.

Badalamenti, A., and Langs, R. (1990). An empirical investigation of human dyadic systems in the time and frequency domains. *Behavioral Science* 39:100–114.

Bakeman, R., and Brown, J. (1977). Behavioral dialogues: an approach to the assessment of mother–infant interaction. *Child Development* 48:195–203.

Bakhtin, M. (1981). *The Dialogic Imagination*. Austin: University of Texas Press.

Baldwin, J. M. (1902). *Development and Evolution*. New York: Macmillan.

Balint, M. (1992). *The Basic Fault*. Evanston, IL: Northwestern University Press.

Baron-Cohen, S. (1991). Precursors to a theory of mind: understanding attention in others. In *Natural Theories of Mind: Evolution, Development and Simulation of Everyday Mindreading,* ed. A. Whiten, pp. 233–251. Oxford: Basil Blackwell.

Basch, M. (1977). Developmental psychology and explanatory theory in psychoanalysis. *Annual of Psychoanalysis* 5:229–263.

Bates, E. (1976). *Language and Content: The Acquisition of Pragmatics*. New York: Academic Press.

———— (1979). *The Emergence of symbols: Cognition and Communication in Infancy*. New York: Academic Press.

Bateson, M. C. (1971). The interpersonal context of infant vocalization. *Quarterly Progress Report Research Laboratory of Electronics* 100: 170–176.

Beebe, B. (1999). Organizing principles of interaction in infant research and adult treatment. Award speech, given at the Division of Psychoanalysis, American Psychological Association, New York, NY. April 1999.

———— (2000). Co-constructing mother–infant distress: the microsynchrony of maternal inpingement and infant avoidance in the face-to-face encounter. *Psychoanalytic Inquiry* 20(3):421–440.

———— (2003). Brief mother–infant treatment: psychoanalytically informed video feedback. *Infant Mental Health Journal* 24(1):24–52.

———— (2005, in press). Mother–infant research informs mother–infant treatment. *Psychoanalytic Study of the Child, 60*.

Beebe, B., Alson, D., Jaffe, J., et al. (1988). Vocal congruence in mother–infant play. *Journal of Psycholinguistic Research* 17(3):245–259.

Beebe, B., and Jaffe, J. (1999). *Mother–Infant Regulation: Depression and Attachment*. NIMH MH56130 Research Grant, N.Y.S. Psychiatric Institute.

Beebe, B., Jaffe, J., Feldstein, S., et al. (1985). Interpersonal timing: the application of an adult dialogue model to mother–infant vocal and kinesic interactions. In *Social Perception in Infants*, ed. T. Field and N. Fox, pp. 217–247. Norwood, NJ: Ablex.

Beebe, B., Jaffe, J., and Lachmann, F. (1992). A dyadic systems view of communication. In *Relational Perspectives in Psychoanalysis*, ed. N. Skolnick and S. Warshaw, pp. 61–81. Hillsdale, NJ: Analytic Press.

Beebe, B., Jaffe, J., Lachmann, F., et al. (2000). Systems models in development and psychoanalysis: the case of vocal rhythm coordination and attachment. *Infant Mental Health Journal* 21:99–122.

Beebe, B., and Lachmann, F. (1988). The contribution of mother–infant mutual influence to the origins of self- and object representations. *Psychoanalytic Psychology* 5(4):305–337.

——— (1994). Representation and internalization in infancy: three principles of salience. *Psychoanalytic Psychology* 11(2):127–165.

——— (1998). Co-constructing inner and relational processes: self and mutual regulation in infant research and adult treatment. *Psychoanalytic Psychology* 15:1–37.

——— (2002). *Infant Research and Adult Treatment: Co-Constructing Interactions*. Hillsdale, NJ: Analytic Press.

Beebe, B., Lachmann, F., and Jaffe, J. (1997). Mother–infant interaction structures and presymbolic self and object representations. *Psychoanalytic Dialogues* 7(2):133–182.

Beebe, B., and McCrorie, E. (2005, in press). A model of love for the 21st century: literature, infant research, adult romantic attachment, and psychoanalysis. *Psychoanalytic Inquiry*.

Beebe, B., and Stern, D. (1977). Engagement-disengagement and early object experiences. In *Communicative Structures and Psychic Structures*, ed. N. Freedman and S. Grand, pp. 35–55. New York: Plenum.

Beebe, B., Stern, D., and Jaffe, J. (1979). The kinesic rhythm of mother–infant interactions. In *Of Speech and Time: Temporal Patterns in Interpersonal Contexts*, ed. A. Siegman and S. Feldstein, pp. 23–34. Hillsdale, NJ: Lawrence Erlbaum.

Benjamin, J. (1988). *The Bonds of Love: Psychoanalysis, Feminism, and the Problem of Domination*. New York: Pantheon.

——— (1992). Recognition and destruction: an outline of intersubjectivity. In *Relational Perspectives in Psychoanalysis*, ed. N. Skolnick and S. Warshaw, pp. 43–59. Hillsdale, NJ: Analytic Press.

——— (1995). *Like Subjects, Love Objects: Essays on Recognition and Sexual Difference*. New Haven, CT: Yale University Press.

Bernstein, N. (1967). *The Coordination and Regulation of Movements*. London: Pergamon.

Bion, W. (1977). *Seven Servants*. New York: Jason Aronson.

Bornstein, M. (1985). Infant into adult: unity to diversity in the development of visual categorization. In *Neonate Cognition*, ed. J. Mehler and R. Fox, pp. 115–138. Hillsdale, NJ: Lawrence Erlbaum.

Bower, B. (2001). Faces of perception. *Science News* 160(1):10–12.

Bowlby, J. (1969). *Attachment and Loss, Vol. 1.* New York: Basic Books.

Braten, S., ed. (1998). *Intersubjective Communication and Emotion in Early Ontogeny.* Cambridge: Cambridge University Press.

Brazelton, T. B., Tronick, E., Adamson, L., et al. (1975). Early mother–infant reciprocity. In *The Parent–Infant Relationship*, ed. M. A. Hofer, pp. 137–154. New York: Elsevier.

Bretherton, I., and Bates, E. (1979). The emergence of intentional communication. In *New Directions for Child Development*, Vol. 4, ed. I. C. Uzgiris. San Francisco: Jossey-Bass.

Bretherton, I., and Beeghly, M. (1982). Talking about internal states: the acquisition of an explicit theory of mind. *Developmental Psychology* 18:906–921.

Bretherton, I., McNew, S., and Beeghly-Smith, M. (1981). Early person knowledge as expressed in gestural and verbal communication: When do infants acquire a "theory of mind"? In *Infant Social Cognition*, ed. M. E. Lamb and L. R. Sherrod. Hillsdale, NJ: Lawrence Erlbaum.

Bromberg, P. (1998). *Standing in the Spaces: Essays on Clinical Process, Trauma, and Dissociation.* Hillsdale, NJ: Analytic Press.

Bruner, J. (1977). Early social interaction and language acquisition. In *Studies in Mother–Infant Interaction*, ed. H. R. Schaffer, pp. 271–289. New York: Norton.

———— (1986). *Actual Minds, Possible Worlds.* Cambridge, MA: Harvard University Press.

Bucci, W. (1985). Dual coding: a cognitive model for psychoanalytic research. *Journal of the American Psychoanalytic Association* 33:571–608.

———— (1997). *Psychoanalysis and Cognitive Science.* New York: Guilford.

Buck, R. (1984). *The Communication of Emotion.* New York: Guilford.

Capella, J. (1981). Mutual influence in expressive behavior: adult and infant–adult dyadic interaction. *Psychological Bulletin* 89:101–132.

———— (1991). The biological origins of automated patterns of human interaction. *Communication Theory* 1:4–35.

Cassidy, J. (1994). Emotion regulation: Influences of attachment relationships. *Monographs of the Society for Research in Child Development* 59(2–3, Serial no. 240), pp. 2228–2249.

Chapple, E. (1970). *Culture and Biological Man.* New York: Holt, Rinehart and Winston.

Clyman, R. (1991). The procedural organization of emotions: a contribution from cognitive science to the psychoanalytic theory of therapeutic action. *Journal of the American Psychoanalytic Association* 39:349–381.

Cohen, P., and Beebe, B. (2003). The case of Linda and Dan: a collaborative individual and mother–infant treatment. *Journal of Infant, Child, and Adolescent Psychotherapy* 2 (3):1–55.

Cohn, J., Campbell, S., Matias, R., and Hopkins, J. (1990). Face-to-face interactions of depressed and non-depressed mother–infant pairs at 2 months. *Developmental Psychology* 26 (1):15–23.

Cohn, J., and Elmore, M. (1988). Effect of contingent changes in mothers' affective expression on the organization of behavior in 3-month-old infants. *Infant Behavior and Development* 11:493–505.

Cohn, J., and Tronick, E. (1988). Mother–infant face-to-face interaction: influence is bidirectional and unrelated to periodic cycles in either partner's behavior. *Developmental Psychology* 24:386–392.

———— (1989). Specificity of infant response to mother's affective behavior. *Journal of the American Academy of Child and Adolescent Psychiatry* 28:242–248.

Crown, C. (1991). Coordinated interpersonal timing of vision and voice as a function of interpersonal attraction. *Journal of Language and Social Psychology* 10:29–46.

Damasio, A. (1994). *Descartes' Error: Emotion, Reason, and the Human Brain*. New York: Grosset/Putnam.

Davidson, R., and Fox, N. (1982). Assymetrical brain activity discriminates between positive versus negative affective stimuli in human infants. *Science* 218:1235–1237.

DeCasper, A., and Carstens, A. (1980). Contingencies of stimulation: effects on learning and emotion in neonates. *Infant Behavior and Development* 9:19–36.

Demos, V. (1989). A prospective constructivist view of development. *Annual of Psychology* 17:287–308.

Demos, V., and Kaplan, S. (1986). Motivation and affect reconsidered: affect biographies of two infants. *Psychoanalysis and Contemporary Thought* 9:47–72.

Di Pelligrino, G., Fadija, L., Fogassi, L., et al. (1992). Understanding motor events: a neurophysiological study. *Experimental Brain Research* 91:176–180.

Dimberg, U., Thunberg, M., and Elmehed, K. (2000). Unconscious facial reactions to emotional facial expressions. *American Psychological Society* 11:86–89.

Dissanyake, E. (1992). *Homo Aestheticus*. New York: Free Press.

Downing, G. (2001). *Changing procedural representations*. Submitted manuscript.

Duncan, S., and Fiske, D. (1977). *Face-to-Face Interaction*. Hillsdale, NJ: Lawrence Erlbaum.

Dunham, P., and Dunham, F. (1990). Effects of mother–infant social interactions on infants' subsequent contingency task performance. *Child Development* 61:785–793.

Ehrenberg, D. (1992). *The Intimate Edge*. New York: Norton.

Eibl-Eibesfeldt, I. (1989). *Human ethology*. New York: Aldine de Gruyter.

Eigen, M. (1993). *The Electrified Tightrope*. Northvale, NJ: Jason Aronson.

Ekman, P., Freisen, W., and Ancolli, S. (1980). Facial signs of emotional experience. *Journal of Personality and Social Psychology* 39:1125–1134.

Ekman, P., Levenson, R., and Friesen, W. (1983). Autonomic nervous system activity distinguishes among emotions. *Science* 221:1208–1210.

Emde, R., Biringen, Z., Clyman, R., and Oppenheim, D. (1991). The moral self of infancy: affective core and procedural knowledge. *Developmental Review* 11:251–270.

Fadiga, L., Fogassi, L., Pavesi, G., and Rizzolatti, G. (1995). Motor facilitation during action observation: a magnetic stimulation study. *Journal of Neurophysiology* 73:2608–2611.

Fagen, J., Morrongiello, B., Rovee-Collier, C., and Gekoski, M. (1984). Expectancies and memory retrieval in three-month-old infants. *Child Development* 55:936–943.

Fairbairn, W. (1952). *Psychoanalytic Studies of Personality*. London: Routledge & Kegan Paul.

Fantz, R., Fagen, J., and Miranda, S. (1975). Early visual selectivity as a function of pattern variables, previous exposure, age from birth and conception, and expected cognitive deficit. In *Infant Perception*, ed. L. Cohen and P. Salapatek, New York: Academic Press.

Feldstein, S., and Welkowitz, J. (1978). A chronography of conversation: in defense of an objective approach. In *Nonverbal Behavior and Communication*, ed. A. Siegman and S. Feldstein, pp. 329–377. Hillsdale, NJ: Lawrence Erlbaum.

Fernald, A. (1987). Four-month-old infants prefer to listen to motherese. *Infant Behavior and Development* 8:181–195.

Field, T. (1981). Infant gaze aversion and heart rate during face-to-face interactions. *Infant Behavior and Development* 4:307–315.

——— (1995). Infants of depressed mothers. *Infant Behavior and Development* 18:1–13.

Field, T., Healy, B., Goldstein, S., and Guthertz, M. (1990). Behavior state matching and synchrony in mother–infant interactions of nondepressed versus depressed dyads. *Developmental Psychology* 26(1):7–14.

Field, T., Woodson, R., Greenberg, R., and Cohen, D. (1982). Discrimination and imitation of facial expressions by neonates. *Science* 218:179–181.

Flavell, J. (1988). The development of children's knowledge about the mind: from cognitive connections to mental representation. In *Developing Theories of Mind*, ed. J. W. Astington, P. L. Harris, and D. R. Olson, pp. 244–267. Cambridge, UK: Cambridge University Press.

Flavell, J., Green, F., Herrera, C., and Flavell, E. (1991). Young children's knowledge about visual perception: lines of sight must be straight. *British Journal of Developmental Psychology* 1:89–103.

Fogel, A. (1993). Two principles of communication: co-regulation and framing. In *New Perspectives in Early Communicative Development*, ed. J. Nadel and L. Camaioni. London: Routledge.

Fonagy, P. (1991). Thinking about thinking: some clinical and theoretical considerations in the treatment of the borderline patient. *International Journal of Psycho-Analysis* 72:639–656.

——— (1994). Mental representations from an intergenerational cognitive science perspective. *Infant Mental Health Journal* 15(1):57–68.

——— (1995). *The role of mentalization in attachment, emotional development, and in borderline personality disorder.* Paper presented at the Rapaport–Klein Meeting, Austin Riggs Center, June 9.

Fosshage, J. (2000). Interaction in psychoanalysis: a broadening horizon. *Psychoanalytic Dialogues* 5:459–478.

Freud, S. (1911). Formulations on the two principles of mental functioning. *Standard Edition* 12:218–226. London: Hogarth Press, 1958.

——— (1913). On the beginning of treatment. (Further recommendations on the technique of psycho-analysis 1). *Standard Edition* 12:133–134. London, Hogarth Press.

——— (1914). On negation. *Standard Edition* 12:218–226. London: Hogarth Press.

Frie, R., and Reiss, B. (2001). Understanding intersubjectivity: psychoanalytic formulations and their philosophical underpinnings. *Contemporary Psychoanalysis* 37(2):297–328.

Frye, D., Zelazo, P., and Burack, J. (1998). Cognitive complexity and control: I. Theory of mind in typical and atypical development. *Current Directions in Psychological Science* 7(4):121–126.

Frye, D., Zelazo, P., and Palfai, T. (1995). Theory of mind and rule-based reasoning. *Cognitive Development* 10(4):483–527.

Gadamer, H. (1979). *Philosophical Hermeneutics.* trans. D. E. Linge. Berkeley: University of California Press.

Gergeley, G., and Watson, J. (1998). Early social-emotional development: contingency perception and the social-biofeedback model. In *Early Social Cognition,* ed. P. Rochat, pp. 101–136. Hillsdale, NJ: Lawrence Erlbaum.

Gerhardt, J., Sweetnam, A., and Borton, L. (2000). The intersubjective turn in psychoanalysis: a comparison of contemporary theorists. Part I: Jessica Benjamin. *Psychoanalytic Dialogues* 10(1):5–42.

Ghent, E. (1989). Credo: the dialectics of one-person and two-person psychologies. *Contemporary Psychoanalysis* 25:200–237.

Gianino, A., and Tronick, E. (1988). The mutual regulation model: the infant's self and interactive regulation coping and defense. In *Stress and Coping,* ed. T. Field, P. McCabe, and N. Schneiderman, pp. 47–68. Hillsdale, NJ: Lawrence Erlbaum.

Gill, M. (1982). *Analysis of Transference, Vol 1: Theory and Technique.* New York: International Universities Press.

Goldman, A. (1989). Interpretation psychologized. *Mind and Language* 4:161–185.

Gopnik, A. (1990). Developing the idea of intentionality: children's theories of mind. *Canadian Journal of Philosophy* 20:89–114.

Gopnik, A., and Meltzoff, A. (1997). *Word, Thoughts and Theories.* Cambridge, MA: MIT Press.

Gottman, J. (1979). *Marital Interactions.* New York: Academic Press.

Grafton, S., Arbib, M., Fadiga, L., and Rizzolatti, G. (1996). Localization of grasp representations in humans by positron emission tomography. 2: Observation compared with imagination. *Experimental Brain Research* 112:103–111.

Grigsby, J., and Hartlaub, G. (1994). Procedural learning and the development and stability of character. *Perceptual Motor Skills* 79:355–370.

Habermas, J. (1970). A theory of communicative competence. In *Recent Sociology*, 2nd ed., ed. H. Dreitzel. New York: Macmillan.

——— (1979). *Communication and the Evolution of Society*. London: Heinemann.

Haith, M., Hazan, C., and Goodman, G. (1988). Expectation and anticipation of dynamic visual events by 3.5-month-old babies. *Child Development* 59:467–479.

Harris, A. (1992). Dialogues as transitional space: a rapproachment of psychoanalysis and psycholinguistics. In *Relational Perspectives in Psychoanalysis*, ed. N. Skolnick and S. Warshaw, pp. 119–146. Hillsdale, NJ: Analytic Press.

Harrison, A. (1998). The case of Sophie. *Infant Mental Health Journal* 19(3):309–314.

Heimann, M. (1989). Neonatal imitation, gaze aversion, and mother–infant interaction. *Infant Behavior and Development* 12:493–503.

Heller, M., and Haynal, V. (1997). A doctor's face: mirror of his patient's suicidal projects. In *The Body in Psychotherapy*, ed. J. Guimon, pp. 46–51. Basel, Switzerland: Karger.

Hoffman, I. (1998). *Ritual and Spontaneity in the Psychoanalytic Process: A Dialetical-Constructivist View*. Hillsdale, NJ: Analytic Press.

Holstege, G., Bandler, R., and Sapir, C., eds. (1997). *The Emotional Motor System*. Amsterdam: Elsevier.

Holtz, P. (2001). *Patterns of coordinated interpersonal timing of the vocal behaviors of patients and therapists, therapists interpretive accuracy, and the patient's immediate progress in brief psychodynamic psychotherapy*. Fielding Institute.

Hubley, P., and Trevarthen, C. (1979). Sharing a task in infancy. In *Social Interaction during Infancy: New Directions in Child Development*, vol. 4, ed. I. C. Uzgiris, pp. 57–80. San Francisco: Jossey-Bass.

Isabella, R., and Belsky, J. (1991). Interactional sychrony and the origins of infant–mother attachment: a replication study. *Child Development* 62:373–384.

Izard, C. (1971). *The Face of Emotion*. New York: Appleton-Century-Crofts.

Jacobs, T. (1991a). The inner experience of the analyst: their contributions to the analytic process. *International Journal of Psycho-Analysis* 74:7–14.

——— (1991b). The interplay of enactments: their role in the analytic process. In *The Use of the Self*, ed. T. Jacobs, pp. 31–49. Madison, CT: International Universities Press.

Jaffe, J., Beebe, B., Feldstein, S., et al. (2001). Rhythms of dialogue in infancy. *Monographs of the Society for Research in Child Development* 66, serial no. 264, no. 2.

Jaffe, J., and Feldstein, S. (1970). *Rhythms of Dialogue*. New York: Academic Press.

Jaffe, J., Stern, D., and Peery, C. (1973). "Conversational" coupling of gaze behavior in prelinguistic human development. *Journal of Psycholinguistic Research* 2(4):321–329.

Jasnow, M., and Feldstein, S. (1986). Adult-like temporal characteristics of mother–infant vocal interactions. *Child Development* 57: 754–761.

Jeannerod, M. (1994). The representing brain: neural correlates of motor intention and imagery. *Behavioral and Brain Science* 17:187–245.

Kendon, A. (1980). Gesticulation and speech: two aspects of the process of utterance. In *The Relationship of Verbal and Nonverbal Communication*, ed. M. R. Key. New York: Mouton.

Klinnert, M., Campos, J., Sorce, J., et al. (1983). The development of social referencing in infancy. In *Emotion: Theory, Research, and Experience, Vol. 2: Emotion in Early Development*, ed. R. Plutchik and H. Kellerman. New York: Academic Press.

Knoblauch, S. (1997). Beyond the word in psychoanalysis: the unspoken dialogue. *Psychoanalytic Dialogues* 7:491–516.

———— (2000). *The Musical Edge of Therapeutic Dialogue*. Hillsdale, NJ: Analytic Press.

———— (2001). Nonverbal implicit dimensions of interaction: a discussion of Hazel Ipp's clinical case. In *Progress in Self Psychology*, vol. 17, ed. A. Goldberg, pp. 79–86. Hillsdale, NJ: Analytic Press.

Knoblauch, S., Rustin, J., Sorter, D., and Beebe, B. (1999). *Intersubjectivity, infant research and therapeutic action*. Paper presented at the American Psychological Association, Division of Psychoanalysis, New York City, April 14–18.

Kohlberg, L. (1969). Stage and sequence: the cognitive developmental approach to socialization. In *Handbook of Socialization Theory and Research*, ed. D. A. Goslin, pp. 347–480. Chicago: Rand-McNally.

Kohut, H. (1977). *The Restoration of the Self*. New York: International Universities Press.

———— (1984). *How Does Analysis Cure?* Chicago: University of Chicago Press.

Koulomzin, M., Beebe, B., Anderson, S., et al. (2002). Infant gaze, head, face, and self-touch at four months differentiate secure vs. avoidant attachment at one year: a microanalytic approach. *Attachment and Human Development* 4(1):3–24.

Kugiumutzakis, G. (1985). *The origin, development and function of early infant imitation*. Unpublished Ph.D. paper, Uppsala University.

——— (1993). Intersubjective vocal imitation in early mother–infant interaction. In *New Perspectives in Early Communicative Development*, ed. J. Nadel and L. Camaioni. London: Routledge.

LaBarre, F. (1995). Aspects of self: from systems to ideas. In *The Self in Infancy: Theory and Research*, ed. P. Rochat, pp. 95–115. New York: Elsevier Science B.V.

——— (2001). *On Moving and Being Moved: Nonverbal Behavior in Clinical Practice*. Hillsdale, NJ: Analytic Press.

Lachmann, F., and Beebe, B. (1996). Three principles of salience in the organization of the patient–analyst interaction. *Psychoanalytic Psychology* 13(1):1–22.

Laird, J. (1984). The real role of facial response in the experience of emotion. *Journal of Personality and Social Psychology* 47:909–917.

Langer, S. K. (1967). *Mind: An Essay on Human Feeling*, vol. I. Baltimore: Johns Hopkins Press.

Langhorst, B., and Fogel, A. (1982). *Cross validation of microanalytic approaches to face-to-face interaction*. Paper presented at the International Conference on Infant Studies, Austin, TX.

Levenson, R., Ekman, P., and Friesen, W. (1990). Voluntary facial action generates emotion-specific autonomic nervous system activity. *Psychophysiology* 27(4):363–384.

Levinas, E. (1974). *Otherwise Than Being*. Pittsburgh, PA: Duquesne University Press.

Lewin, K. (1935). *A Dynamic Theory of Personality*. New York: McGraw-Hill.

Lewis, M. (1995). Aspects of self: from systems to ideas. In *The Self in Infancy: Theory and Research*, ed. P. Rochat, pp. 95–115. New York: Elsevier Science B.V.

——— (1999). Social cognition and the self. In *Early Social Cognition: Understanding Others in the First Months of Life*, ed. P. Rochat, pp. 81–98. Mahwah, NJ: Lawrence Erlbaum.

Lewis, M., and Brooks, J. (1975). Infants' social perception: a constructionist view. In *Infant Perception: From Sensation to Cognition*, vol. 2, ed. L. Cohen and P. Salapatek, pp. 101–148. New York: Wiley-Interscience.

Lewis, M., and Feiring, C. (1989). Infant, mother and mother–infant interaction behavior and subsequent attachment. *Child Development* 60:831–837.

Leyendecker, B., Lamb, M., Fracasso, M., et al. (1997). Playful interaction and the antedants of attachment: a longitudinal study of Central American and Euro-American mothers and infants. *Merrill Palmer Quarterly* 43(1):24–47.

Lichtenberg, J., Lachmann, F., and Fosshage, J. (1992). *Self and Motivational Systems*. Hillsdale, NJ: Analytic Press.

Loewald, H. (1980). *Papers on Psychoanalysis*. New Haven, CT: Yale University Press.

Lyons-Ruth, K. (1996). Attachment relationships among children with aggressive behavior problems: the role of disorganized early attachment patterns. *Journal of Consulting and Clinical Psychology* 64:32–40.

——— (1998). Implicit relational knowing: its role in development and psychoanalytic treatment. *Infant Mental Health Journal* 19:282–291.

——— (1999). The two-person unconscious: intersubjective dialogue, enactive relational representation, and the emergence of new forms of relational organization. *Psychoanalytic Inquiry* 19:576–617.

MacKain, K., Stern, D., Goldfield, A., and Moeller, B. (1985). The identification of correspondence between an infant's internal affective state and the facial display of that affect by another. Unpublished manuscript.

Main, M., and Hesse, E. (1992). Disorganized/disoriented infant behavior in the strange situation, lapses in the monitoring of reasoning and discourse during the parent's Adult Attachment Interview, and dissociative states. In *Attachment and Psychoanalysis*, ed. M. Ammaniti and D. Stern, pp. 80–140. Rome: Guis, Laterza & Figli.

Malatesta, C., Culver, C., Teman, J., and Shepard, B. (1989). The development of emotion expression during the first two years of life. *Monographs of the Society for Research in Child Development* 54, serial no. 219, nos. 1–2.

Mandler, J. (1988). How to build a baby: on the development of an accessible representation system. *Cognitive Development* 3:113–136.

——— (1991). *The foundation of symbolic thought in infancy*. Paper presented at the Society for Research in Child Development, Seattle, April.

Maratos, O. (1982). Trends of development of imitations in early infancy. In *Regressions in Mental Development: Basic Phenomena and Theories*, ed. T. G. Bever, pp. 81–101. Hillsdale, NJ: Lawrence Erlbaum.

McCrorie, E. (2000). Our voicings (unpublished paper). Providence College, RI.

McLaughlin, J. (1991). Clinical and theoretical aspects of enactment. *Journal of the American Psychoanalytic Association* 39:595–614.

Mead, G. H. (1934). *Mind, Self, and Society*. Chicago: University of Chicago Press.

Meltzoff, A. (1985). The roots of social and cognitive development: models of man's original nature. In *Social Perception in Infants*, ed. T. Field and N. Fox, pp. 1–30. Norwood, NJ: Ablex.

————— (1990). Foundations for developing a concept of self: the role of imitation in relating self to other and the value of social mirroring, social modeling, and self practice in infancy. In *The Self in Transition: Infancy to Childhood*, ed. D. Cicchetti and M. Beeghley. Chicago: University of Chicago Press.

Meltzoff, A., and Gopnik, A. (1993). The role of imitation in understanding persons and developing a theory of mind. In *Understanding Other Minds*, ed. S. Baron-Cohen, H. Tager-Flusberg, and D. Cohen, pp. 335–366. New York: Oxford University Press.

Meltzoff, A., and Moore, M. (1977). Imitation of facial and manual gestures of human neonates. *Science* 198:75–78.

————— (1994). Imitation, memory, and the representations of persons. *Infant Behavior and Development* 17:83–99.

————— (1998). Infant intersubjectivity: broadening the dialogue to include imitation, identity and intention. In *Intersubjective Communication and Emotion in Early Ontogeny*, ed. S. Braten, pp. 47–62. Cambridge, UK: Cambridge University Press.

Millar, W., and Watson, J. (1979). The effects of delayed feedback on infancy learning re-examined. *Child Development* 50:747–751.

Mitchell, S. (1997). *Influence and Autonomy in Psychoanalysis*. Hillsdale, NJ: Analytic Press.

————— (2000). *Relationality*. Hillsdale, NJ: Analytic Press.

Modell, A. (1984). *Psychoanalysis in a New Context*. New York: Independent University Press.

Mounoud, P. (1995). From direct to reflexive (self-knowledge): a recursive model. In *The Self in Infancy*, ed. P. Rochat. Amsterdam: Elsevier.

Muller, U., and Overton, W. (1998). How to grow a baby: a reevaluation of image-schema and Piagetian approaches to representation. *Human Development* 41:71–111.

Murray, H. (1938). *Explorations in Personality*. New York: Science Editions.

Murray, L., and Trevarthen, C. (1985). Emotional regulation of interactions between two-month-olds and their mothers. In *Social Perception in Infants*, ed. T. Field and N. Fox, pp. 177–197. Norwood, NJ: Ablex.

Nagy, E., and Molnar, P. (1994). "Homo imitans" or "homo provocans"? *International Journal of Psychophysiology* 18(2):28.

Newson, J. (1977). An intersubjective approach to the systematic description of mother–infant interaction. In *Studies in Mother–Infant Interactions*, ed. H. R. Schaffer. New York: Academic Press.

Ogden, T. (1982). *Projective identification and psychotherapeutic technique*. New York: Jason Aronson.

——— (1986). *The Matrix of the Mind: Object Relations and the Psychoanalytic Dialogue*. Northvale, NJ: Jason Aronson.

——— (1989). *The Primitive Edge of Experience*. Northvale, NJ: Jason Aronson.

——— (1994). *Subjects of Analysis*. Northvale, NJ: Jason Aronson.

——— (1995). Analyzing forms of aliveness and deadness of the transference-countertransference. *International Journal of Pscyho-Analysis* 76:695–709.

Orange, D., Atwood, G., and Stolorow, R. (1997). *Working Intersubjectively: Contextualism in Psychoanalytic Practice*. Hillsdale, NJ: Analytic Press.

Ornstein, P., and Ornstein, A. (1984). Understanding and explaining: the empathic vantage point. *Progress in Self Psychology* 1:43–61.

Overton, W. (1994). Contexts of meaning: the computational and the embodied mind. In *The Nature and Ontogenesis of Meaning*, ed. W. Overton and D. Palermo. Hillsdale, NJ: Lawrence Erlbaum.

Pally, R. (1997a). How the brain actively constructs perceptions. *International Journal of Psycho-Analysis* 78:1021–1030.

——— (1997b). Memory: brain systems that link past, present and future. *International Journal of Psycho-Analysis* 78:1123–1234.

——— (1998). Emotional processing: the mind–body connection. *International Journal of Psycho-Analysis* 79:349–362.

——— (1999). *Mirror neurons*. Unpublished manuscript. Los Angeles, CA.

——— (2000). *The mind–brain relationship*. London: Karnac.

———— (2001). A primary role for nonverbal communication in psycho-analysis. *Psychoanalytic Inquiry* 21:71–93.

Papousek, H., and Papousek, M. (1977). Mother and the cognitive head start. In *Studies in Mother–Infant Interaction*, ed. H. R. Schaffer, pp. 63–85. New York: Academic Press.

———— (1987). Intuitive parenting: a dydactic counterpart to the infant's precocity in integrative capacities. In *Handbook of Infant Development*, 2nd ed., ed. J. Osofsky, pp. 669–720. New York: Wiley.

Perry, B. (1996). Childhood trauma, the neurobiology of adaptation, and "use-dependent" development of the brain: how "states" become "traits." *Infant Mental Health Journal* 16(4):271–291.

Piaget, J. (1954). *The Construction of Reality in the Child*. New York: Basic Books.

Poppel, E. (1994). Temporal mechanisms in perceptions. *International Review of Neurobiology* 37:185–202.

Reese, H., and Overton, W. (1970). Models of development and theories of development. In *Life-Span Developmental Psychology*, ed L. Goulet and P. Baltes, pp. 115–145. New York: Academic Press.

Rizzolatti, G. (1994). Nonconscious motor images. *Behavioral and Brain Science* 17:220.

Rizzolatti, G., and Arbib, M. (1998). Language within our grasp. *Trends in Neuroscience* 21:188–194.

Rizzolatti, G., Camarda, R., Gallese, V., and Fogassi, L. (1995). Premotor cortex and the recognition of motor actions. *Cognitive Brain Research* 3:131–141.

Rizzolatti, G., Camarda, R., Matelli, M., et al. (1996). Localization of grasp representations in humans by PET: 1. Observation vs. execution. *Experimental Brain Research* 111:246–252.

Ruesch, J., and Bateson, G. (1951). *Communication: The Social Matrix of Psychiatry*. New York: W. W. Norton.

Rustin, J. (1997). Infancy, agency, and intersubjectivity. *Psychoanalytic Dialogues* 7:43–62.

Rustin, J., and Sekaer, C. (2001). *The neuroscience of memory: clinical applications*. Paper presented at the American Psychological Association, Division of Psychoanalysis, Santa Fe, NM, April 25.

Ryan, J. (1974). Early language development. In *The Integration of a Child into a Social World*, ed. M. P. M. Richards, pp. 185–213. Cambridge, UK: Cambridge University Press.

Sameroff, A. (1983). Developmental systems: contexts and evolution. In *Mussen's Handbook of Child Psychology*, vol. 1, ed. W. Kessen, pp. 237–294. New York: Wiley.

Sander, L. (1977). The regulation of exchange in the infant–caretaker system and some aspects of the context–content relationship. In *Interaction, Conversation, and the Development of Language*, ed. M. Lewis and L. Rosenblum, pp. 133–156. New York: Wiley.

———— (1995). Identity and the experience of specificity in a process of recognition. *Psychoanalytic Dialogues* 5:579–593.

Sandler, J. (1987). *From Safety to Superego*. London: Karnac.

Schore, A. (1994). *Affect Regulation and the Origin of the Self: The Neurobiology of Emotional Development*. Hillsdale, NJ: Lawrence Erlbaum.

———— (1997). Interdisciplinary developmental research and a source of clinical models. In *The Clinical Significance of Early Development: Implications for Psychoanalytic Intervention*, ed. M. Moskowitz, C. Monk, and S. Ellman, pp. 1–72. Northvale, NJ: Jason Aronson.

Shane, M., Shane, E., and Gales, M. (1998). *Intimate Attachments: Toward a New Self Psychology*. New York: Guilford.

Shields, P., and Rovee-Collier, C. (1992). Long-term memory for context-specific category information at six months. *Child Development* 63:245–259.

Silverman, D. (1994). From philosophy to poetry: changes in psychoanalytic discourse. *Psychoanalytic Dialogues* 4:101–128.

———— (1999). Bridging natural science and hermeneutics: An oxymoron or a conjunction? *Psychoanalytic Dialogues* 9:597–608.

Slavin, M., and Kriegman, D. (1992). *The Adaptive Design of the Human Psyche*. New York: Guilford.

Sorter, D. (1994). Therapeutic action and procedural knowledge: a case study. *International Forum of Psychoanalysis* 4:65–70.

Sperry, R. (1952). Neurology and the mind–brain problem. *American Scientist* 40:291–312.

Spitz, R. (1963). The evolution of the dialogue. In *Drives, Affects, and Behavior*, vol. 2, ed. M. Shur. New York: Independent University Press.

Squire, L., and Cohen, N. (1985). Human memory and amnesia. In *Neurobiology of Learning Memory*, ed. J. M. G. Lynch and N. Weinberger, pp. 3–64. New York: Guilford.

Stern, D. (1971). A microanalysis of mother–infant interaction. *Journal of the American Academy of Child Psychiatry* 19:501–517.

———— (1977). *The First Relationship.* Cambridge, MA: Harvard University Press.

———— (1985). *The Interpersonal World of the Infant.* New York: Basic Books.

———— (1989). The representation of relational patterns: developmental considerations. In *Relationship Disturbances in Early Childhood*, ed. A. Sameroff and R. Emde, pp. 52–69. New York: Basic Books.

———— (1994). One way to build a clinically relevant baby. *Infant Mental Health Journal* 15(1):9–25.

———— (1995). *The Motherhood Constellation.* New York: Basic Books.

Stern, D., Hofer, L., Haft, W., and Dore, J. (1985). Affect attunement: the sharing of feeling states between mother and infant by means of intermodal fluency. In *Social Perception in Infants*, ed. T. Field and N. Fox. Norwood, NJ: Ablex.

Stern, D., Jaffe, J., Beebe, B., and Bennett, S. (1975). Vocalizing in unison and in alternation: two modes of communication within the mother–infant dyad. *Annuals of the New York Academy of Science* 263:89–100.

Stern, D., Sander, L., Nahum, J., et al. (1998). Non-interpretative mechanisms in psychoanalytic therapy. *International Journal of Psycho-Analysis* 79:903–921.

Stolorow, R. (1997). Dynamic, dyadic, intersubjective systems: an evolving paradigm for psychoanalysis. *Psychoanalytic Psychology* 14:337–346.

Stolorow, R., and Atwood, G. (1992). *Contexts of Being.* Hillsdale, NJ: Analytic Press.

Stolorow, R., Atwood, G., and Brandchaft, B. (1994). *The Intersubjective Perspective.* Northvale, NJ: Jason Aronson.

Stolorow, R., Brandchaft, B., and Atwood, G. (1987). *Psychoanalytic Treatment: An Intersubjective Approach.* Hillsdale, NJ: Analytic Press.

Sullivan, H. (1940). *Conceptions of Modern Psychiatry.* New York: Norton.

———— (1953). *The Interpersonal Theory of Psychiatry.* New York: Norton.

Taylor, C. (1991). *The Ethics of Authenticity.* Cambridge, MA: Harvard University Press.

Teicholz, J. (1999). *Kohut, Loewald and the Postmoderns: A Comparative Study of Self and Relationship.* Hillsdale, NJ: Analytic Press.

Thomas, E., and Martin, J. (1976). Analyses of parent–infant interaction. *Psychological Review* 83(2):141–155.

Tomkins, S. (1962). *Affect, Imagery and Consciousness, Vol. 1: The Positive Affects.* New York: Springer.

——— (1963). *Affect, Imagery and Consciousness, Vol. 2: The Negative Affects.* New York: Springer.

Trehub, S. (1990). The perception of musical patterns by the human infant. In *Comparative Perception, Vol. 1: Mechanisms*, ed. I. M. Berkeley and W. Stebbins, pp. 429–459. New York: Wiley.

Trevarthen, C. (1974). The psychobiology of speech development. In *Language and Brain: Developmental Aspects*, ed. E. Lenneberg. *Neurosciences Research Program Bulletin* 12:570–585.

——— (1977). Descriptive analyses of infant communicative behavior. In *Studies in Mother–Infant Interaction*, ed. H. R. Schaffer, pp. 227–270. London: Academic Press.

——— (1979). Communication and cooperation in early infancy: a description of primary intersubjectivity. In *Before Speech: The Beginnings of Human Communication*, ed. M. Bullowa, pp. 321–347. London: Cambridge University Press.

——— (1980). The foundations of intersubjectivity. In *The Social Foundations of Language and Thought*, ed. D. R. Olson, pp. 216–242. New York: W.W. Norton.

——— (1984). Emotions in infancy: regulators of contacts and relationships with persons. In *Approaches to Emotion*, ed. K. Scherer and P. Ekman, pp. 129–157. Hillsdale, NJ: Lawrence Erlbaum.

——— (1988). Universal cooperative motives: how infants begin to know language and skills and culture. In *Acquiring Culture: Cross-cultural Studies in Child Development*, ed. G. Jahoda and I. M. Lewis, pp. 37–90. London: Croom Helm.

——— (1989). Development of early social interactions and the effective regulation of brain growth. In *Neurobiology of Early Infant Behavior*, 55 ed., ed. C. Von Euler, H. Forssberg, and H. Langercrantz, pp. 191–216. New York: Stockton.

——— (1993a). The function of emotions in early infant communication and development. In *New Perspectives in Early Communicative Development*, ed. J. Nadel and L. Camaioni, pp. 48–81. London: Routledge.

——— (1993b). The self born in intersubjectivity: the psychology of an infant communicating. In *The Perceived Self: Ecological and Interpersonal Sources of Self-knowledge*, ed. U. Neisser, pp. 121–173. New York: Cambridge University Press.

——— (1998). The concept and foundations of infant intersubjectivity.

In *Intersubjective Communication and Emotion in Early Ontogeny*, ed. S. Braten. Cambridge, UK: Cambridge University Press.

Trevarthen, C., and Hubley, P. (1978). Secondary intersubjectivity: confidence, confiding and acts of meaning in the first year. In *Action, Gesture and Symbol: The Emergence of Language*, ed. A. Lock, pp. 183–229. London: Academic Press.

Trevarthen, C., Kokkinaki, T., and Fiamenghi, G. (1999). What infants' imitations communicate: with mothers, with fathers, and with peers. In *Imitation in Infancy*, ed. J. Nadel and G. Butterworth, pp. 127–185. Cambridge, UK: Cambridge University Press.

Tronick, E. (1989). Emotions and emotional communication in infants. *American Psychologist* 44:112–119.

——— (1998). Dyadically expanded states of conciousness and the process of therapeutic change. *Infant Mental Health Journal* 19(3):290–299.

Tronick, E., Als, H., and Adamson, L. (1977). Structure of early face-to-face communicative interactions. In *Before Speech*, ed. M. Bullowa, pp. 349–372. Cambridge, UK: Cambridge University Press.

Tronick, E., Als, H., and Brazelton, T. (1980). The infant's communicative competencies and the achievement of intersubjectivity. In *The Relationship of Verbal and Nonverbal Communication*, ed. M. R. Key, pp. 261–273. The Hague: Mouton.

Tronick, E., and Cohn, J. (1989). Infant–mother face-to-face interaction: age and gender differences in coordination and the occurrence of miscoordination. *Child Development* 60:85–92.

Uzgiris, I. C. (1981). Two functions of imitation during infancy. *International Journal of Behavioral Development* 4:1–12.

von Holst, E., and Mittelstaedt, H. (1950). Das reafferenzprinsip. *Natur Wissenschafter* 37:256–272.

Vygotsky, L. (1962). *Thought and Language*. Cambridge, MA: MIT Press.

Walton, G., and Bower, T. (1993). Newborns form "prototypes" in less than 1 minute. *Psychological Science* 4(3):203–205.

Warner, R. (1988). Rhythm in social interaction. In *The Social Psychology of Time*, ed. J. McGrath, pp. 63–88. London: Sage.

Warner, R., Malloy, D., Schneider, K., et al. (1987). Rhythmic organization of social interaction and observer ratings of positive affect and involvement. *Journal of Nonverbal Behavior* 11:57–74.

Webster's New Collegiate Dictionary. (1977). Springfield, MA: G. & C. Merriam Company.

Weil, E. (1958). The origin and vicissitudes of the self-image. *Psychoanalysis* 1:15–18.

Wellman, H. M. (1990). *The Child's Theory of Mind.* Cambridge, MA: MIT Press.

Werner, H. (1948). *Comparative Psychology of Mental Development.* New York: Harper & Row.

Werner, H., and Kaplan, S. (1963). *Symbol Formation.* New York: Wiley.

White, R. (1959). Motivation reconsidered: the concept of effectance. *Psychological Review* 66:297–323.

Winnicott, D. (1958). *Collected papers: through paediatrics to psychoanalysis.* London: Tavistock.

———(1965). *Maturational Processes and the Facilitating Environment.* New York: International Universities Press.

——— (1971). *Therapeutic Consultations in Child Psychiatry.* London: Hogarth.

——— (1974). *The Mirror Role of the Mother and Family in Child Development: Playing and Reality.* Middlesex, England: Penguin.

Winton, W. (1986). The role of facial response in self-reports of emotions: a critique of Laird. *Journal of Personality and Social Psychology* 50: 808–812.

Wolf, N., Gales, M., Shane, E., and Shane, M. (2001). The developmental trajectory from amodal perception to empathy and communication: the role of mirror neurons in this process. *Psychoanalytic Inquiry* 21(1):94–112.

Younger, B. A., and Cohen, L. B. (1985). Developmental change in infant's perception of correlations among attributes. *Child Development* 57:803–815.

5

Discussion of Forms of Intersubjectivity in Infant Research and Adult Treatment

THEODORE J. JACOBS

This important book is about frontiers in communication, the frontiers opened up by the pioneering studies of Meltzoff, Trevarthen, Stern, Beebe, and their colleagues.

These studies, which investigate, analyze, and illuminate modes of communication in the mother–infant dyad, give us new and vitally important information, not only about these earliest communications and their implications for the kinds of attachment that form between mother and child, but about basic and enduring patterns of nonverbal behavior. These patterns, which are laid down from birth on, underlie the verbal system and, throughout life, continue to modify, alter, complement, or negate the spoken word.

I will discuss these issues not as a researcher or an expert in infant development, but as a practicing adult and child analyst who has a particular interest in nonverbal communication in the analytic situation.

I will divide my comments into four parts. In the first, in order to provide some background for my subsequent discussion of nonverbal elements in analysis and to put the analytic study of nonverbal behavior into historical context, I will offer a brief review of analytic contributions to the understanding of nonverbal phenomena.

Second, I will comment on the relevance to analytic treatment both of the research reported in this volume and Beatrice Beebe's unique case study.

Third, drawing on my clinical experience and previous writings on the subject, I will describe how I have attempted to utilize the nonverbal behavior of both patient and analyst to enhance my understanding of the analytic process. In discussing these clinical examples, I will attempt to show how the kind of infant-mother observational research studies reported in this volume can both enlarge the clinician's perspective on nonverbal behavior and assist him in understanding the multi-faceted communications between patient and analyst that form the essence of the analytic process.

Finally, I will offer a few thoughts about the ongoing neglect of nonverbal phenomena in analysis today. In doing so, I will comment on certain problems in analytic education, as well as aspects of theory and technique.

PSYCHOANALYTIC CONTRIBUTIONS TO NONVERBAL PHENOMENA

From its earliest beginnings to the present time, the role of nonverbal communication in analysis has been consistently underappreciated. To be sure, over the years there have been important contributions to our understanding of one or another aspect of the nonverbal behavior of patient and/or analyst, but these contributions have not resulted in the integration of the nonverbal dimension into either our theory or our technique. Such integration remains a task for the future, one that will be substantially aided by knowledge gained from studies of the nonverbal behavior not only of infants, but of older children and adults as well.

One root of the problem, I believe, stems from the historical fact that although Freud was a keen observer of nonverbal behavior in his patients, he did not elaborate on or develop this aspect of analytic work. That he understood its importance and could write about it with a novelist's eye for evocative detail is well illustrated by the way he describes Frau Emmy Von N (Breuer and Freud 1898).

> This lady, when I first saw her, was lying on a sofa with her head resting on a leather cushion. She still looked young and had finely-cut features, full of character. Her face bore a strained and painful expression, her eyelids were drawn together and her eyes cast down; there was a heavy frown on her forehead and the naso-labial folds were deep. She spoke in a low voice as though with difficulty and her speech was from time to time subject to spastic interruptions amounting to a stammer. [pp. 48–49]

Among Freud's followers, it was Wilhelm Reich (1933) who made the most significant contributions to our understanding of the role that nonverbal communication plays in the analytic situation. His focus was on the way in which defensive processes and character traits were revealed in muscular tension, body posture, voice, and movement.

> Apart from the dreams, associations, slips and other communications of the patient(s). . . , their attitude, that is the *manner* in which they relate their dreams, commit slips, produce their associations and make their communications, deserves special attention. The manner in which the patient talks, in which he greets the analyst or looks at him, the way he lies on the couch, the inflection of the voice, the degree of conventional politeness, all these things are valuable criteria for judging the latent resistances against the fundamental rule. [p. 45]

Reich's work fell under a cloud, however, because of the untenable ideas he promulgated later in his career. Partially because of that unfortunate situation as well as the fact that the early psychoanalysts were preoccupied with building the foundations of their science, further explorations of the nonverbal realm of analysis were not undertaken for some time. It was not, in fact, until the 1950s that a few papers on this topic began to appear in the literature. At that time Deutsch (1952) reported on his observations of patients' movements on the couch and demonstrated that the emergence of certain themes in the verbal material were regularly preceded by particular movement patterns. Cataloging a wide array of nonverbal phenomena, Feldman (1959) called attention to the importance of gestures and mannerisms in both the clinical situation and everyday life. The same year, Meerloo (1959) demonstrated that, as a result of the regression stimulated by the analytic situation, the substitution of nonverbal behavior for the verbalization of ideas and feelings takes place with some frequency. "In the motor and gestural area," he pointed out, "rhythmic stroking, plucking, picking and scratching, chronic rigidity, restless tossing or sudden change in position become the means of expression of such thoughts and ideas. In states of deep regression, infantile rhythmic movements can be observed" (p. 77).

Needles (1959) also emphasized the regressive nature of nonverbal behavior in analysis. Focusing on the phenomenon of gesticulations, he pointed out that such behavior occurs with greater frequency when patients are in states of emotional distress. In this condition, he maintained, they are more likely to utilize developmentally earlier modes of communication to express their feelings.

In discussing the nonverbal communications that occur in analysis, Shapiro (1979) noted that such communications regularly accompany the patient's verbalizations, in effect creating a dual message system. This fact "becomes important," he stated, "when one notices that an individual may be saying one thing while doing another" (p. 85).

Using films, tape recordings, and one-way screen observations, researchers such as Scheflen (1963, 1965) and Birdwhistell (1962) demonstrated the important role played in therapy by the nonverbal interactions of patients and therapist. These studies, along with the work of Jackson (1962) on communicative processes, were among the first to emphasize the interactive quality of such behavior and the way that it punctuates, regulates, and augments the verbal exchanges. This work anticipated the later findings of infant–mother observational research as well as the current interest in enactments taking place in both patient and analyst.

Increased analytic experience with young children, borderline patients, and individuals who have suffered trauma in the preverbal period, stimulated interest among analysts in nonverbal communication. Rangell (Panel 1969) described the way unconscious content is revealed in a wide variety of nonverbal phenomena. Making use of kinetic, mimetic, postural, and vocal channels, these include body language, affective states, and symptomatic acts. Adatto (1970) focussed on snout-hand behavior in a patient as an example of the repetitive reliving of the past in the form of a motor pattern that could be traced back to early biological origins. Zetzel (Panel 1969) commented on the importance of differentiating between behavior that conveys a specific nonverbal message and that which represents condensations of many levels of meaning that have developed over a long period of time.

Mittelmann (1957) studied the role of motility in development and emphasized the value of utilizing data from the motor sphere in analytic work. Such data, he pointed out, include the patient's observable movements during the hours, memories expressed through motor behavior, and dreams with motor content. Anthony (Panel 1977) expressed the modern view, endorsed in contemporary researches, that verbal and nonverbal systems are complementary. Each modality, he believed, offers a commentary on the other. To understand this infracommunicational system, he suggested, methods need to be devised to help order the data. Mahl (Panel 1977) presented clinical work illustrating the way bodily movements and other nonverbal behaviors occurring in analysis anticipate and facilitate the recall of significant memories. Lilleskov (Panel 1977) raised the question of whether nonverbal behavior should be interpreted. Much depends, he concluded, on the degree to which such behavior is resistive and the extent to which it is communicative. The important question to be considered with regard to each manifestation of nonverbal behavior is whether interpretation of that behavior will facilitate or impede the analytic process.

In more recent times, Anthi (1983) has emphasized the value of exploring preverbal experiences in analysis: "It is of vital importance for psychoanalysis as a science and as a clinical method of treatment to explore the uncharted region of preverbal life so fundamental to psychic development" (p. 34). And for Anthi, as for others interested in this early developmental period, the key to understanding it lies in the decoding and comprehension of the nonverbal behavior of adult patients.

MacDougall (1979) has made the same point in discussing the analytic treatment of patients who have suffered severe trauma in the preverbal period. Such patients are often unable to communicate their feelings verbally, she says, and will do so through action and somatic symptoms. Difficult to comprehend, the messages conveyed by such nonverbal communications can sometimes be understood by means of the analyst's countertransference reactions, and particularly by his tuning in to his affective and bodily responses.

Sandler (1987), too, has been interested in the nonverbal behavior of the analyst. Describing a situation in which a highly stressful event took place in her life while she was treating a young woman patient, she demonstrated that her emotional response to this event had a direct, but unconscious, influence on the emerging analytic material.

Weil (1984) has described the phenomenon of visual communication between patient and analyst that, in her view, takes place with some frequency in the treatment of the more disturbed patient. In such cases, she maintains, the nonverbal messages conveyed through visual contact assist the patient in regulating tension and contribute to the development of a holding environment in the broadest sense.

Focusing on the nonverbal interplay between himself and a patient that occurred in the course of an analysis, McLaughlin (1987) demonstrated how such activity actualizes and amplifies the primary verbal data of the analytic dialogue. And in a later contribution (1992), he presents evidence that links kinesic phenomena occurring in an analytic patient to certain developmental vicissitudes of her early years. He concludes this paper with a view of analysis that reflects the thinking of increasing numbers of colleagues—a view that stresses the important part played by non-verbal communication in the analytic process. "Effective analytic experience," he says, "is a prolonged enactment or actualization in which nonverbal behaviors have an essential role" (p. 159).

McLaughlin (1992) has also made another important statement about the place of the nonverbal in the communications of everyday life.

> We constantly provide stamp and signature for what we are and for what we feel through our postures, gestures, facial expressions, voice qualities, and the rest. That to a varying extent we are forever signers, as well as speakers, because we spent so many years in rapt mimetic absorption of our world, before we had words to supplement these alternative ways of knowing and telling. And that we do not lose or relinquish these ways just because there are times when words are better. [pp. 159–160]

In important contributions Kramer (1992) demonstrated that unresolved separation-individuation issues are often expressed in adult life through posture, gesture, bodily habitus, and personal hygiene; while Akhtar (1992) showed that children who have difficulty attaining appropriate distance between self and object representations often, in adulthood, develop fantasies of being tethered and attempt, through their behavior, to regulate and control the physical distance between themselves and others.

Until quite recently the literature on nonverbal behavior contained few contributions focusing on the visual sphere, particularly on the part of the analyst. The analyst's use of his eyes, however, plays an important role in analytic technique.

In a previous communication (1991) I discussed the visual system as an inherent part of the analytic instrument in the following way:

> Visualization in the analytic situation is analogous to the phenomenon in the auditory sphere that has been variously termed

evenly suspended or *freely hovering attention*. Just as the analyst listens with equal attention to all of the patient's verbalizations and tries not to fix any particular aspect of the material in mind or make a conscious effort to concentrate on it, so he observes all of the patient's nonverbal behavior. Looking as he listens, he takes in and registers what he sees, but does not focus on any particular bodily movement or facial expression. The visual imagery that he registers makes contact via associative pathways with visual aspects of memory and stimulates the recall of memories that are linked with the patient's nonverbal communications. Often it stimulates in the analyst kinesic behavior and autonomic responses that are reactions on an unconscious level to nonverbal messages. Thus the analyst's visual perceptions join with his auditory perceptions to stimulate in him responses that draw on unconscious visual and auditory memory. In practice, both visual and auditory spheres play vital roles in the registration and processing of analytic data. Both are essential parts of the analytic instrument. [pp. 49–50]

It is a paradox that although the study of transference has been elevated to a fine art, rarely in courses on technique are students taught to observe those small, barely perceptible, and often fleeting interactions between patient and analyst that can be of the greatest significance. I will return to this issue presently.

In my own training I was fortunate to have Dr. Annie Reich as one of my supervisors. Influenced by her former husband, Wilhelm Reich, Annie Reich made a point of positioning her chair so that she could see the patient as he lay on the couch. I was quite amazed, in fact, to see that Dr. Reich's chair was placed at a right angle, rather than behind, the couch.

"If you sit behind the patient, you can see nothing," Reich said to me, "and you miss vital material."

In my own work, I prefer to place my chair at about a 45-degree angle from the couch, just out of sight of the patient, but positioned so that I can view the patient's body, and enough of her face so that I can pretty well judge her facial expression.

RELEVANCE TO PSYCHOANALYTIC TREATMENT OF *FORMS OF INTERSUBJECTIVITY IN INFANT RESEARCH AND ADULT TREATMENT*

To my mind the studies reported in this book constitute landmark contributions to our understanding not only of the mind of the infant and the complex communications that take place between mother and child from birth on, but the origins of the dialogic aspects of human psychology.

Quite remarkable are the infant's capacities to read and respond to the mother's emotional state, including feelings about the child that are not in conscious awareness. This view of the infant, that of a baby ready to respond to vocal and bodily cues from the mother, is a very different one from the image of the passive infant wrapped in an autistic cocoon, described by Mahler. Prior to the work of Stern (1985), Beebe and Stern (1977) and others, this later view of the infant was accepted without question and was widely taught to students of human development.

While the studies in this book are invaluable in expanding, as well as correcting, our knowledge of infancy and the earliest patterns of communication between mother and child, a fundamental question remains for the clinician: To what extent and in what way are these studies relevant to analytic work with older children and adults? Few analysts would disagree with McLaughlin's (1992) observation that throughout life the nonverbal system continues to operate behind and within the verbal one, but just how in the analysis of older children and adults nonverbal behavior relates to the verbalizations of patient and analyst and to what extent it conveys centrally important, as opposed to incidental, information about the patient—a view taken by a number of classically trained analysts—remain to be explored. Some analysts maintain that the reason the nonverbal exchanges between patient and analyst have not become a central focus of study is precisely because they are of minor importance compared to the verbal material, and the information they yield, while interesting, is in no way essential to understanding the patient.

Others, including Deutsch (1952), McLaughlin (1992), Kramer (1992), Chused (1991), Akhtar (1992), and myself (Jacobs 1991), among others, view nonverbal communication as a vital and vitally important part of the communicative process in analysis. From this perspective, to dismiss or overlook it, is to blind oneself to information that not only regularly alters, modifies, and punctuates the verbal material, but at times contradicts the verbal message.

In recent years, interest in nonverbal communication has focused less on the posture, gestures, and movements of patient and analyst during analytic hours and more on the phenomenon called enactments, which includes behaviors that take place within and outside the consulting room.

The literature on enactments has grown so large and the use of the word so varied that it threatens to become one of those terms whose meaning has become so diffuse as to render it of little value.

Although I was quite astonished to discover this fact, apparently I was the one who first used the term *enactment* in an analytic context. I did so in my 1986 paper entitled "On Countertransference Enactments." At the time I was searching for a substitute for the term *acting out*, one that had not only become shopworn but increasingly was used in a pejorative way. In fact, it had become impossible to speak of acting out without communicating—or being heard as communicating—a judgmental attitude.

Thinking that the term was in common usage in psychoanalysis as well as in ordinary speech, I described certain behaviors on the part of patient and/or analyst as enactments. Since its meaning has become so general and imprecise, perhaps it would be useful for me to clarify what I had in mind when, in 1986, I used the term enactment.

What I was attempting to describe were communications in the form of behavior on the part of patient and/or analyst that arose out of the transference–countertransference interactions but that were also re-editions of behaviors or psychological experiences of the past. Thus, for me, enactments always included an aspect of reenactment. Today the term is often used to designate mutually interacting behaviors of patient and analyst. While it is true that both participants in analysis regularly communicate a great deal through behavior, and, in fact, analytic treatment can be defined, in McLaughlin's words, as a "continuous series of enactments," each of which must be analyzed, it is also true that enactments may be carried out without the participation, at least initially, of the other.

The patient who comes late for his session because he fears that I will criticize him for reading *Playboy* magazine is enacting both a present-day fantasy and reliving, through his behavior, his fear of being criticized by his father for his sexual interests.

The root of enactments and, indeed, of all nonverbal communication in our adult patients undoubtedly lies in the kind of mutually regulating and self-regulating behaviors described in this book. The illuminating analyses of the nonverbal interactions presented here give us an invaluable window on the way in which mother and baby respond—and alter their responses—in reaction to the behavior, facial expressions, and vocalizations of the other. We see here the origins of a nonverbal communicative system, that, although altered by developmental factors, remains a fundamental ingredient in the nonverbal communications of adults.

Recent work by Feldstein (1998) has demonstrated that individuals, including infants and mothers, are highly sensitive to vocal rhythms and that the messages conveyed through rhythm are significant in influencing the responses of one person to the other. The same, I believe, can be said for tonal qualities as well as for the syntax, timing, and inflections of speech. When I was a resident in psychiatry I had the privilege of working with Dr. Albert Scheflen, who came to our program as a visiting professor. As is well known, Scheflen was very much interested in studying nonverbal behavior in psychotherapy and, as an exercise, had the residents observe therapy sessions from behind a one-way screen with the sound system turned off. All that we, the observers, were permitted to see were the postures, gestures, and movements of patient and therapist.

It was remarkable to me to discover how much one could understand about both the patient's mood and feelings and the responses of both participants to one another from this nonverbal behavior alone. When the relationship between them was positive and the patient experienced empathy on the part of the therapist, there regularly occurred a mirroring by the patient of the therapist's posture and movements. The postures of both appeared relaxed, with legs uncrossed and arms held in an open position. When tension developed, patient and analyst shifted away from the other, their legs were often crossed, and their bodies appeared rigid and taut. While there was no perfect matching, there was sufficient correspondence between the nonverbal behaviors of patient and analyst to suggest that much was resonating unconsciously with parallel movement to communications, both verbal and otherwise, received from the other.

Presently I will describe similar behaviors in a patient and myself during a session in which negative feelings and the repair of those feelings were played out in posture and movement as well as in words.

Clearly in the behavior of adults we see traces of the kinds of movement—ones indicating rapport and attunement on the one hand and alienation on the other—that the authors of this book have described so well. Behind the bodily movements of patient and analyst that suggest rapport we can detect the positive—and joyful—actions and reactions of mothers and infants who are in tune with one another. On the other hand, in the aversive movements away from each other that often take place when patient and analyst are in a state of misattunement, we can detect the avoidant maneuvers or the chase-and-hide game observed in infant–mother pairs who are poorly attuned to one another.

This is not to say that the nonverbal behaviors of adults duplicate those of infants and mothers. Clearly this is not the case, nor is such exact correspondence claimed by researchers in the field. Rather one detects certain similarities that suggest that certain nonverbal behaviors in infant–mother pairs inform and help shape that of adults in interaction with one another.

What we do not yet understand—and what it would be most important to study—is the impact of development on nonverbal communication. Developmental studies in this area are largely lacking at this time and as a result, we do not know how, and in what way, nonverbal communication is altered or is not substantially affected by the progressing shifts from infancy to adulthood.

Without such information it is not possible to know whether, and in what way, the kinds of reciprocal mother–infant behavior described in this book are carried over into later childhood. In the anal sadistic phase, for instance, or in the oedipal period, nonverbal communication must play a vital role, not only in the sending and receiving of key messages concerning the feelings of parents and children about one another, but in continually influencing the nature of their relationship. Such nonverbal messages must interact with the verbal ones and must help foster or resolve key conflicts at these crucially important times of life.

The same may be said of later childhood and adolescence. We know comparatively little about nonverbal communication and its impact on development at these times of life. Yet we know, for instance, that nonverbal communication is a major pathway in adolescence for the expression of moods, attitudes, identifications, beliefs, and conflicts. To varying degrees the same may be said of the phases of adulthood as well as old age. We need rather urgently to study nonverbal behavior developmentally if we are to understand the contribution of the nonverbal world to neurosis, conflict, sublimation, and character formation. Such studies will help us also to learn more about the role that nonverbal communication plays in the analytic situation, particularly with regard to the question of therapeutic action.

Until we have such information, it will be difficult to disprove the contention of certain traditionally trained analysts that analysis is primarily a verbal treatment, and that, at best, a patient's nonverbal behavior provides a clue, but only a clue, to certain psychological experiences of infancy and early childhood. These colleagues contend that such material is inevitably speculative and is therefore not sufficiently reliable to form the basis for interpretation or accurate reconstruction. Nor can one disprove the contention that nonverbal, and, especially, preverbal material, as it appears in analysis, plays a comparatively small role in understanding the centrally important oedipal period. The same argument holds for other phases of childhood when verbalization clearly overshadows and conceals the more primitive nonverbal elements. It remains for researchers in the future to expand our knowledge of nonverbal communication throughout the life cycle, and in addition, to assess more precisely than we can do now its contribution to the analytic process.

In her case study, Beatrice Beebe has made a good start at doing just that. Her thoughtful, innovative, and creative work with Dolores has demonstrated, as no case report before has done, how vitally important in human psychology is the mental representation of the mother's face, especially when early trauma has taken place.

It is quite remarkable to learn how closely, how minutely, Dolores observed Beebe's face and responded to the slightest alterations in it. This material recalls the comments of the late Ernst Gombrich (1963), the well-known art historian, who, through the study of artistic representations of the human form, intuitively grasped the unique power possessed by the image of the face:

> We know that there are certain privileged motifs in our world to which we respond almost too easily. The human face may be outstanding among them. Whether by instinct or very early training, we are certainly ever-disposed to single out the expressive features of a face from the chaos of sensations that surrounds it and to respond to its slightest variations with fear or joy. Our whole perceptual apparatus is somehow hypersensitized in this direction of physiognomic vision and the merest hint suffices for us to create an expressive physiognomy that "looks" at us with surprising intensity. [p. 6]

Dolores, of course, is a patient who suffered profound trauma in childhood, including the loss of the one person who was a sustaining and nurturing figure. Her persistent focus on the face, and also on Beebe's vocal qualities, are directly traceable to her efforts to recapture the lost object as well as to the work of coming to terms with that devastating loss.

What we do not understand well enough as yet is the role that nonverbal communication, particularly that involving the face and voice, plays in the treatment of less troubled patients. That it does play a significant role is beyond question. Every clinician can observe how closely patients observe our faces and listen to the tone and inflection of our words. And we can trace their reactions to these nonverbal communications in their associations, fantasies, and dreams.

What we do not yet understand is how these nonverbal elements relate to the verbal material and, even more important, how they are embedded in and are expressed by the patient's neurosis. Only further research, and especially the kind of careful and precise study that Beatrice Beebe carried out in her treatment of Dolores, will show us how the nonverbal elements contribute to, and help shape, such matters as free association, the interweaving of transference and countertransference, and the process of working through.

In her clinical work with Dolores, Beebe combined her remarkable ability to work in, and to decipher, the nonverbal sphere with the more traditional—and invaluable—approach of uncovering and interpreting those creations of the mind that contributed so much to the patient's difficulties.

It was Dolores's fantasies and unconscious beliefs regarding her role in, and responsibility for, her foster mother's abandoning her, as well as for her subsequently being abused, that played a key role in her troubles. And it was Dolores's continual scrutinizing of Beebe's face that helped uncover this core fantasy, a fantasy that, in turn, lent meaning to her nonverbal behavior. Thus both elements, the patient's nonverbal behavior and the unconscious beliefs that are clearly related to it, lie at the heart of Dolores's difficulties. To work quite exclusively with one aspect of the patient's psychology and to leave unattended the other, an error that for some years was made by analysts who were solely interested in the verbal realm, is to unnecessarily limit understanding of the patient's communications and hence of the analytic process.

Nonverbal behavior, however, like other aspects of communication, can be used defensively to screen out and protect against the awareness of those conflicts, fantasies, and memories that induce anxiety, depressive feelings, and other unwelcome affects. This aspect of nonverbal behavior, its use in the service of defense, was not emphasized in Beebe's case report. We do not know, therefore, to what extent, or in what way, Dolores may have unconsciously employed her focus on Beebe's face and voice not only as a way of reliving and recovering her traumatic past, but protectively to screen out, for instance, aspects of her psychology, her sexuality, her competitiveness, and her aggression.

In any case, one must be aware of the fact that nonverbal behavior, like other behaviors, is a compromise formation that contains a mix of elements, including significant defensive operations. So valuable is nonverbal communication as a pathway to the forgotten past that one may forget the fact that it may also be utilized protectively to screen out, and keep at bay, conflict and fantasies that the patient—and at times the analyst—may wish to avoid.

ILLUSTRATIONS OF MY APPROACH TO NONVERBAL BEHAVIOR IN THE ANALYTIC PROCESS

I wish now to turn to some illustrations of the way that the nonverbal interactions of patient and analyst that take place in the treatment of neurotic individuals may contribute to our understanding of the covert communications that regularly flow beneath the surface of the analytic dialogue.

My first example concerns Ms. C, a professional woman, who suffered from deep feelings of inferiority. In one session, after she had spoken of feeling enclosed in a small shell, I had the visual image of her being wrapped in a cocoon. Utilizing the material of the hour and the fantasy I had had in association to it, I offered the interpretation that Ms. C seemed to be expressing the idea that she lived in a cocoon that she was struggling to break out of. This notion of herself, I added, seemed not only to be a long-standing one that had helped shape many of her experiences in life, but was her way of expressing feelings that she was having right now with me in this session. It was also a view of herself, I said, that she seemed to want me to share.

In response, Ms. C was silent for several minutes. Then she curled into herself, pulled up her legs and lowered her head. The thought occurred to me that with these movements she was pantomiming being wrapped into a cocoon. While this may, in fact, have been true, I failed at that time to recognize the aversive nature of Ms. C's movements. Feeling hurt by what I had said, she was retreating into a protective shell.

Following these transactions, Ms. C seemed to withdraw emotionally. She remained quiet for long periods of time and when she did speak, focused on the events of everyday life.

In light of this behavior, I came to understand that for some time Ms. C had been conveying important messages via her bodily responses, and that in her treatment I had not recognized the importance of this mode of communication. I realized that my focus had been almost exclusively on our verbal exchanges. I had paid comparatively little attention to the array of messages that were being transmitted nonverbally as accompaniments to, commentaries on, and sometimes contradictions of the verbal material.

Now in order to better understand what had transpired, and was continuing to transpire, between Ms. C and myself, I began to pay close attention not only to the covert meanings contained within our words, but to these nonverbal messages. Conveyed through posture, gesture, and movement, in facial expressions, in the tone, syntax, and rhythm of speech, and in the pauses and silences that punctuated the hours, these unconscious communications anticipated both subsequent conscious recognition in patient and analyst of the affects and fantasies to which they referred and the later verbalization of this material.

As I observed Ms. C and myself in interaction, I became aware of certain patterns in our movements. Often reciprocal and cuing off one another, these movements were enacted in a repetitive manner, almost like a familiar dance.

It became clear, for instance, that in connection with the mobilization of certain emotions, Ms. C and I engaged in predictable behavior. Thus, in sessions if we began to feel negatively toward one another—not a rare occurrence in light of Ms. C's tenacious resistances and the feelings of frustration that they evoked in me—each of us would unconsciously and automatically carry out particular movements.

Typically, for instance, during periods of silence Ms. C would rotate her body slightly to the left, fold her arms across her chest, and turn her head toward the wall.

On my side, I became aware at such times that I would turn my body slightly to the right, away from Ms. C and in a direction opposite to her movement. I would also lean back in my chair, and for brief intervals would close my eyes when listening.

After a period of time ranging from several minutes to a half-hour or more, not infrequently Ms. C would again reposition herself. She would draw up her legs, flex her knees, and let her arms fall to the side. At the same time, she would roll on her back so that she was no longer facing the wall. Then she would begin to speak in a quiet, modulated voice and in a tone that seemed placating or appeasing. At these times, there was about her a muted, but definite, seductive quality.

In response, I would find myself turning back toward Ms. C. I would lean forward in my chair and when offering an intervention would speak in a tone that came close to matching hers.

In addition to my effort to communicate understanding and empathy in this way, there was in my action, I believe, a resonant response to Ms. C's seductive behavior.

Although at the time I did not appreciate the significance of these nonverbal enactments, which conveyed negative emotions, efforts at repair, and a covert sexuality between Ms. C and myself, later, upon reflection, I realized that they anticipated the conscious registration of emerging feelings in both patient and analyst. They operated, in other words, as an early signal system for affects that were approaching, but had not yet reached, consciousness. Had I been aware of the studies reported in this book, I might have understood the way that our behaviors not only regulated our interactions, but served to self-regulate affects in each of us that were experienced as potentially threatening to our stability and self-esteem. Many years ago, as I have mentioned, Deutsch (1952) demonstrated that certain nonverbal behaviors regularly predicted and anticipated the appearance of particular themes in the patient's subsequent material.

If, as happened later in the analysis, I was able to observe these nonverbal communications in Ms. C and myself and decipher their meaning, it often became possible to gain access to the underlying affects and fantasies. Gaining conscious awareness of these responses, in turn, helped me both to contain them better and to utilize them interpretively.

When, on the other hand, I overlooked the nonverbal interactions taking place in sessions, the related affects often grew in intensity, with the result that the increased feeling of pressure from within not infrequently led to the living out of troublesome countertransference enactments, ones that caused much difficulty in Ms. C's treatment.

In another case I was working with a woman, Ms. A, who suffered from depression. Her mood disorder was closely connected to long-standing feelings of anger, anger that often remained outside of awareness and that was expressed by means of critical attacks on others.

As in the case of Ms. C, nonverbal communication played out in posture, gesture, and movement in this treatment offered early clues to nascent affects in both patient and analyst, affects that, on my side, were at times enacted in an unhelpful way. Whenever, for instance, Ms. A launched one of her typically veiled attacks on me, her words would be accompanied by particular actions. As she spoke, Ms. A would move toward the edge of her chair, her upper body would be thrust out and angled forward, and her head, with chin leading, would follow suit. This posture was one of belligerence, but curiously mixed with a kind of provocativeness that, at times, I experienced as covertly sexual.

I, on the other hand, would sit leaning back in my chair, leaning as far back, in fact, as I possibly could in what clearly was an involuntary retreat from Ms. A's poorly concealed aggression and provocative behavior.

After she had given vent to her feelings in this way, Ms. A would straighten up, slide backward in her seat, and, appearing drained, would remain quiet for several minutes.

In response, I would move forward, my body no longer angled backward, and I would resume my usual listening posture. These seesaw movements, backward and forward, advance and retreat, communicating anger, a breach between Ms. A and myself, and efforts to heal that breach, punctuated the sessions and were reliable markers for what, at any given time, was transpiring between my patient and myself.

Had I been able at the time to understand the importance of such movements and their connection to those patterns of communication established in infancy, so well described in this book, it would have been possible, I believe, for me, early on, to identify and explore the underlying feelings of irritation and rising anger experienced by both patient and analyst before they spilt over into the kind of nonverbal enactment that was the cause of considerable trouble in this treatment.

If, in fact, such nonverbal elements can be identified and explored as they appear, it is often possible for the analyst, through introspection and attunement to what is rising from within, to monitor, better contain, and early on make interpretive use of some of his countertransference responses, rather than unconsciously enacting them and attempting, after the fact, to grasp the meaning and significance of such enactments. Increasing the scope of his awareness, then, to include the movement patterns of patient and analyst as they emerge in the analytic hour is, I believe, a valuable tool in the analyst's ongoing efforts to turn his subjective reactions into useful insights rather than automatic actions.

Our growing knowledge of the nonverbal behavior not only of infants and mothers, but of older children and adolescents, will make such awareness increasingly available to clinicians.

NEGLECT OF NONVERBAL PHENOMENA
IN PSYCHOANALYTIC EDUCATION TODAY

Finally, in light of the research and clinical material reported in this book and the experiences of my own that I have described, I will comment briefly on what I believe to be a major deficiency in psychoanalytic education today.

Despite the clear evidence that nonverbal transactions are of the greatest importance in analysis, instruction in this aspect of clinical work remains minimal. In many institutes, in fact, it is nonexistent.

In the training analysis, too, the nonverbal dimension of communication is often overlooked. Many senior analysts, though highly experienced in other aspects of analysis, have had comparatively little experience in the decoding and interpretation of nonverbal data. Often uncomfortable in working with this mode of expression, they tend to slight it in favor of the more familiar and more congenial verbal material. As a consequence, communications that are conveyed through posture, gesture, movement, and other bodily means often go unrecognized.

When such a situation occurs in the analysis of a candidate, the minimization or omission of material from the nonverbal realm has wide reverberations for the young analyst's technique. Having experienced little understanding and effective interpretation of his own nonverbal communications in analysis, and having been exposed to little teaching about the subject in supervision or in courses on technique, the candidate can be expected neither to appreciate the importance of the nonverbal dimension in analysis nor to develop competence in working with it. The result, all too often, is that in his clinical work the candidate uses his ears to the virtual exclusion of his eyes, focuses single-mindedly on the verbal material, and sooner or later develops a scotoma for material expressed in bodily language or through other nonverbal means. In this way a significant deficiency in analytic technique is transmitted from one generation of analysts to the next.

MacDougall (1979) has commented on this issue and has pointed out that the unconscious assimilation of the attitudes, values, and way of working of our teachers and mentors not infrequently contributes to the development of significant resistances in the analyst, making it difficult for us to hear all that is being transmitted by our patients. MacDougall's focus, like that of most authors who have written on the topic, is on the internalization of attitudes, values, and ways of thinking that are actively taught at our institutes. Although she does not discuss the effect on candidates of what is omitted, doubtless she would agree that what is not taught and not spoken of is of equal importance in shaping the young analyst's approach to his work.

My own experiences as a student, although they took place many years ago, are not atypical of the difficulties that today's candidates face when, seeking to better understand the nonverbal transactions that form a significant part of the analytic material, they include descriptions of such nonverbal behavior in their reports.

Exposed as I was in my residency to the pioneering work of Scheflen (1963, 1965) on the role of nonverbal behavior in psychotherapy, I made a point of including such material in my reports to supervisors. It stirred mild interest in some teachers, very little in others. The clear wish of most supervisors was to move on to the verbal associations, that is, to the material that they regarded as truly analytic, that was familiar to them, and that they could understand. Sometimes, in fact, I felt as though I were being cast in the role of the Egyptian archeologist, with my supervisor playing his Israeli counterpart, in the story about those two rival leaders of teams digging in the Sinai.

"We have discovered that our people had a highly sophisticated communications system," the Egyptian proudly announced one day, "because in our excavation we discovered buried telephone wires." "That is nothing," the Israeli retorted. "We know that the ancient Hebrews had a far more sophisticated system, a wireless one in fact, because in our dig we found no wires at all."

Although today we have learned that communication in the analytic situation is a highly complex affair taking place on several levels and via several modalities at once, we are just beginning to investigate the complicated transactions that take place between analyst and patient in each hour. For many students of analysis as well as their teachers, this is a comparatively uncharted area, one that requires new ways of observing and new ways of thinking about what we observe. From that perspective, the exploration of the nonverbal dimension in analysis constitutes one of its few remaining frontiers. It is an area that promises to yield information of great value—information that will enrich our understanding not only of our patients' verbal communications, but of the entire analytic process.

To the growing body of knowledge essential for any practitioner of analysis and analytic psychotherapy, the studies reported in this book have made an invaluable contribution. Invaluable, too, is the work of Beatrice Beebe and her co-authors, not only in bringing this important research to the attention of the analytic community but by adding to and advancing it through their own creative efforts. All of us who toil in the rough and rocky terrain of clinical practice are deeply appreciative to them for putting together this important volume, one that expands our understanding of the origins of human communication and, in doing so, contributes so much to our analytic education.

REFERENCES

Adatto, C. (1970). Snout-hand behavior in an adult patient. *Journal of the American Psychoanalytic Association* 18:823–830.

Akhtar, S. (1992). Tethers, orbits, and invisible fences: clinical, developmental, sociocultural, and technical aspects of optimal distance. In *When the Body Speaks*, ed. S. Kramer and S. Akhtar, pp. 22–57. Northvale, NJ: Jason Aronson.

Anthi, P. R. (1983). Reconstruction of preverbal experiences. *Journal of the American Psychoanalytic Association* 31:33–58.

Beebe, B. (1986). Mother–infant mutual influence and precursors of self and object representations. In *Empirical Studies of Psychoanalytic Theories, Vol. 2*, ed. J. Mashing, pp. 27–48. Hillsdale, NJ: Analytic Press.

Beebe, B., and Stern, D. (1977). Engagement–disengagement and early object experiences. In *Communicative Structures and Psychic Structures*, ed. N. Freedman and S. Grand, pp. 35–55. New York: Plenum.

Birdwhistell, R. L. (1962). An approach to communication. *Family Process* 1(2):194–201.

Breuer, J., and Freud, S. (1898). Studies on hysteria. *Standard Edition* 2.

Chused, J. F. (1991). The evocative power of enactments. *Journal of the American Psychoanalytic Association* 39(1):605–640.

Deutsch, F. (1952). Analytic posturology. *Psychoanalytic Quarterly* 21:196–214.

Feldman, S. (1959). *Mannerisms of Speech and Gestures in Everyday Life*. New York: International Universities Press.

Feldstein, S. (1998). Some non-obvious consequences as of monitoring time in conversations. In *Progress in Communication Sciences, Vol. 14*, ed. G. A. Barnett and M. T. Palmer, pp.163–190. Norwood, NJ: Ablex.

Gombrich, E. H. J. (1963). *Meditations on a Hobby Horse and Other Essays on the Therapy of Art*. London: Phaidon.

Jackson, D. (1962). Psychoanalytic education in communication processes. *Science and Psychoanalysis* 5:129–145.

Jacobs, T. (1986). On countertransference enactments. In *The Use of the Self: Contertransference and Communication in the Analytic Situation*, pp. 139–156. Madison, CT: International Universities Press.

——— (1991). The interplay of enactments: their role in the analytic press. In *The Use of the Self*, ed. T. Jacobs, pp. 31–49. Madison, CT: International Universities Press.

Kramer, S. (1992). Nonverbal manifestations of unresolved separation-individuation in adult psychopathology. In *When the Body Speaks*, ed. S. Kramer and S. Akhtar, pp. 2–19. Northvale, NJ: Jason Aronson.

MacDougall, J. (1979). Primitive communication and the use of counter-transference. *Contemporary Psychoanalysis* 14:173–209.

McLaughlin, J. T. (1987). The play of transference. *Journal of the American Psychoanalytic Association* 35:557–582.

——— (1992). Nonverbal behaviors in the analytic situation: the search for meaning in nonverbal cues. In *When the Body Speaks*, ed. S. Kramer and S. Akhtar, pp. 132–161. Northvale, NJ: Jason Aronson.

Meerloo, J. a. M. (1959). Psychoanalysis as an experiment in communication. *Psychoanalysis and Psychoanalytic Review* 46:75–89.

Mittelmann, B. (1957). Motility in the therapy of children and adults. *Psychoanalytic Study of the Child* 12:284–311.

Needles, W. (1959). Gesticulation and speech. *International Journal of Psycho-Analysis* 40:229–294.

Panel (1969). Nonverbal communication in the analysis of adults, A. Soslich, reporter. *Journal of the American Psychoanalytic Association* 17:955–967.

——— (1977). Nonverbal aspects of child and adult psychoanalysis, R. K. Lilliskov, reporter. *Journal of the American Psychoanalytic Association* 25:693–705.

Reich, W. (1933). *Character Analysis*. New York: Orgone Institute Press, 1945.

Sandler, A. M. (1987). Dialogue without words: some nonverbal aspects of the psychoanalytic encounter. *Israel Journal of Psychiatry and Religious Science* 20(1–2):193–203.

Scheflen, A. E. (1965). Quasi-courtship behavior in psychotherapy. *Psychiatry* 28:245–257.

——— (1963). Communication and regulation in psychotherapy. *Psychiatry* 26:126–136.

Shapiro, T. (1979). *Clinical Psycholinguistics*. New York: Plenum.

Stern, S. N. (1985). *The Interpersonal World of the Infant*. New York: Basic Books.

Weil, M. (1984). The role of facial expressions in the holding environment. *International Journal of Psychoanalytic Psychotherapy* 10:76–89.

A *Neuroscience Perspective on* Forms of Intersubjectivity in Infant Research and Adult Treatment

REGINA PALLY

From the brain only, arise our pleasure, joys, laughter and jests, as well as our sorrows, pains, griefs and tears. Through it we think, see, hear and distinguish the ugly from the beautiful, the bad from the good, the pleasant from the unpleasant.
— attributed to Hippocrates, fifth century, B.C.

Consciousness and its sidekick, language, are new kids on the evolutionary block—unconscious processing is the rule rather than the exception. We will not begin to fully understand the workings of human unconscious processes until we turn away from the use of verbal stimuli and verbal reports.
— LeDoux 1996, p. 71

INTRODUCTION

This book makes an important contribution to psychoanalytic work. Beebe, Knoblauch, Rustin, and Sorter provide a deeper understanding of *intersubjective interaction* within psychoanalytic treatment. Following their description of adult and infant theories of intersubjectivity, the authors offer in Chapter 3 their own model, "forms of intersubjectivity." The case of Dolores poignantly illustrates their model in the clinical setting.

My discussion focuses on their model, forms of intersubjectivity, and adds a neuroscience perspective. Let me begin by making clear the limitations of this endeavor. Neuroscience research does not in general study the rapidly changing, ongoing face-to-face interactions that are central to these authors' work. Neuroscience relies heavily on animal data. Neuroscience experiments tend to involve people *interacting with inanimate objects*. The occasions of person-to-person exchange tend to be static, or "one-way."

Despite these limitations, neuroscience data are relevant to a number of questions, each of which is addressed in a separate section: (1) Nonverbal, implicit modes of processing "bridge the gap" between infant research and adult treatment; (2) The value of the model "forms of intersubjectivity"; (3) The importance of temporal concepts such as contingency and prediction; and (4) The relative importance of implicit vs. explicit dimensions of therapeutic action.

NONVERBAL, IMPLICIT MODES OF PROCESSING "BRIDGE THE GAP" BETWEEN INFANT RESEARCH AND ADULT TREATMENT

I first became impressed with the relevance of neuroscience to psychoanalysis through the work of Damasio (1994), LeDoux (1994), and Brothers (1989, 1992) who emphasize the importance of the mind–body connection and emotion to adaptation. The centrality of emotion, including the bodily aspects of emotion, is particularly significant in interpersonal relationships. It points to the importance of nonverbal, implicit mechanisms in much of what psychoanalysts address, for example transference, countertransference, the influence of the past on the present, "repetition," and unconscious defense (Pally 1998, 2000, 2001, 2002, 2004 in press).

The authors argue that via preverbal, presymbolic action sequences, infants implicitly learn "expectancies" of how relationships "go." They also argue that similar mechanisms are evident in the work with adults at the implicit, nonverbal level. In this, they are aligned with the work of Lyons-Ruth (1998, 1999) and Stern and colleagues (1998) in which the procedural memory of action sequences serves as a form of "implicit relational knowing." We know without even being aware how to greet one another or say good-bye, how to play around or joke, and how to enter a romantic encounter. Whereas infants operate at a preverbal, presymbolic, and prereflective level, organized around affect and action schemas, psychoanalytic work with adults tends to operate at a verbal, symbolic, and reflective level. The mind develops along a trajectory from earlier levels of cognition, that is, preverbal, presymbolic, to later forms, which retain elements of earlier experience at an implicit nonverbal, nonsymbolic level of emotion and behavior. They suggest that nonverbal, implicit processes in adults serve as a bridge between infant research and adult treatment.

What is the evidence? It is well recognized that during gestation and extending into infancy, primate and human brains undergo periods of exuberant growth and overproduction of "neural connections" (dendrites and synapses), followed by attrition and pruning back of these connections (Fuster 2003). The attrition phase results in the fine-tuning of cognitive and behavioral capacities. While much of this process is genetically determined, there is a general consensus that some of it is, at least in part, *experience-dependent* (for a review see Schore 1994). Additionally, the infant brain possesses an immature hippocampus and, as a result, does not retain an autobiographical memory of events that occur before about 3 years of age (Nelson 2000). Thus, the adult brain differs in significant ways from that of the infant. However, a number of lines of evidence indicate that events which occur at a preverbal, presymbolic level in infancy continue to influence the individual into adult life. This influence occurs via alterations of neurotransmitters, hormones, and "neural connections," affecting emotional regulation and procedural memory, all of which function in adults *without* words or conscious awareness.

Before addressing these points, some clarification of terms is necessary. Neuroscientists use the term "nonconscious" rather than "unconscious." The psychoanalytic term "unconscious" implies that experience is repressed or split off for defensive purposes. Neuroscientists do not typically address repression or other defenses. Instead nonconsciousness and consciousness are seen as existing on a continuum from the fully nonconscious, to the barely imperceptible, to consciousness only of the present moment, to "reflective" consciousness. Reflective consciousness involves awareness of one's own conscious processes, past, present, and future, and it makes possible all higher cognitive processes, such as symbolic representation, language, and theory of mind abilities.

"Implicit" is an umbrella term that refers to *all* nonconscious processes, including learning, memory, behavior, and interactive influences. Neuroscientists use the term "procedural" when referring to the implicit aspects of *motor* processes. They use the terms "emotional" conditioned learning or "emotional" memory for implicit *affective* processes, and "priming" for the implicit aspects of *perception*. Implicit is considered nonverbal by definition, since spoken language requires consciousness. (A clinical exception is a phenomenon of "sleep talking," which may not even be remembered upon awakening.) But there can be an implicit dimension to spoken language, such as rhythm intonation and intensity. While generally implicit, the nonverbal can become conscious. Nonverbal refers to motor behavior such as gesture and facial expression, as well as changes in body physiology and arousal such as quivering of the voice, dilation of the pupils, pallor or flushing of the skin, and tearing. The terms "nonverbal" and "implicit" will be used with the above distinctions understood.

Nonverbal, Implicit Processes Are the Usual Mode of Brain Functioning

One reason that nonverbal implicit mechanisms are significant for adult treatment and may serve as a bridge between infant research and adult treatment is that *at all stages of development*, from infancy throughout the life span, the *vast majority of brain activity* occurs entirely outside of conscious awareness and therefore is nonverbal and implicit (Crick 1994, Damasio 1995, Edelman 1992). Consciousness and spoken language account for only a very small percentage of the brain activity involved in perception, behavior, emotion, memory, planning, decision making, learning, and interaction. I will emphasize the nonconscious, nonverbal aspects of learning and interaction, since these are most relevant in the current context.

Psychoanalysts do recognize unconscious, nonverbal elements of analytic treatment but typically focus on their *symbolic* communicative function (Jacobs 1994). Neuroscience, on the other hand, emphasizes that nonconscious, nonverbal processes *influence* arousal level, emotion, and behavior *between* interacting individuals. Research suggests that many nonverbal behaviors are innately designed nonconsciously to trigger a nonverbal behavior in others (Eibl-Eibesfeldt 1980). In animals, a threat display in one animal triggers submissive behavior in others; a male mating display triggers "presentation" displays in females. In humans, a direct stare at a stranger signals danger and impedes the other's approach behavior; a smile signals friendly intent and beckons the other to approach; and crying triggers comforting behaviors in others.

This nonverbal level of interaction also regulates the biology in each member of the dyad, including neurotransmitter levels, hormones, and autonomic nervous system functioning, all of which support behavior and emotion and contribute to attachment, cognitive functioning, and physical health (Damasio 1994, Davidson et al. 2000, Hofer 1984, 1996, Panksepp 1998).

A set of experiments by Ekman illustrates how nonverbal behaviors *influence* the self and others (Ekman 1990, 1993). When human subjects are instructed to contract specific muscles (without being told the particular emotion associated with those muscle movements), a high percentage of subjects actually report feeling that particular emotion and demonstrate the autonomic changes associated with it. Additionally, when one person observes the facial expression of another, at the implicit level the observer's brain matches the motor elements of the partner's expression (Dimberg et al. 2000). This motor activity becomes implicitly linked, in the observing person, with autonomic changes, somatic sensations, and emotional feelings that are associated with the facial expression. In this way, when one person sees the emotional expression of another, the person *recreates* as his own *internal state* the bodily processes of the other and the emotional experience of what the other "feels." This is one important aspect of empathy (Damasio 1994, 1995). In addition to "implicit matching," when an individual also "explicitly" (i.e., consciously) matches the facial expression of another, there is an *enhancement* of this internal state and therefore increased empathic capacity (Carr et al. 2003).

Damasio (1994, 1999) argues that the orbitofrontal region (OFC) of the prefrontal cortex *represents* the memory of these body responses as part of the emotional memory of events. These bodily memories implicitly influence how the individual will respond to a current situation: his feelings, behaviors, and decisions. The OFC and ventromedial prefrontal cortex (VMPFC) are involved in emotional learning, which predicts the occurrence of *future* positive and negative events, that is, rewards and punishments (Damasio 1994). The review work of Schore (1994) indicates that mother–infant face-to-face affective exchanges result in the early stages of maturation of these prefrontal regions, beginning at about 3 months of age. In the case of Dolores, these brain circuits seem to have learned to anticipate abandonment and disappointment.

A subcortical structure, the amygdala, uses implicit processes exclusively to appraise and respond to threat or reward, to predict the circumstances under which they are likely to occur, and to initiate adaptive physiological and behavioral responses. Hyman (1998) demonstrates that the amygdala is activated in response to visualizing fearful faces, even when a subject does not consciously realize that she has seen a face. By presenting a brief fearful stimulus to subjects, immediately followed by a longer neutral *masking* stimulus, the subjects do not consciously report seeing a fearful face. However, the subjects "indicate" that they have experienced it, albeit nonconsciously, as reflected in increased activity in the amygdala on fMRI and alterations of arousal and visceral changes such as heart rate or sweating. In another experiment, subjects receive a mild shock paired with the presentation of a *neutral* face. Subsequently, subjects respond to the neutral face in the same way they do to the shock, that is, with fear and withdrawal, without being consciously aware of the connection. Such implicit "social" learning can also be studied using electrical scalp recordings and facial electromyograms (Bunce et al. 1999, Shevrin 2001, Wong et al. 1997). This work indicates that associative or conditioned learning about faces, that is, whether a facial expression will be associated with positive or negative experiences, can occur at the implicit level.

Shevrin, a neurophysiologist and analyst, along with his colleagues, emphasizes that implicit learning can occur in parallel with conscious awareness (Wong et al. in press). Many studies indicate that *in order to change* an implicitly learned, conditioned "autonomic" visceral response to a stimulus, the subject must be made conscious of the stimulus. However, the work of Shevrin and colleagues suggests that even though conscious attention to the new stimulus occurs, the *learning of a new association* can occur at a nonconscious, implicit level. Another study by Rose (Rose et al. 2002) shows that while a subject is *consciously* learning the flexible rules for performing a task, *implicitly* embedded rules can also be learned *at the same time*, but outside conscious awareness.

A gambling experiment simulates real-life learning situations in which people are dealing with the uncertainty of receiving positive or negative consequences (Bechara et al. 1997). Using normal human subjects, this experiment emphasizes the degree to which people can *implicitly* learn about what events are likely to turn out positively and negatively and yet be unaware, at least initially, of the factors that influence them to choose either advantageous or disadvantageous responses. The "players" are given four decks of cards and a loan of $2000 facsimile U.S. bills, and are asked to play so that they can lose the least amount of money and win the most. Turning each card carries an immediate reward ($100 in decks A and B and $50 in decks C and D). Unpredictably, however, the turning of some cards also carries a penalty (which is large in decks A and B and small in decks C and D). Playing mostly from the disadvantageous decks (A and B) leads to an overall loss. Playing from the advantageous decks (C and D) leads to an overall gain. The players have no way of predicting when a penalty will arise in a given deck, no way to calculate with precision the net gain or loss from each deck, and no knowledge of how many cards they must turn to end the game (the game is stopped after 100 card selections). While playing, each player is monitored for skin conduction response (SCR), a measure of *implicit* physiologic change and emotional arousal. After encountering a few losses, subjects generate SCR's *before* selecting a card from the bad decks and begin to avoid the decks with large losses. Subjects begin to choose advantageously *before they consciously know why* or are able to verbally explain which strategy works best. Moreover, subjects generate *anticipatory* skin conduction responses whenever they ponder a choice that turns out to be risky *before* they know *declaratively*, in words, that it is a risky choice. These results suggest that *nonconscious* knowledge guides behavior *before* conscious knowledge does. Particularly relevant for psychoanalysis, the researchers believe that without the help of such *nonconscious* biases, overt conscious knowledge may be insufficient to ensure advantageous behavior. In relation to the work with Dolores, this suggests that the implicit mechanisms in the preliminary stages of treatment may have facilitated her subsequent conscious awareness of what was happening.

Throughout development, plasticity is evident in implicit learning systems (Davidson et al. 2000). When predictive contingencies *change*, such that "old" dangers or rewards are no longer present, the extinction or "unlearning" of old responses can occur (Quirk et al. 2003). Such extinction, which can occur without conscious awareness, nevertheless involves active "new" learning and memory encoding for new associations and predictions. For example, a rat is trained to fear a sound because it receives a shock right after the sound. As a result, the rat anticipates danger when hearing the sound and jumps with fear *before* any shock occurs. For extinction to occur, the sound is played over and over but without a shock. The rat now learns that nothing happens after a shock: no need to do anything. Both learned responses remain, and the rat now has *two* possible responses to the sound. At any given moment only one is expressed while the other is inhibited. The rat's prefrontal cortex can "select" a new "do nothing" response and inhibit the old fear response. Under situations of stress, such as illness, loss, or changed context, for example a new cage, the old fear response can reemerge (Quirk et al. 2003). Similarly in humans, after long periods of remission, a successfully treated phobia can reemerge with the death of a loved one, or a job loss (Nadel and Land 2000).

What this implies is that in the case of Dolores, early implicitly encoded experiences of abandonment, along with the loss of love and safety, cause Dolores to be frightened and withdraw from intimate interactions. With Dr. Beebe, she begins to learn and engage in a new kind of interaction at an implicit, emotional-procedural level, where the face is no longer associated with abandonment and emotional desolation. What neuroscience research suggests is that the old responses remain, leaving her susceptible to "emotional retreat" under stress.

The fact that so much in the brain occurs nonconsciously and without words suggests that "emotional non-verbal exchange may play at least as much importance in analytic treatment as does verbal exchange" (Pally 2000, p. 99). Analysts and patients may influence one another's body sensations, imagery, thoughts, behaviors, and even words, through nonconsciously processed nonverbal cues of emotion, such as autonomic changes (flushing, dry mouth) and behaviors (facial expression, posture, gesture). These nonverbal cues are evident in the analyst as well as in the patient. Since the brain is organized so that individuals impact each other so much at the nonverbal level, this work suggests that *how* the analyst communicates may be as important for therapeutic action as *what* the analyst says. Additionally, *how* the analyst behaves and feels may be as much an indicator of what is going on unconsciously *in the patient* as anything that is consciously known by either individual.

Experiences of Early Childhood Can Have a Long-lasting Effect on Adult Functioning

Another explanation for thinking of nonverbal, implicit processes as a bridge between infancy and adulthood is that experiences that happen during early childhood can have a life-long effect on functioning at the nonconscious, nonverbal level of behavior, emotion, and arousal. The newborn brain continues to develop rapidly through the first few years of life (Yamada et al. 2000). Environmental exposures, including types and degrees of stimulation, affect the number and density of neuronal synapses (Greenough et al. 1987). The types and intensity of visual and auditory experiences that children have early in life may have profound influences on brain development (for review, see Christakis et al. 2004).

The factors most likely to have long-lasting effects and to be particularly resistant to change are those highly associated with survival (Don't touch a hot stove! Don't run into the street!), those associated with very intense affect or arousal (e.g., high elation, romantic love, trauma, neglect), or those that occur at a very young age. Early interactions in which important skills are learned, such as how vigilant to be to mother's changing affect, how dependent to be on her for regulation, what to do to be comforted, how to avoid overstimulation, how to get attention or to get praise, appear to involve all three factors of survival, intense affect, and developmentally early. Interactions that promote attachment have a survival function, serving to keep the infant close to the protecting caretaker, as well as fostering affective and physiologic regulation. These interactions are frequently repeated and often involve high affect states. Therefore, these early experiences can become deeply engrained in neural circuitry and they tend to remain stable over time. Many sources of data, both animals and human, suggest that what occurs during infant–maternal interactions can have long-lasting, even permanent effects that continue into adult life.

Animal studies demonstrate how the "type" of maternal care can have lifelong effects on an offspring's emotional temperament, behavior, and biology (Suomi 1999). For example, naturally occurring differences in maternal care among rats have been demonstrated by Meaney (2001). At one end of the spectrum are naturally highly nurturing mothers who exhibit a high degree of licking their pups (HiMC). At the other end are naturally poor mothers who exhibit low degrees of licking their pups (LoMC). Genetically pure strains of rats can be bred such that these traits will be genetically determined. HiMC mothers have offspring with characteristic traits. They are calm, freely explore their environment, have low levels of cortisol, have high levels of gluccocorticoid receptors (GR's), and the females, when they grow up, are HiMC themselves. On the other hand, LoMC mothers have offspring that are fearful, have reduced exploratory behavior, have high levels of cortisol, have low GR's, and the female offspring grow up to be LoMC. Foster rearing experiments illustrate how environmental experiences can influence outcome and lead to permanent lifelong patterns of emotional traits and responses to stress. Half the pups of a HiMC mother are put in the nest of a LoMC mother and reared by her. Similarly, half of the pups of a LoMC mother are put in the nest of the HiMC mother and reared by her. Each mother has *half* of her own biologic offspring and *half* of the biologic offspring of the other mother. Results show that *all* pups reared by HiMC resemble each other. They are calm, explore freely, are low in cortisol, are high in GR's, and female offspring grow up to be HiMC. Similarly, *all* pups reared by LoMC resemble each other. They are fearful, do not explore freely, are high in cortisol, are low in GR's, and the females grow up to be LoMC.

Foster care experiments involving monkeys also emphasize the lifelong impact of mothering (Suomi 1999). A baby monkey who is highly fearful will not function well in the troop. If reared by a foster mother who is very nurturing, the monkey will turn out calm and will rise to a high level in the troop. Even normal maternal care is better than none. Baby monkeys with a genetic predisposition to impulsivity, exhibit that trait only if they are *peer* raised but *not* if raised by the *mother*. With respect to temperament features such as fearfulness and impulsiveness, for which there is a genetic predisposition, these studies suggest that a good environment can have an ameliorative effect on a genetically vulnerable individual, while a poor environment can increase the likelihood that a genetic vulnerability will be expressed.

Human studies show that having a depressed mother during infancy can have similar permanent, negative, and biologic effects on human babies (Newport et al. 2002a,b). These biologic profiles (i.e., abnormal cortisol and GR levels) predispose such individuals to maladaptive coping responses to stress later in life and make them more likely to develop psychiatric conditions, such as posttraumatic stress disorder (PTSD), depression, and anxiety (Raison and Miller 2003). Studies with children who have been abused or neglected also show lifelong impairments (Raison and Miller 2003, Silk 1998, 2000, Teicher 2000). When abused children are exposed to facial images, they are more likely to perceive danger even when it is not there. They do not look for evidence to disconfirm their view and, therefore, chronically respond as if danger is imminent (Pollak and Kistler 2002). When they grow up, they continue to be hypervigilant and more likely to perceive danger even in neutral interpersonal situations (van der Kolk 2003, Yehuda 2001). As adults, abused or neglected children are more likely to suffer from PTSD, depression, anxiety, affect dysregulation, interpersonal difficulties, and physical illness. These individuals tend to become too emotionally over-aroused even with relatively benign levels of stress.

These experiments indicate that very early experiences can lead to permanent changes at emotional, behavioral, and biological levels. Very early maternal care is not remembered consciously but is represented, at the implicit level, in the person's neural brain circuitry, evident in adulthood as physical sensations, perceptions, emotions, nonverbal emotional expressions, and patterns of interpersonal interaction. In the case of Dolores, what this suggests is that her early loss of the "good face mother," together with many abusive experiences, inclined her to a tendency to become fearful of emotional connectedness with others.

Adult Linguistic and Reflective Capacity Are
Built upon Preverbal, Nonsymbolic, Affective,
and Behavioral Interactions

Nonverbal gestures, which operate *very rapidly* at an *implicit* level, organize all spoken conversation (Kendon 1992). For example, when a group of people are having a conversation, *moving* in the rhythm of the speaker's vocalizations is a signal that one wants to enter the conversation. When the speaker wants to change the topic of conversation, a nonverbal gesture is sent out that serves as a "trial balloon." If the others *consent* to the change, they signal back with a nonverbal gesture. All of this goes on *before* the speaker switches the topic. In many respects this is what the authors are describing in their detailed account of mutual influence in vocal rhythms and turn-taking that occurs between mothers and infants. This early interactive behavior then develops into verbal exchange, with the nonverbal embedded within the verbal, albeit at a nonconscious, implicit level.

Language is a uniquely human capacity. Evolutionary biologists, linguists, and neuroscientists maintain that it did not emerge in its present form until approximately 50,000 years ago (Calvin 2004, Deacon 1997, Tomasello 1999). Although other primates do not have language, they appear to have some of the basic neural circuitry onto which human linguistic capacity is added. Early human ancestors, such as Homo Erectus (about 1.8 million years ago) and even *early* Homo Sapiens (about 100,000 years ago), probably did not have language as we know it. While just exactly *how* language evolved is not known, one theory (and remember it is only a theory) holds that it began with H. Erectus in the form of gestures and grunts with one- to three-word phrases emerging in *early* H. Sapiens, and finally complex, syntactic speech emerging in *modern* H. sapiens. It is an intriguing theory because it parallels the development of language in children that seems to follow a similar pattern, from nonverbal to one- to three-word phrases to verbal syntactic expression, with earlier stages making possible, and remaining embedded in, subsequent stages.

Neuroscientists have identified that a certain subset of neurons in brain regions that subserve social behavior may be the basis for the evolution of language from our primate and early human ancestors, as well as for the individual development of language from infancy to adulthood (Gallese 2003, Rizzolatti and Arbib 1998). What is also relevant to psychoanalysis is that this same system is involved in *nonlinguistic* capacities, such as imitation, empathy, intuition, and understanding the intentions of others, all of which are in place prior to the development of spoken language (Arbib 2002, Gallese 2003, Iacoboni et al. 1999). Many studies, both animal (using single cell recordings) and human (using fMRI), demonstrate that when we observe the goal-directed or intentional behavior of others, such as pointing at an object or picking up an apple to eat, or even moving our lips to speak, the pre-motor system (where behaviors are planned within our own brain) becomes active *without our being aware*, in the same way it would if we were performing that same intentional act (Iacoboni et al. 1999, Rizzolatti et al. 1996). This *implicitly* operating pre-motor system is called the "mirror neuron" system. Mirror neurons are labeled as such because they are neurons that become active when observing or performing an intentional act.

The mirror system underlies many human abilities. The *pre-motor* mirror system can readily signal the *primary* motor system to act, making possible *nonconscious* imitation. This process explains how we learn to perform skills or to act, in social situations, from watching others without any explicit instruction (Tessari et al. 2002). The mirror neuron system provides a means for recognizing a most fundamental aspect of relatedness, that others are like self, which underlies all aspects of social functioning, imitation, empathy, and language (Carr et al. 2003, Meltzoff and Gopnik 1993, Tomasello 1999). In humans, mirror neurons form part of a circuit. Mirror neurons are found in the pre-motor region of the brain, which includes Broca's speech area. These mirror neurons link to *primary motor cortex* (overt muscle movement), the *temporal cortex* (recognition and naming of observed action), the *limbic system* (emotion, intentions, and memory), the *prefrontal cortex* (executive functions, e.g., higher abstract thought, decision-making, planning, inhibition of impulses), and the *parietal cortex* (somatic sensation and spatial mapping).

Together, these systems enable us to know what others feel and intend from watching them act. When the pre-motor mirror system matches and represents the behavior of others, it sets up *inside a person* the behaviors and feelings of others (Carr et al. 2003, Gallese 2003). For this reason, when one person watches another's behavior, the person can know the other's intention, because he knows what he would intend if he were performing that same behavior. When watching another's facial expression of emotion or other emotional behaviors, one can know what the other feels, because one's own limbic system knows what one's feeling would be when making that same emotional expression with its concomitant facial muscle feedback.

Neuroscientists distinguish between mimicry, a reflexive matching of behavior found in all primates, and imitation, which occurs only in humans and involves behavioral matching along with an intended goal (Tomasello 1999). In *imitation*, overt expression occurs, but for the most part during action observation, overt expression of behavior is inhibited by the prefrontal cortex (Rizzolatti and Arbib 1998). When what is observed is of particular interest or emotionally meaningful, however, the brain of the "observer" allows a *very brief motor expression*, which will be recognized by the other member of the dyad and helps explain why especially empathic individuals are more likely to show overt muscle movement of the face and body as they match the affects of others. It appears that more empathic individuals match and express more of the emotional behavior of others, which probably leads them to feel the feelings of others more readily, and to intuit their intentions more, as well as to show by a little overt expression that they "get it," that is, understand (Chartrand and Bargh 1999, Tessari et al. 2002).

This mirror neuron system is probably the basis for much of what analysts refer to as internalization and identification, where we literally take in and may even perform what others feel and do. This may also explain why young children, whose prefrontal monitoring system is still quite immature, may misattribute the emotional states and intentions of others. For example, if a caretaker is very impatient or disgusted with a child, the child may misattribute these feelings. The child may subjectively experience feeling impatient or disgusted with him/herself and not be aware that the source of the feeling is from the parent.

From a developmental perspective, it appears that aspects of the mirror neuron system are already in place at birth. It is proposed that the mirror system contributes to language development and theory of mind. Symbols are arbitrary and have no direct similarity to the things they represent (Deacon 1997). Because a symbol is abstract and not concrete, it can stand for many things simultaneously. The word *bank* can mean a specific bank such as Bank of America, bank in general, the bank of a river, or to bank on something (count on it). Symbol formation begins somewhere around 9 months of age (Tomasello 1999). Once the child is able to point to objects of interest and follow with eye gaze when mother points to objects, the dyad can engage in *joint attention* to the object and the *sharing of interest* in the object. When the baby points at a cookie and grunts, the situation is ambiguous. The pointing and grunt can mean "I want to eat that cookie," "What a yummy looking cookie," or simply "Look at the cookie." Mother might say "Oh yes, that is a yummy looking cookie" or "Oh yes, you want to eat the cookie. Here it is." In fact, continued grunting may serve as a signal and may not stop until she "gets" the intended meaning correctly.

It is this delicate interplay within the interaction that links together the motor act of pointing, the joint attention, the mother's labeling with words, *one* of several possible meanings, and that, ultimately, underlies symbolization and facilitates language development. Pointing is also an early stage in the development of theory of mind, as the 9-month-old infant can recognize that when the mother points, she has the *intention* of sharing attention with the baby (Nelson 2000, Tomasello 1999). Not until about 5 years of age does theory of mind really begin to mature such that a child is able to understand that people have beliefs and desires that may differ from their own (Nelson 2000). What is suggested by this developmental sequence of events is that a continuum exists in which higher mental functions that are found in adults are grounded in the action-observation system and emotional matching system that begins in infancy and childhood.

Could it be that by actually getting to view Dr. Beebe's face by watching the videotape, Dolores's mirror neuron system is activated and she is able to have a different emotional, visceral, and behavioral response? In this way, she is able to decenter from her own automatic, traumatic response to faces (avoid looking) and to shift to paying attention and taking in emotional responsiveness. Perhaps the video gave her some distance from her immediate and traumatic experience so she could pay attention. She needs to do this privately, have control over it, and do it over and over as much or little as she wants. In addition, perhaps Dolores's imitation of Dr. Beebe's face evoked through her own muscle feedback the feeling of being cared for, which activated the attachment system that had been so traumatized in Dolores.

THE VALUE OF THE MODEL "FORMS OF INTERSUBJECTIVITY"

There are a number of related points within this model that I will address from a neuroscientific perspective: regulation is interactive, an extensive range of variable patterns of interactive regulation exists, a flexible balance between self- and other regulation is optimal, and temporal factors such as contingency and predictability are critical in mother–infant interactions.

Regulation Is Interactive

The authors' central goal is the refinement of a theory of interaction for psychoanalysis, and interactive regulation is one of their central concepts. Neuroscience research has shown that the human brain develops and functions *only* through interactions with the environment. These interactions are mediated through bodily processes of physical movement, emotional behavior, and physiologic changes, such as flushing and quivering of the voice (Clark 1997, Damasio 1999, Edelman 1989, Edelman and Tononi 2000, Freeman 2000, 2003, Fuster 2003). In this sense *there is no such thing as an isolated individual.* Organisms survive *only* in relation to an environment, *influencing* that environment and in turn being *influenced by* it. Therefore, people cannot be properly studied outside the context of their environments.

At birth the human brain is immature, having only a basic and rough outline of neural circuitry, determined primarily by genetic programs. Further development and maturation occur after birth, primarily *in response to the individual's own interactions with the environment* (Edelman 1989). For example, when exposed to an environment rich in tactile stimulation (e.g., kangaroo care, massage, nonnutritive sucking), preterm infants show increased brain and body size and leave the hospital more quickly than babies who do not receive this stimulation (Field 2003). The most salient environment leading to brain growth and mental development is the *relationship with caretakers* (Schore 1994, Tomasello 1999).

The cortex of the brain is *innately organized to interact with the world*, in a cyclic fashion, called the "perception–action" cycle (Fuster 2003). Each behavior leads to some type of sensory consequence, a *change* in sensory input, either "in the world" or "in the self." In turn, each new input to the sensory cortex activates premotor cortical regions involved in the planning and preparation for movement, which influence subsequent behavior. These interactions can lead to the physical growth of new neural connections that are the fundamental elements of brain development. Through these interactions, the brain stores in *implicit memory systems* the *temporal sequences* of *what sensory and motor events tend to follow one another.* The brain encodes these sequences at the implicit level as "expectancies" or "predictions" of what to anticipate in relation to the self and the world.

For example, when a person lifts a cup of coffee to drink, "self" consequences include proprioceptive sensations (i.e., where the body and its parts are located in space) and visceral sensations (e.g., sense of tension on joints and muscles, stretching of the skin, heat from the coffee). "Self" consequences involve one's own body changes in response to interactions, encoded in parietal and limbic regions. "World" sensory consequences include the distance of the cup to the mouth and the angle at which the cup is viewed. These consequences are processed in sensory association areas and in the parietal cortex. "World" inputs provide information about the objects and people we encounter. Self and world inputs are processed in distinct brain systems but eventually are integrated in the prefrontal cortex.

Neuroscientists have made the remarkable discovery that the brain organizes an individual's interactions more in accordance with implicit predictions than actual events. This is because it takes time for *actual* sensory consequences of an action to reach the brain and lead to a reaction, often *too much time* for the brain to operate efficiently and smoothly in the rapidly changing world of the objects and people it encounters.

The influence of predictions can be dramatic. In repeated interactions like lifting a coffee cup or the routines of conventional social behavior, such as smiling and shaking hands in greeting, the inner sense of where the body is located in space is derived from *where the brain predicts the body will be.* The brain guides the next action based on the predicted, not the actual. As a result of implicit predictions, a smile of greeting is planned in advance and *ready to go*, as one person approaches another, enabling the person to smile at the appropriate moment.

These implicitly operating predictions influence not only how we behave, but also our subjective experience of how we behave. In one experiment (Schwartz et al. 2004), during the first "control condition," subjects view a computer screen with a circle on it. Subjects are instructed to trace the outline of the circle with a cursor that is visible on the screen, by rotating a handle out of view underneath the table. The *gain* between cursor and handle is such that, when the cursor traces a circular path on the screen, the handle also follows a circular path. In the second "experimental condition," unbeknown to the subjects, the *gain* on the handle is now altered so that when the handle moves in an elliptical shape, the cursor nevertheless moves in a circle. Now when the subject sees the circle, the brain predicts the hand will move in a circle, and "pre-motor" predictive activity is set in motion. This predictive activity correlates with subjective experience of circular motion, not the actual movement of the hand that is elliptical. Thus subjective experience can be more affected by predicted than actual events, and the brain can actually make a mistake.

The authors' claim that human interaction is, and *must be*, dynamic and changing, is also supported by neuroscience research. Despite the fact that in general neuroscientists have not yet studied the rapidly changing events of human ongoing face-to-face interactive regulation, there are a number of neuroscience findings relevant to this issue. Neuroimaging data indicate that changes in a stimulus maintain conscious attentive focus at the level of prereflective or primary consciousness and correspond to an increase in neural activity. Studies in animals show that neural activity quickly decreases, that is, *habituates*, in response to a stimulus that remains *static* and *unchanging* (Kandel et al. 1991). As an example, a baby will show interest at the *onset* of a stimulus, but with *continued presence* of the stimulus, the baby quickly loses interest and stops attending. At the neural level the loss of interest corresponds to habituation and a decrease in neural activity for that stimulus. An increase of neural activity leads to the growth and strengthening of neural connections, and a decrease can lead to an attrition or pruning back of connections (Clark 1997, Damasio 1999, Freeman 2000, Kandel et al. 1991). Changes in stimulus presentation during mother–infant interaction enhance growth of brain circuits for features of face, voice, gesture, and affect so important for social functioning.

What is the evidence that conscious attention (at the level of prereflective or "primary" consciousness) enhances the kind of brain activity necessary for the growth of neural connections? Conscious attention to a stimulus enhances blood flow and glucose metabolism in cortical regions specialized for that stimulus (Corbetta et al. 1991). For example, in a PET scan study, subjects are shown a number of moving objects. PET scans measure glucose metabolism in the brain, which is an indirect measure of blood flow and a direct measure of brain activity. All the objects are the same shape. Subjects are asked to attend to their color, or to their direction of motion. Although *shapes* are identical, brain activity differs depending on what *feature* is consciously attended to. In looking for *motion*, the greatest activity is in area V5 of the visual cortex, an area specialized for motion detection. In attending to *color*, the greatest activity is in area V4, an area specialized for color detection. In looking at *faces*, activity is greater in the temporal region, a facial recognition area, when subjects must decide *if the two faces are the same person or not*. Activity is greater in the parietal area, a spatial location area, when asked to determine the *spatial location* of the faces. Attention to sensory inputs also leads to an increased *firing rate* (how many electrical waves per second) of neurons *within* sensory regions (Desimone and Duncan 1995, Miller and Cohen 2001), and increased *entrainment* or *synchrony* (firing at the same rate) of firing *within* and *between* cortical areas, such as sensory cortex, prefrontal cortex and motor cortex (Fried et al. 1997, Roelfsema et al. 1997). Both forms of increased firing enhance *integration* of brain function.

One neuroscience area of research that more closely resembles human interactive regulation is that which studies the uniquely human ability for *accurate* ballistic throwing and tracking of ballistic trajectories. This ability allowed our early human ancestors to run and throw rocks or spears while hunting moving prey. This same ability is used in many sports. A tennis player watches a ball's trajectory as it leaves the opponent's racket, runs to the ball, and swings his own racket for a hit. At the level of the brain, *non*conscious processes are able to monitor the ball's movement and coordinate these with rough movement guidance of torso and limbs for the "expected" trajectory of the ball. However, for more *accurate fine-tuning* of the movement, more *accurate* racket contact, and precise accommodation to *unexpected* changes in trajectory from a gust of wind, some degree of conscious monitoring is required (Schall 2001).

All of this data taken together suggest that by promoting dynamic flux within the interaction, such that stimuli and arousal states do not remain static, mothers and babies are facilitating mutual attention and awareness of one another, so that the baby continues to receive the kind of sensory stimulation needed to maximize brain maturation and integration.

Patterns of Interactive Regulation Vary

The authors present an expanded view of intersubjectivity in infancy in which they argue that the full range of patterns of interactive regulation provides the broadest definition of the presymbolic origins of intersubjectivity, with correspondence being only one of many critical patterns. From the neuroscience perspective, in order to function adaptively, the brain needs a *variable repertoire* of *possible* ways of responding, and the ability *flexibly* to *select* among these options. The mother–infant relationship sets the stage for this adaptation by providing the infant with a broad range of patterns of interactions upon which to build neural circuitry. The authors describe self- and other regulation patterns that include positive and negative affect matching, affect difference, coordination of direction of affect change, degrees of coordination of vocal rhythms, and distress regulation. A baby who experiences the optimal degree of these variable patterns of interaction will be able to sustain the kind of brain growth necessary to develop an optimal and flexible repertoire of ways of engaging with partners and coping with varying encounters in the future.

One critique the authors make of infant theorists Meltzoff, Trevarthen, and Stern is that too little attention has been paid to difference. Similarity of behaviors, or "matching," is important, for example, in situations where creating the experience of being understood is involved, particularly in an affect range from interest through positive to exuberance. But difference is also important, particularly in distress states. If, for example, the mother actually matches the infant's distress, behaving *as distressed as* the infant, rather than *somewhat less,* her soothing may fail.

Posner and Rothbart (1998) have studied the effects of human mother–infant interaction on attention shifts in the infant's subsequent development of affect regulation. They theorize that when the mother matches the infant's negative state just a little and then moves to a different, more positive, state, this "partial matching" may enable the infant to shift by matching the mother's more positive state. Gergeley and Watson (1998) have a similar theory. Posner and Rothbart (1998) suggest that while the caretaker is more responsible for regulating affect states in the infant in the beginning of life, these interactions lead to neural encoding and the development of the infant's own circuits for independent affect regulation. In reviewing neuroscience research, Schore (1994) also points out that brain tracts responsible for affect regulation (which link brainstem, subcortex, and prefrontal cortex) develop in response to the changing contours of positive and negative affect states during face-to-face encounters. In the vocal exchanges documented in the work of Jaffe and colleagues (2001), and in Beebe and colleagues (2000), described in Chapter 3, changes in temporal rhythm most likely stimulate the prefrontal cortex, a brain region specifically sensitive to the *temporal* aspect of experience, and therefore critical to brain functions such as narrative memory, planning, conversational exchange, and linguistic syntax (Deacon 1997, Fuster 2003).

A Flexible Balance Exists Between Self- and Other Regulation

Neuroscientists emphasize that *both* variability (a broad range of possible responses) and flexibility (being able to choose and select among response options) are important for human adaptation. Children learn not only behaviors, but a *set* of flexible and context-sensitive rules to guide behavior. In other words, they learn what behavior to use and when. This type of rule-guided learning occurs both nonconsciously and consciously. Some behavioral rules apply to all situations. Others apply only to particular contexts. Some rules are quite flexible and shifting. For example, children learn the general rule "do not talk to strangers," but then must learn that there are subtle contextual variations under which this rule does not apply. When on the street alone, definitely "do not," but when on the street with Mommy and she talks to someone, who is a *stranger* to the child, it is okay to talk to them. As development proceeds children develop hierarchical repertoires of *possible* responses for given circumstances and are able to prioritize them according to current emotions (joyful, sad, angry), goals (I want to study for a test), biologic needs (I need to sleep), or social needs (I am lonely and need to call a friend).

These neuroscience ideas lend support to the authors' proposal that *interactive* regulation is optimally balanced with *self*-regulation, that optimal social functioning involves the *flexibility to shift between* self- and interactive regulation in a figure-ground fashion, with neither excessive. For example, certain children seem to lack this flexibility. Based on the work of Jaffe and colleagues (2001), the authors describe excessive monitoring or "interactive vigilance" associated with insecure-disorganized patterns of attachment. They propose that excessive monitoring of the partner may occur at the expense of self-regulation; reciprocally, excessive preoccupation with self-regulation may occur at the expense of interactive sensitivity, which can result in social withdrawal (Beebe and Lachmann 2002, Beebe and McCrorie 1996).

At the beginning of the treatment this lack of flexibility was evident in Dolores, who was very withdrawn and relied mostly on her own extreme forms of self-regulation, such as her lowered head and avoidance of eye contact, to manage her distress.

THE IMPORTANCE OF TEMPORAL FACTORS, SUCH AS CONTINGENCY AND PREDICTABILITY

The authors argue that the emphasis on matching or correspondence in the infant theories of intersubjectivity may lead to a static conceptualization of intersubjectivity. Instead, the authors emphasize the *temporal* nature of interactive regulation, that is, mutual influences (contingencies) over time, which lead to predictable patterns. For the baby to experience the mother's response as *con-*

tingent on the response of the baby, the mother must respond to the baby within an *optimally* brief window of time. For a response to be *predictable*, the brain must be able to detect a *degree of statistical probability* that it will occur, meaning a likelihood greater than chance. Neuroscientists have concluded that the capacity to perceive temporal relationships, such as recognition of contingency and detection of probabilities and predictability, is a fundamental property of the mammalian brain. The human brain organizes its experience from a temporal perspective, because self and environment are normally in continual flux.

What Is Important About Contingency?

The authors argue that matching the behavior of the other is different from *contingently* matching it. Contingency enables a sense of agency, of impact. Contingency is what allows the child to learn: "What changes happens because of *me*," vs. "What happens independently of *me*." When the other's response occurs *contingent* on one's own, the response is attributed to one's own effort, not to that of the other (Haggard et al. 2002, 2003). When a child pushes a ball, and it moves, the child ascribes the movement as due to his own effort, and not that of the ball. If the ball moves too quickly or slowly, the source of movement will be experienced as *external* to the child. When a baby smiles or cries and Mother's empathic responsiveness is contingent on the behavior of the baby, the baby feels Mother understands and experiences having an impact on Mother.

Predictions Enhance Adaptation, but Can Bias Experience Toward the Past

By being able to predict future events, an animal is in a more advantageous position to respond to the ever-changing flux in the *self* and in the *world* of objects and others. For a complete review of prediction with respect to psychotherapy, see Pally (2004 in press). The brain learns from interactions with the physical and social world what events *tend to follow one another*; the brain stores this *probabilistic* learning in implicit memory, in the form of *predictions*. Based on this learning, even *before* an event occurs, the brain has already made a prediction about what is *most likely* to occur. As a result of this prediction, the brain triggers physiologic, perceptual, emotional, behavioral, and interpersonal processes in accordance with what is predicted. This allows the individual to recognize events and respond to them more quickly and efficiently when they do occur.

In this way, for example, during the interaction with Mother, the infant is learning sequences such as "When I smile, mother smiles back," or "When she jiggles me, I feel overaroused, so I turn away," or "When I slow down, she slows down too." As Beebe and Lachmann (1988) described, "Once symbol formation develops, experiences in matching affect and interpersonal timing may contribute to expectations in the older child or adult of being attuned, known, or on the same wavelength. We infer an experience not only of 'I reflect you,' but also of 'I change with you, we are going in the same direction, I experience myself as tracking you and being tracked by you'" (p. 323). The infant stores this learning in the form of predictions, which it relies on for future interactive encounters.

Predictive mechanisms serve as a bias to alter a person's body physiology, behavior, emotion, and perception in the direction of what is predicted. In perception, for example, the brain takes a few bits of sensory data and predicts what the whole object is, then activates the sensory system to enhance the likelihood of perceiving the expected object (Grossberg 1999). In performing routine habits or skills, as the brain performs one movement it predicts the next step and activates the motor processes for that predicted action (Graybiel 1998, Graybiel et al. 1994). This is why in one's daily routine of getting ready and going to work, one often fails to do some nonroutine task, like taking clothes to the cleaners. If the brain predicts a certain emotion will occur as a result of some situation, limbic centers are set in motion to "rev up" that emotion before the situation occurs (LeDoux 1996, Schultz and Dickinson 2000).

The biasing affects of predictions can also lead to *maladaptive* repetition of earlier forms of relatedness, as old predictive biases subjectively shape current feelings and behavior. When a baby views the mother's face, the baby experiences "world" changes (mother's face) and "self" changes (body physiologic responses of arousal or calming). When her beloved and loving foster mother's face disappeared, Dolores experienced "self" changes in the form of alterations of body physiology, emotion, and behavior, which led to the subjective state of no longer being a *lovable, good, responded to* Self. Early on, she most likely tried again and again to remember the good face, but to no avail. It is absent and she gives up. The sequence might be something like: Dolores tries to remember the loving face loving her; no loving face appears; painful and dysregulated affects; the self is experienced as not good. This experience, encoded as a temporal sequence of motor actions, which is followed by sensory consequences and associated affects, leads to predictions that then organize subsequent behavior *and* subjective experience. Since this learning occurs so early in her life it becomes particularly deeply engrained. When Dolores interacts with other faces, these predictions will *predominate* as factors that guide her behavior with others. Even though Dr. Beebe uses a loving and empathically responsive face, Dolores behaves with Dr. Beebe's face according to predetermined predictions. Her predictions of loss, disappointment, and distress probably also influence how she *subjectively experiences* her interactions with Dr. Beebe. Even when Dr. Beebe provides an empathically responsive face, Dolores nevertheless subjectively feels a sense of loss, disappointment, and distress. Dolores cannot *pay attention* to Dr. Beebe's face. Instead, Dolores responds to the predicted face.

A rather dramatic example of the biasing effect of prediction occurs with "fear conditioning" during trauma. If a woman is assaulted by a man with a beard in the parking lot near her work, when presented with a man, or even simply a beard, or a parking lot, her brain will predict that danger is imminent. Her heart will race and she will shake with fear even though no danger occurs. The more repeated the sequence, the more strongly the predictive mechanisms take hold, and the more difficult the habitual emotional response is to change.

The authors discuss the findings of Jaffe and colleagues (2001) showing that degrees of temporal coordination between mother and infant, and stranger and infant, predict later attachment outcomes. When vocal rhythms are excessively *or* insufficiently predictable (coordinated), attachment outcomes are insecure; midrange coordination predicts secure outcomes. When behavioral responses remain overly coordinated and rigidified, change and new learning may be impeded. On the other hand, when the interactions are not predictable enough, nothing can be taken for granted, so to speak; the attention and consciousness systems are overly engaged and overloaded. In order to counteract this overinvolvement of consciousness and attention, the baby may become disengaged or detached. This too interferes with new learning and change since this system is easily overwhelmed and soon becomes unavailable for learning cognitive and motor tasks. The consequence therefore is a child who is overly vigilant and rigid, or a child who is somewhat detached because nothing is reliable enough. Because these less than optimal predictive modes have such an impact on the development of neural circuitry, they can have a permanent effect on the child's interpersonal style of relating and attachment styles.

Predictions are particularly relevant to the issue of transference experience. Predictions are based on past experience and implicitly organize current perceptual, motor, emotional, physiologic, and social cognition systems in terms of what is predicted, *before* the event actually occurs. What is particularly important to transference and countertransference is that both members of the dyad are influenced by the other *at the same time*: each partner's predictive biases influence the encounter (Miller and Turnbull 1986). If the brain predicts a certain emotion will occur as a result of some gesture or facial expression of the partner, limbic centers are set in motion to "rev up" that emotion before the gesture or expression occurs (LeDoux 1996, Schultz and Dickinson 2000). With respect to infants and mothers, predictions can take the form of "When I smile, Mother smiles back and I feel good" or "When Mother smiles, I am overstimulated and I turn away." As a result of predictive mechanisms, simply looking at Mother's face can give a sense of calm. These automatically generated predictions or expectancies may place some limitations on the degree to which an individual will remain responsive to the unique interactive events *within a particular encounter.*

In the case of Dolores, very early she learned to anticipate loss, disappointment, and distress in intimate encounters, and that she may be better off avoiding them. This early learning is deeply ingrained. Dolores is heavily biased by her early experience toward repeating this pattern over and over. Looking at an important face is *predicted* to result in feelings of loss, abandonment, or terror, so she avoids such faces over and over. But, if she does look at an important person's face, such as that of Dr. Beebe, she may automatically feel the predicted distress feelings. The fact that early trauma can result in a permanent emotional oversensitivity to certain events may help explain other features of Dolores's case. Despite being highly intelligent, reflective, and competent in many arenas, in intimate relationships Dolores becomes flooded with painful affects and presumably stress hormones, such as cortisol and adrenaline. These negative affects and stress hormones may leave her overly vigilant for danger, compromising her ability to think and feel in intimate interpersonal encounters.

The study of coordination of mother and infant vocal rhythms (Jaffe et al. 2001) exemplifies how the behavior of each member of a dyad is predictable from that of the other. Each learns to predict the other's response, in response to her own behavior. In other words, "When I do *this*, you will do *that*." In the clinical situation, at the nonconscious level, both patient and analyst are making predictions based on the behavior of the other: What is the likelihood that I will I be soothed or distressed?, that I will be appreciated or devalued?, that I will be loved or rejected?—and both are reacting accordingly. Transference–countertransference configurations emerge that contain underlying nonconscious expectations of the patient and the analyst, and the defenses that are mobilized against these *expected* outcomes.

To understand the transference the analyst often tracks temporal sequences between the analyst's behavior and that of the patient. Even before the analyst understands what the temporal sequence "means," the analyst may draw the patient's attention to a particular pattern to engage the patient in the exploration process. For example, the analyst smiles as she opens the door to the waiting room, but the patient avoids eye contact with the analyst when walking into the room. The analyst offers an empathic comment, but the patient's response is defensive. The analyst's tracking of these sequences might be shared with the patient, helping to bring into joint shared attention aspects of the relationship that reflect the patient's implicit way of knowing others.

Dolores, for example, expects that when she looks at Dr. Beebe's face, she may see the "monster-face." As a result, Dolores's whole mind and body are primed for that event. She feels anxious and bad *before* any looking has occurred. She therefore avoids looking, even though Dr. Beebe's face is so available and attuned to Dolores. Early in the treatment, frequently the only kind of intervention Dr. Beebe makes is an observation about this kind of temporal sequence of events, providing Delores a sense of being known.

The attachment process is a learning experience that generates predictions. A child learns what will happen if, for example, the child smiles, becomes distressed, becomes separated, needs attention, becomes self-focused, or pursues his own curiosity. What will the parent do: smile, shout, sigh, look anxious, or ignore him? Children learn to predict how to best engage the parent in responding to their needs, and what they need to do, for example, to keep connected, be soothed, or avoid being overstimulated. This learning activates neurotransmitters and leads to actual growth of "neural circuitry," which forms the basis for how these events are represented in the brain. The earlier in life an experience occurs and the closer it is associated with survival, the more likely the circuitry becomes deeply engrained and difficult to change.

Attachment is a "survival" process and thus predictions formed about what to expect in relationships that occur during this time period can be entrenched. Deeply engrained predictions make therapeutic change difficult. For example, a child who was very harshly reprimanded, or shamefully humiliated by parents, may *always* have the tendency toward feelings of fear and anxiety with authority figures. Such feelings may leave a person with an involuntary, automatic maladaptive style of behavior. Perhaps the person chronically avoids asserting himself with professors, employers, and spouse. For example, as much as Dolores longs for intimacy, she tends to avoid it. She had a deeply loving relationship with the first good mother, but her emotional survival was threatened by the loss of this mother. Her emotional and physical survival felt threatened during the period she spent with the abusive mother. By the time she arrived at the home of her adoptive family, the intimacy she longs for is very difficult to achieve.

THE RELATIVE IMPORTANCE OF IMPLICIT VS. EXPLICIT ASPECTS OF THERAPEUTIC ACTION

Traditional psychoanalytic approaches have been more concerned with verbal symbolic elements of the exchange than nonverbal and implicit. For therapeutic change to occur, traditional approaches have assumed that conscious reflection *must* be engaged. The conflicts, feelings, and beliefs that resist change and result in a repetition of old ways of relating interpersonally must be brought into conscious awareness, through interpretation and insight.

Beebe and colleagues argue otherwise. Their work is a contribution to the recent growing awareness among psychoanalytic theorists of the important therapeutic role of implicit, nonconscious, and nonverbal aspects of the exchange. Their work argues for the importance of both levels, implicit and explicit, within the psychoanalytic treatment process. There are a number of lines of neuroscience evidence that support their view.

The brain maintains a balance between *stability* and *change*, keeping things the same as much as possible while allowing for change when necessary (Damasio 1999, Freeman 2000). Every morning on awakening one wants to be able to remember when one was born, how to tie one's shoes, and how people converse, even as other things change, such as one's age, shoe size, or school.

The authors' discussion of Jaffe and colleagues' (2001) identification of a *mid-range* level of predictability of the coordination of vocal rhythms associated with secure infant attachment outcomes is consistent with the neuroscience perspective of a balance between stability and change. All mothers have moods that naturally fluctuate, changing in *un*expected ways, so that they cannot always attend empathically to the infant's needs. From a neuroscience perspective, why would a mid-range level of predictability between partners predict a more secure outcome for the child? A baby must have the potential to adapt both to the familiar nature of the mother and to her unexpected changing moods and concerns. The brain too needs an optimal level of predictability. When predictability is excessive, the individual may be too automatic, rigid, and inflexible; when predictability is insufficient, efficiency is lost and the person may become overwhelmed with doubt as to how to respond.

It is well known that nonconscious processes are far more rapid than conscious ones. Nonconscious processes occur approximately within 20–100 milliseconds after an event occurs. For this same event to achieve conscious awareness, as long as 500 milliseconds may be necessary (Libet 1993). From the neuroscience perspective, processes that maintain stability tend to operate nonconsciously. This is the likely explanation for why events such as interactive regulation, in which changes occur rapidly from moment-to-moment, operate nonconsciously: consciousness is too slow and cumbersome. This may also explain work by Shevrin and his colleagues (2002) who conclude that repressive processes, which resist change, occur nonconsciously. Their experiments suggest that repression occurs *within the time difference between nonconscious and conscious awareness*, such that defensive operations are set in motion *before* one is even aware of what one is defending against.

Processes that *facilitate change* can operate nonconsciously, as well, particularly if those changes occur in an *expected* or *predictable* fashion (Posner and Rothbart 1998). When the brain is dealing with ongoing change that is *un*expected or *un*predictable, however, consciousness typically is *required*. Whether or not implicit processes are sufficient for change, or whether conscious awareness needs to be involved in change, is critical to understanding therapeutic action.

In my discussion thus far, I have used findings from neuroscience to illuminate the nonconscious implicit level of how an individual responds to his environment, and how the brain can learn new things and change. Neuroscience data suggest that therapeutic action may begin nonverbally, at the implicit level, providing a milieu of trust and safety, so necessary for a therapeutic process to unfold. In the next phase therapeutic action may involve the co-construction of new ways of being with another, also created nonverbally/implicitly, before they become conscious and can be put into words. This is what for the most part appears to be happening in the early stages of the treatment of Dolores. She senses *at an implicit level* that something is different from what she expects is happening with Dr. Beebe, and she even begins to engage differently, before being aware of any change. I think it is at this implicit level that she begins to watch the videotape, not yet able to apprehend why she is drawn to it. As Beebe explains, Dolores struggles with "multiple, inconsistent, and often contradictory [preverbal] implicit relational models, stemming from her three primary caregiving situations.... In the course of treatment [Dr. Beebe] and [Dolores] together, [through the use of nonverbal affective and vocal rhythm exchanges] developed a fourth model, in which [they] struggled to integrate in the same person the good mother and the abandoning mother and [they] also developed ... new ways of relating" (Chapter 4, pp. 141–142).

However, neuroscience research also indicates an important and specific role for consciousness in therapeutic change. For example, in many instances we drive without paying conscious attention to our driving, operating fully on automatic pilot, as long as the route is familiar and the traffic moves along as expected. When an *un*expected shift in the traffic occurs, and we have to make a choice to slow down or speed up, and select among possible and often competing options, consciousness is engaged. Consciousness is required to figure out more *precisely* what is happening and to *accurately* decide and choose whether or not to turn the wheel, put on the brakes, or put on the gas. Research in neuroscience is now beginning to describe just how nonconscious processing differs from conscious processing, such that each is uniquely adapted to different kinds of situations (Freeman 2000). Key features of each type of processing are listed below:

Nonconscious/Implicit Systems

- Rapid, efficient, automatic, involuntary, rough, approximate responses
- Poor perceptual detail or discrimination (the color red)
- Behaviors are *repeated* over and over, in the same way
- Handles vast arrays of information simultaneously, in parallel
- From an evolutionary survival perspective, for the stable, familiar, and expected aspects of life the brain utilizes implicit processing whenever possible. (For example, homeostatis processes that maintain life, heart rate, respiration, blood pressure, gastrointestinal movement, are regulated *only* nonconsciously.)

Conscious/Explicit Systems

- Slow, inefficient, deliberate, voluntary, precise, finely tuned responses
- Good perceptual specificity and discrimination (a specific red, e.g. burgundy, scarlet, cranberry)
- Behaviors contain *precise* fine tuning and flexibility

- Handles essentially one thing at a time, in serial, is easily overwhelmed
- From the evolutionary survival perspective, consciousness is reserved only for very particular situations, where implicit mechanisms no longer suffice

Consciousness tends to be called on for situations of

(a) *Novelty* (never been experienced before)
(b) *Unpredicted* or *unexpected* (in the current circumstances)
(c) *Conflicted* (Should I take the last piece of chicken or be polite and leave it for someone else?)
(d) *Ambiguous* (I can't tell if that woman wearing the red hat is my friend or not)
(e) When a *Decision* or *Choice* must be made, to *Resolve* an ambiguity or conflict.

The Importance of Context in Therapeutic Action

To consider the issue of whether or not therapeutic action involves nonconscious or conscious processes, it is helpful to remember that learning itself is very contextually driven. Something learned *in one context* will tend to be applied whenever that particular context is present. Context can include affect state, arousal, or body physiology state, and environmental sensory details, such as location, colors, sounds, or people.

Most animals are quite limited in such discrimination of context. Whenever you put on your walking shoes, your dog may come over, wag its tail, and expect to go out for a walk, no matter how often you disappoint it, by leaving without taking the dog. Chimps have better discrimination.

Human beings *are unique in the animal kingdom* for being able to learn a whole repertoire of possible responses for the same contextual situation, and to be able to flexibly shift among them. The young child learns that "Mommy always responds to crying," but later learns "Perhaps not after bedtime." Some of this can occur without explicit conscious attention. But in situations with conflict or ambiguity, which require resolution, accuracy, detail, reflection, and voluntary selective choice, *consciousness is required*.

A child who lives in a "good *enough*" environment develops optimal flexibility between implicit automatic responses and conscious reflective ones. This child will implicitly "know" that there is a baseline of safety even in uncertainty, and that it is okay to *voluntarily select* a nonhabitual response for a particular situation. A child well-schooled to leave Mommy alone when she is on the phone will still feel safe enough to shout and bother her if an injury occurs. If there is conflict or ambiguity a healthy child will be able to utilize conscious reflective thinking to decide what to do. A less fortunate child may inhibit such seemingly acceptable and adaptive responses if the environment has not provided enough flexibility or regularity.

Although the brain is able to formulate a wide *repertoire of possible* responses to a particular situation, in certain instances responses compete, and only one can "win." In *overt* action (such as gesture or facial expression), *conscious* perception, or spoken language, we perform only one action at a time, we *consciously* perceive only one thing at a time, and we can say only one word at a time.

A number of factors that we are entirely *unaware* of drive the competition among possible responses. For one thing, repetition plays a role. A response that has more often been repeated will tend to dominate the competition. This is why when you hear someone say, "Mary had a little . . . ," even though the person says "jam" or "ham," most people will respond as if they heard "lamb." This is why when you pass a colleague in the hall, you say "How are you?" and walk on by, as if they have said "Fine, how are you?, even though they say "Not so good!" It takes conscious awareness to voluntarily stop, pay attention to what they have actually said, and to ask "What is the matter?" In psychoanalytic treatment we often say in effect, "You have been doing it the *old* way, *automatically*, for a long time. The more times you try and act in a *new* way, the more it will eventually become *second nature*. Change takes time."

Survival and intense emotion also play a role in competition among possible responses. Feelings of danger tend to dominate over all other emotions. Once having learned to cope with traumatic circumstances, an individual may be particularly resistant to responding calmly, even when circumstances are safer. For Dolores a face may be "automatically" dangerous and to be avoided. Whether it is an empathically responsive face or not, was generally not well distinguished by her.

What does this imply for therapeutic action? What facilitates the development of new, more flexible ways of responding in a patient's current repertoire? Dr. Beebe provided a new type of interaction, one that was contingently responsive to slight shifts in Dolores's nonverbal behavior, although this responsiveness often occurred out of awareness of both partners. This form of responsiveness enhanced emotional regulation and feelings of trust, safety, and control in the patient. Dolores learned these new ways of relating at the implicit level. She came to feel safer, before she could express this in words.

However, to maximize the likelihood that a patient will be able to apply this new learning to other relationships, or during periods of stress such as separation even within the therapeutic relationship, it is also important to explicitly recognize, in words, what is going on. Conscious explicit mechanisms differ significantly from nonconscious implicit ones, in ways that allow for a greater likelihood of flexible and deliberate choice. With explicit processing, despite similarities between a current situation and a prior traumatic one, old responses developed for coping with trauma can be inhibited, and newly learned more adaptive ones can be activated.

A number of factors promote conscious explicit processes. One factor is verbalization. Putting experience into words *requires* consciousness. This is why people often are reluctant to put painful experiences into words. The experience enters more into conscious awareness and feels more real. When Dolores starts to tell Dr. Beebe of her early trauma, she *feels it more acutely* and once again starts to withdraw.

Time can also promote conscious explicit processing. By taking time to reflect on a perception, or delaying a bit between perceiving something and reacting to it, one is more able to employ consciousness. For example, as we listen to another person speak, as each word emerges only part of our brains listen consciously. Much of the brain is also *nonconsciously* listening and generating a number of possible replies. A person may say "I-had-a-terrible-weekend-because-my-wife-was-so. . . . With each word, the *listener's* brain generates a number of possible replies, all of which compete. As the sentence nears its end, the number of possible replies decreases considerably. When the last word is spoken and the pause occurs, a "winner" is selected. The *listener* now gives only one of those possible replies, as a function of whether the *speaker's* last word was "sick," "mean," or "depressed." The listener's response may be totally askew if the speaker's last word turns out to be something entirely unexpected, such as "My wife was so loving." Since the competitive "weaning down" of possible utterances occurs nonconsciously, the listener may not even know exactly what he is going to say until he says it.

Consciousness makes a valuable contribution by enhancing a feeling of integration and wholeness in a person's sense of self. Llinas (2001) argues that the *synchronization* of brain circuitry involved in conscious processing facilitates connectedness *among* the many modular brain regions, such as different sensory regions for sight, sound, smell, and touch, emotional limbic regions, motor regions, and prefrontal ones for decision making and reasoning. While sensory stimulation can lead to brain maturation, only conscious awareness of stimulation creates the experience of whole scenes of experience, and an integrated sense of self, such as being a continuous center of one's experience (Llinas 2001).

The brain has a nonconscious bias to perceive, feel, and behave in the expected way, just as with my example of "lamb" vs. "ham" and "jam." Some people notice the unexpected word and others do not. The brain can sometimes nonconsciously monitor a mismatch between an expected event and the actual occurrence. But conscious awareness may be able to enhance this monitoring (Posner 1994). Neuroimaging studies indicate that the anterior cingulate cortex is a good candidate for this monitoring system (Posner 1994, Posner and Rothbart 1998). When mismatch is detected, the anterior cingulated is activated. In experiments using fMRI, when subjects are shown "color words" on a computer screen (e.g., *red, green*) and asked to name either the *color of the ink* of the written word, or the *written word* itself (e.g., read the word "red" written in green ink), if they make a mistake and notice it, the anterior cingulate is activated. If they do not notice it, the anterior cingulate is not activated. If the experimenter subsequently points out the mistake, the cingulate becomes active. Conscious attention helps detect otherwise unnoticed errors of perception by enhancing activity in attended areas, and by discriminating more sensory details, thereby increasing accuracy.

Focal attention can, however, be excessive, with negative consequences. The executive focal attention system develops in the first year of life, in the prefrontal cortex, primarily to regulate emotion. For example, a baby can shift attention away from Mother by looking away, turning the head away, or turning the whole body away. But infants of 12 months or younger may show more extreme shifts of attention described as "stilling" or "freezing," which are associated with disorganized attachment patterns (Lyons-Ruth 1998). In the older child or adult, such extreme attentional shifts can result in powerful dissociative states, so commonly found with childhood neglect and abuse, and adult trauma. These dissociative states were characteristic of Dolores early in the treatment.

The executive focal attention system is relevant to therapeutic action. Direction of one's focal attention determines what aspect of the world, body, or self one attends to. Focal attention can keep us very much in the present, helping to correct perceptual or behavioral errors and to more flexibly regulate emotion. Or, as with Dolores, focal attention can keep us detached from the present, rigidly grounded in the past.

In the clinical setting, through implicit forms of interaction, the patient may begin to trust the analyst and even begin to engage in a new way, often well before either patient or analyst is consciously aware, or can verbalize what is going on. This appears to have happened in the case of Dolores. It probably contributed to her watching the videotapes repeatedly at home. Dolores implicitly "knew" something different was going on with Dr. Beebe *in the office*. Although she could not yet utilize this knowledge in the office, it nevertheless affected her and she wanted to view the tapes over and over to figure it out.

Unfortunately, the biases that occur as a result of the brain's predictive mechanisms may interfere with a patient being able to grasp, even at the implicit level, that something unexpected has occurred. For this reason, people are more inclined to perceive what they expect than to perceive what is actually occurring. With those patients who do not seem to be able to detect, even at an implicit level that something different is happening, it may require the analyst to recognize this and to offer some way of drawing the patient's attention to it.

What neuroscientists now recognize is that habitual avoidance from danger behaviors, or habitual approach behaviors to obtain rewards, can be learned implicitly and even unlearned implicitly. The habitual response does not however disappear. When stress occurs, or old reminder contexts recur, old habitual responses reemerge. Dolores will probably remain vulnerable to her struggles for the rest of her life. Perhaps as a result of her relationship with Dr. Beebe, she may be able to operate, much of the time, in a new way. However, probably there will be many times when she needs to call up her powers of self-reflection and symbolic understanding of her situation. With enough motivation and effort she will be able to bring to bear what she has learned with Dr. Beebe in times of stress.

From a clinical perspective, engaging focal attention and the consciousness system to notice the pattern of interaction, both what is expected and what is unexpected, is a critical therapeutic tool. This consciousness may facilitate choice and behavioral and affective control, enhance neural growth and plasticity, and ultimately promote therapeutic change. During the working-through phase new ways of interacting are fragile and old ways still dominate. Outside the therapeutic setting it may still be very difficult to integrate new ways of functioning. When the patient is under stress, such as a separation, the old ways may once again dominate.

SUMMARY AND CONCLUSIONS

The authors have provided a detailed analysis of different meanings of the term "intersubjectivity" within both infant research and adult treatment. By using a dyadic systems view of the integration of self- and interaction regulation they have given us a unifying framework within which to compare different theorists. Self- and interactive regulation are defined as contingencies or predictabilities over time, within the person's own behavior and between the behaviors of the two partners. Their concept of "forms of intersubjectivity," which includes distinctions between presymbolic and symbolic as well as implicit and explicit forms, provides an inclusive approach relevant to all theories of intersubjectivity, but one which requires us to be far more differentiated in our thinking. They have clarified and enriched our understanding of this complex and often confusing term.

They emphasize that nonverbal/implicit forms of interaction serve as a bridge from infant research to adult treatment. In my discussion I have highlighted some of the new features of their model "forms of intersubjectivity." I found particularly important their emphasis on the importance of *interactive* regulation, and on having a number of varied ways of interacting that are flexible and responsive to change. I also found most valuable their discussion of the temporal or contingent and predictable nature of interaction, and their presentation of research documenting that most parameters of regulation occur within an optimal band or mid-range of functioning.

Their model is consistent with what we know about brain functioning in neuroscience research. Findings from neuroscience emphasize that the infant brain and mind is immature, and that brain circuitry grows and matures in relation to experiences with the environment, particularly the caretaking environment. These findings also emphasize the survival value of variations of "forms" in all biologic and social domains, and of the ability flexibly to shift between forms as the situation calls for. Neuroscience research supports the idea that a number of preverbal, presymbolic experiences in infancy can be embedded in adult brain systems and continue to affect the person's functioning throughout life. Furthermore neuroscience research has documented that prediction is one of the most fundamental of brain functions. The ability to maintain a balance between homeostasis and stability, vs. change and plasticity, critical to adaptive functioning, corresponds to their concept of a continuum of degrees of predictability or regulation. Too much predictability resists change; too little predictability resists stability. Finally, neuroscience research supports the idea that therapeutic change operates with a two-fold process, one implicit and one explicit. The implicit mechanism operates automatically entirely outside of conscious awareness. The explicit mechanism involves conscious awareness, voluntary efforts, and the potential for verbalization.

This two-fold process of therapeutic action implies that the analyst needs to attempt to become aware of the implicit aspects of the patient's as well as her own affect and behavior. Becoming aware is often difficult, but potentially offers the important benefit of being able to speak about and reflect on implicit aspects of the exchange. This two-fold process of therapeutic action suggests that in the treatment setting the analyst functions both to *enact* and to *reflect on* the interaction.

By being more aware of the subtle, varied, and complex dimensions of implicit forms of intersubjectivity described in this book, the analyst may be able to become more empathically responsive, and may be able to contribute to more optimal forms of self- and interactive regulation in the implicit mode. A shift in the patient's material may reflect issues organized in the explicit mode, such as an internal conflict about anxiety or aggression, or may reflect interactive influences in the dyad organized in the implicit mode, where for example for a split-second the analyst looked uncomfortable as the patient made an angry comment. By becoming more aware of both modes of processing, the analyst can choose what aspect of the process to attend to and potentially to share with the patient. The nonverbal, procedural, implicit, biologic elements of the relationship are critically important in making sense of the symbolic meanings of the patient's material.

Similarly, in a well-functioning analysis the patient, as well, enacts as well as reflects, at times drawing the analyst's attention to something unnoticed by the analyst. For example, the patient comments on the analyst's tendency to shift in the chair, or to talk too softly.

Stern (1985) notes that "[t]he advent of language is a mixed blessing" (p. 178), because language is inadequate to the task of communicating internal states. Language permits abstract reasoning, self-reflection, the ability to imagine the past and plan for the future. But, he argues, language also causes a rupture between what one says and how one feels, the verbalizable self and the experiencing self. By privileging verbal communication, psychoanalysis accentuates this rupture and sacrifices the understanding of states that are difficult to verbalize. According to Jacobs (1994), one root of this problem is that while Freud was an astute observer of nonverbal communication, his theories developed more in relation to spoken communication.

It is fair to say that neuroscience data is in agreement with the idea that the analyst can provide a new way of relating that adds to the patient's repertoire of possibilities, as Beebe described in the treatment of Dolores. In the treatment setting, implicit, nonverbal, nonsymbolic elements of experience *do* operate, simultaneously and in conjunction with explicit, verbal, symbolic elements. The question is, Can the analyst harness these elements of the exchange for the benefit of the treatment?

In the elegant and sensitive work that goes on between Dr. Beebe and Dolores both modes of therapeutic action are articulated. In the beginning of treatment but lasting well into the later years as well, the implicit/nonverbal modes of how Dr. Beebe relates to Dolores, such as various forms of matching and distress regulation, provide ways for Dolores to experience that this situation is far safer than what she has experienced before. These implicit/nonverbal modes facilitate connecting to, understanding, and communicating with a brilliant and sensitive but nevertheless very detached, isolated, and shut-down patient. To my mind, these implicit/nonverbal modes may be the precondition for any therapy to occur.

In addition, over time Dolores and Dr. Beebe engage in rather amazingly attuned and articulate verbal exchanges, understanding this new "safer sense" and the new "sense of the possibility of real hope." The consciousness system *certainly did not* and *could not* have acted alone, before a first implicit, nonconscious level of organization occurred. Similarly, a purely nonconscious implicit mode did not and could not have succeeded alone. As the analysis progressed Dolores was more and more able to gain mastery over her catastrophic predictions and fears, as well as her defenses against psychic, emotional, and behavioral withdrawal. The integration of conscious awareness and verbalization, and nonconscious implicit emotional modes (rhythmic, gestural, visceral), was critical to the success of this treatment.

Early in the treatment, much of Dolores's new learning seems to occur without conscious awareness. When Dolores watches the videotapes, she may be receiving positive affective signals from Dr. Beebe's face. She may be imitating and repeating different body and vocal rhythms. She can repeat these interactions over and over as much as she likes. Although clearly she consciously asks Dr. Beebe for the tapes and she must consciously set up the videotape to watch it, the actual initial route of learning may be outside of awareness. She may not even realize what is different about what she sees, or what she is taking in from watching. It does, however, have a calming effect and enhances her trust of the therapist. Dr. Beebe and Dolores herself then begin to direct conscious focal attention to the nature of the videotaped interactions, using words to describe what they see, and reflecting on the meaning of those words, using the explicit or declarative system of the hippocampus. Eventually, as Dolores and Dr. Beebe describe to each other and imagine reexperiencing these implicit interactions, for Dolores they become more strongly encoded in the basal ganglia, and more likely to dominate over competing patterns, and thus activated more often automatically and habitually.

Patients such as Dolores, who have had disordered interactions with early caretakers, bring certain expectancies and ways of relating to the interaction with the analyst. As the analyst interacts differently from early caretakers, in both the implicit and explicit modes, the patient's way of interacting with the analyst as well as with others can dramatically change. To what degree this change can occur without conscious awareness and reflection is a matter of dispute within psychoanalysis, as the authors indicate. Consistent with the position taken by Beebe, Knoblauch, Rustin, and Sorter, in this discussion I have argued for a two-fold theory of implicit and explicit modes of therapeutic action.

Unfortunately, the neuroscience study of consciousness is still in its infancy. Little data are available on the real-life, rapid, face-to-face interactions that are the subject of this book. Therefore the neuroscience data are not available to fully resolve our questions of the relative role and importance of implicit vs. explicit modes of change. Similarly, questions such as, "How does new learning take place? How is new learning implemented? When does old learning continue to predominate or intrude, despite new learning?" are only beginning to be understood by neuroscientists. Fortunately, as the result of more creative experiments using the fMRI scanner, which can more closely simulate interpersonal interactions, neuroscientists are quickly gaining ground. Perhaps in the not-too-distant future neuroscientists will study real-life face-to-face interactive regulation between individuals, and will have even more to offer us as analysts.

REFERENCES

Arbib, M.A. (2002). Language evolution: the mirror system hypothesis. In *The Handbook of Brain Theory and Neuronal Networks*, ed. M. A. Arbib, pp. 606–611. Cambridge, MA: MIT Press.

Beebe, B., Jaffe, J., Lachmann, F., et al. (2000). Systems models in development and psychoanalysis: the case of vocal rhythm coordination and attachment. *Infant Mental Health Journal* 21:99–122.

Beebe, B., and Lachmann, F. (1988). The contribution of mother–infant mutual influence to the origins of self- and object representations. *Psychoanalytic Psychology* 5(4):305–337.

———— (2002). *Infant Research and Adult Treatment: Co-constructing Interactions*. Hillsdale, NJ: Analytic Press.

Beebe, B., and McCrorie, E. (1996). *A model of love for the 21st century*. Paper presented at the Annual Meetings of the Psychology of the Self, Washington DC.

Bechara, A., Damasio, H., Tranel, D., and Damasio, A. R. (1997). Deciding advantageously before knowing the advantageous strategy. *Science* 275:1293–1295.

Brothers, L. (1989). A biological perspective on empathy. *American Journal of Psychology* 146(1):10–19.

———— (1992). Perception of social acts in primates: cognition and neurobiology. *The Neurosciences* 4:409–414.

Bunce, S., Bernat, E., Wong, P. S., and Shevrin, H. (1999). Further evidence for unconscious learning: preliminary support for the conditioning of facial EMG to subliminal stimuli. *Journal of Psychiatric Research* 33:341–347.

Calvin, W. H. (2004). *A Brief History of the Mind*. New York: Oxford.

Carr, L., Iacoboni, M., Dubeau, M., et al. (2003). Neural mechanisms of empathy in humans: a relay from neural systems for imitation to limbic areas. *Proceedings of the National Academy of Sciences of the United States of America* 100:5497–5502.

Chartrand, T. L., and Bargh, J. A. (1999). The chameleon effect: the perception–behavior link and social interaction. *Journal of Personality and Social Psychology* 76:893–910.

Christakis, D. A., Zimmerman, F. J., DiGiuseppe, D. L., and McCarty, C. A. (2004). Early television exposure and subsequent attention problems in children. *Pediatrics* 113: 708–713.

Clark, A. (1997). *Being There*. Cambridge, MA: MIT Press.

Corbetta, M. F., Miezin, S., and Dobmeyer, G. L. (1991). Selective and divided attention during visual discrimination of color, shape, and speed: functional anatomy of positron emission tomography. *Journal of Neuroscience* 11:2383–2402.

Crick, F. (1994). *The Astonishing Hypothesis*. New York: MacMillan.

Damasio, A. R. (1994). *Descartes' Error*. New York: Putnam.

—— (1995). Toward a neurobiology of emotion and feeling: operational concepts and hypotheses. *The Neuroscientists* 1:19–25.

—— (1999). *The Feeling of What Happens*. New York: Harcourt.

Davidson, R. J., Jackson, D. C., and Kalin, N. H. (2000). Emotion, plasticity, context and regulation: perspectives from affective neuroscience. *Psychological Bulletin* 126(6):890–909.

Deacon, T. W. (1997). *The Symbolic Species*. New York: W.W. Norton.

Desimone, R., and Duncan, J. (1995). Neural mechanisms of selective visual attention. *Annual Reviews in Neuroscience* 18:193–222.

Dimberg, U., Thunberg, M., and Elmehed, K. (2000). Unconscious facial reactions to emotional facial expressions. *American Psychological Society* 11:86–89.

Edelman, G. (1989). *The Remembered Present*. New York: Basic Books.

—— (1992). *Bright Air, Brilliant Fire*. New York: Basic Books.

Edelman, G. M., and Tononi, G. (2000). *A Universe of Consciousness: How Matter Becomes Imagination*. New York: Basic Books.

Eibl-Eibesfeldt, I. (1980). Strategies of social interaction. In *Emotion: Theory, Research and Experience*, ed. R. Plutchik and H. Kellerman. New York: Academic Press.

Ekman, P. (1990). Voluntary facial action generates emotion-specific autonomic nervous system activity. *Psychophysiology* 27(4):363–383.

—— (1993). Facial expression and emotion. *American Psychologist*, April, pp. 384–392.

Field, T. M. (2003). Stimulation of preterm infants. *Pediatric Review* 24:4–11.

Freeman, W. J. (2000). *How Brains Make Up Their Minds*. New York: Columbia University Press.

—— (2003). Neurodynamic models of brain in psychiatry. *Neuropsychopharmacology*, supplement 1, S54–63.

Fried, I., MacDonald, K. A., and Wilson, C. (1997). Single neuron activity in human hippocampus and amygdala during recognition of faces and objects. *Neuron* 18:753–765.

Fuster, J. M. (2003). *Cortex and Mind*. New York: Oxford University Press.

Gallese, V. (2003). The roots of empathy: the shared manifold hypothesis and the neural basis of intersubjectivity. *Psychopathology* 36:171–180.

Gergeley, G., and Watson, J. (1998). Early social-emotional development: contingency perception and the social-biofeedback model. In *Early Social Cognition*, ed. P. Rochat, pp. 101–136. Hillsdale, NJ: Lawrence Erlbaum.

Graybiel, A. (1998). The basal ganglia and chunking of action repertoires. *Neurobiology of Learning and Memory* 70:119–136.

Graybiel, A., Aosaki, T., Flaherty, A. W., and Kimura, M. (1994). The basal ganglia and adaptive motor control. *Science* 265:1826–1831.

Greenough, W. T., Black, J. E., and Wallace, C. S. (1987). Experience and brain development. *Child Development* 58:539–559.

Grossberg, S. (1999). The link between brain learning, attention, and consciousness. *Consciousness and Cognition* 8:1–44.

Haggard, P., Clark, S., and Kalogeras, J. (2002). Voluntary action and conscious awareness. *Nature Neuroscience* 5:382–385.

Haggard, P., Martin, F., Taylor-Clark, M., et al. (2003). Awareness of action in schizophrenia. *NeuroReport* 23:1081–1085.

Hofer, M. (1984). Relationships as regulators: a psychobiologic perspective on bereavement. *Psychosomatic Medicine* 46:183–197.

——— (1996). On the nature and consequences of early loss. *Psychosomatic Medicine* 58:570–581.

Hyman, S. E. (1998). Neurobiology: a new image for fear and emotion. *Nature* 393:417–418.

Iacoboni, M., Woods, R. P., Brass, M., et al. (1999). Cortical mechanisms of human imitation. *Science* 286:2526–2528.

Jacobs, T. (1994). Nonverbal communications: some reflections on their role in the psychoanalytic process and psychoanalytic education. *Journal of the American Planning Association* 42:741–762.

Jaffe, J., Beebe, B., Feldstein, S., et al. (2001). Rhythms of dialogue in infancy. *Monographs of the Society for Research in Child Development* 66:2.

Kandel, E. R., Schwartz, J. H., and Jessel, T. M., eds. (1991). *Principles of Neural Science*. New York: Elsevier.

Kendon, A. (1992). The negotiation of context in face-to-face interaction. In *Rethinking Context: Language As an Interactive Phenomenon*, ed. A. Duranti and C. Goodwin, pp. 323–334. Cambridge, UK: Cambridge University Press.

LeDoux, J. (1994). Emotion, memory and the brain. *Scientific American*, June, pp. 50–57.

——— (1996). *The Emotional Brain*. New York: Simon & Schuster.

Libet, B. (1993). The neural time factor in conscious and unconscious events. *Ciba Foundation Symposium* 174:123–137.

Llinas, R. (2001). *I of the Vortex*. Cambridge, MA: MIT Press.

Lyons-Ruth, K. (1998). Implicit relational knowing: its role in development and psychoanalytic treatment. *Infant Mental Health Journal* 19:282–291.

———— (1999). The two-person unconscious: intersubjective dialogue, enactive relational representation, and the emergence of new forms of relational organization. *Psychoanalytic Inquiry* 19:576–617.

Meaney, M. J. (2001). Maternal care, gene expression, and the transmission of individual differences in stress reactivity across generations. *Annual Reviews in Neuroscience* 24:1161–1192.

Meltzoff, A., and Gopnik, A. (1993). The role of imitation in understanding persons and developing a theory of mind. In *Understanding Other Minds*, ed. S. Baron-Cohen, H. Tager-Flusberg, and D. Cohen, pp. 335–366. New York: Oxford University Press.

Miller, D. T., and Turnbull, W. (1986). Expectancies and interpersonal processes. *Annual Review of Psychology* 37:233–256.

Miller, E. K., and Cohen, J. D. (2001). An integrative theory of prefrontal cortex function. *Annual Reviews in Neuroscience* 24:167–202.

Nadel, L., and Land, C. (2000). Memory traces revisited. *Nature Reviews Neuroscience* 1:209–212.

Nelson, K. (2000). Memory and belief in development. In *Memory, Brain and Belief*, ed. D. L. Schacter and E. Scarry, pp. 259–289. Cambridge, MA: Harvard University Press.

Newport, D. J., Stowe, Z. N., and Nemeroff, C. B. (2002a). Parental depression: animal models of an adverse life event. *American Journal of Psychiatry* 159:1265–1283S.

Newport, D. J., Wilcox, M. M., and Stowe, Z. N. (2002b). Maternal depression: a child's first adverse life event. *Seminars in Clinical Neuropsychiatry* 7:113–119.

Pally, R. (1998). Emotional processing: the mind–body connection. *International Journal of Psycho-Analysis* 79:349–362.

———— (2000). *The Mind–Brain Relationship*. New York: Other Press.

———— (2001). A primary role for nonverbal communication in psychoanalysis. *Psychoanalytic Inquiry* 21:71–93.

———— (2002). The neurobiology of borderline personality disorder: the synergy of "nature and nurture." *Journal of Clinical Psychiatry* 8:133–142.

————— (2005, in press). Non-conscious prediction and a role for consciousness in correcting prediction errors. *Cortex.*

Panksepp, J. (1998). *Affective Neuroscience.* Oxford: Oxford University Press.

Pollak, S. D., and Kistler, D. J. (2002). Early experience is associated with the development of categorical representations for facial expression of emotion. *Proceedings of the National Academy of Sciences of the United States of America* 25:9072–9076.

Posner, M. I. (1994). Attention: the mechanisms of consciousness. *Proceedings of the National Academy of Sciences of the United States of America* 91:7398–7403.

Posner, M. I., and Rothbart, M. K. (1998). Attention, self-regulation and consciousness. *Philosophical Transactions of the Royal Society of London* 353:1915–1927.

Quirk, G. J., Likhtik, E., Pelletier, J. G., and Pare, D. (2003). Stimulation of medial prefrontal cortex decreases the responsiveness of central amygdala output neurons. *Journal of Neuroscience* 25:8800–8807.

Raison, C. L., and Miller, A. H. (2003). When not enough is too much: the role of insufficient glucocorticoid signaling in the pathophysiology of stress-related disorders. *American Journal of Psychiatry* 160:1554–1565.

Rizzolatti, G., and Arbib, M. (1998). Language within our grasp. *Trends in Neuroscience* 21:188–194.

Rizzolatti, G., Fadiga, L., Fogassi, L., and Gallese, V. (1996). Premotor cortex and the recognition of motor actions. *Cognitive Brain Research* 3:131–141.

Roelfsema, P. R., Engel, A. K., Konig, P., and Singer, W. (1997). Visuomotor integration is associated with zero time lag synchronization among cortical areas. *Nature* 385:157–161.

Rose, M., Haider, H., Weiller, C., and Buchel, C. (2002). The role of medial temporal lobe structures in implicit learning: an event-related fMRI study. *Neuron* 36:1221–1231.

Schall, J. D. (2001). Neural basis of deciding, choosing and acting. *Nature Reviews Neuroscience* 2:33–42.

Schore, A. N. (1994). *Affect Regulation and the Origin of the Self.* Hillsdale, NJ: Lawrence Erlbaum.

Schultz, W., and Dickinson, A. (2000). Neuronal coding of prediction errors. *Annual Review of Neuroscience* 23:473–500.

Schwartz, A. B., Moran, D. W., and Reina, G. A. (2004). Differential representation of perception and action in the frontal cortex. *Science* 303:380–383.

Shevrin, H. (2001). Event-related markers of unconscious processes. *International Journal of Psychophysiology* 42:209–218.

Shevrin, H., Ghannam, J. H., and Libet, B. (2002). A neural correlate of consciousness related to repression. *Consciousness and Cognition* 11:334–341.

Silk, K., ed. (1998). *Biology of Personality Disorders: Review of Psychiatry.* Washington, DC: American Psychiatric Press.

———— (2000). Overview of biologic factors. *Pediatric Clinics of North America* 23(1):61–75.

Stern, D. (1985). *The Interpersonal World of the Infant.* New York: Basic Books.

Stern, D., Sander, L., Nahum, J., et al. (1998). Non-interpretative mechanisms in psychoanalytic therapy. *International Journal of Psycho-Analysis* 79:903–921.

Suomi, S. J. (1999). Attachment in rhesus monkeys. In *Handbook of Attachment: Theory, Research, and Clinical Application*, ed. J. Cassidy and P. R. Shaver, pp. 181–197. New York: Guilford.

Teicher, M. H. (2000). Wounds that won't heal: the neurobiology of child abuse. *Cerebrum* 2:50–62.

Tessari, A., Rumiati, R. I., and Haggard, P. (2002). Imitation without awareness. *NeuroReport* 13:2531–2535.

Tomasello, M. (1999). *The Cultural Origins of Human Cognition.* Cambridge, MA: Harvard University Press.

van der Kolk, B. (2003). The neurobiology of childhood trauma and abuse. *Child and Adolescent Psychiatric Clinics of North America* 12:293–317.

Wong, P. S., Bernat, E., Bunce, S., and Shevrin, H. (1997). Brain indices of nonconscious associative learning. *Conscious Cognition* 6:519–544.

Wong, P. S., Bernat, E., Snodgrass, M., and Shevrin, H. (in press). Associative learning without awareness. *International Journal of Psychophysiology.*

Yamada, H., Sadato, N., Konishi, Y., et al. (2000). A milestone for normal development of the infantile brain detected by functional MRI. *Neurology* 55:218–223.

Yehuda, R. (2001). Biology of posttraumatic stress disorder. *Journal of Clinical Psychiatry* 62:41–46.

Index